AF505871

A Comparative Vocabulary of Abuan Dialects

HANS WOLFF

Northwestern University Press
Evanston 1969

PUBLISHER'S NOTE

In his Introduction Professor Berry makes it clear that Hans Wolff's posthumous work, <u>A</u> <u>Comparative Vocabulary</u> <u>of</u> <u>Abuan</u> <u>Dialects</u>, is to be seen as "field notes," and he asserts that "nothing more is claimed for them." Northwestern University Press does not ordinarily publish field notes; that it has done so in this instance is wholly attributable to the great esteem in which the Press, like his faculty colleagues, held Hans Wolff. The Press is grateful to the Program of African Studies of Northwestern University for the subsidy in support of manufacturing which has made possible the publication of this work.

Robert Plant Armstrong
Director

INTRODUCTION

From September 1965 to July 1966 Hans Wolff, as is
well known, was in Nigeria carrying out linguistic
research under a grant from the Social Science Research
Council (Joint Committee on African Studies). His main
concern throughout that period was a group of quite
closely related dialects spoken in that part of the
eastern Niger Delta which lies directly inland from the
coastal Kalabari and Nembe. The Abua-Ogbia group, as he
came to call it, consists of the following dialects:
Abua (referred to as A); Odual (Od); Kugbo (Ku), spoken
in four villages in the southern part of Odual; Eastern
Ogbia (EO), spoken on the Kolo Creek; and Western Ogbia
(WO), especially as spoken in the Oloibiri and Anyama
area.

At the time of his death in 1967, he was working
intensively on the data he had collected, and was already
planning a series of journal articles which would deal
both descriptively and comparatively with the phonology
and morpho-syntax of the dialects of the group. These
articles were never written. But he had gone some way
toward assembling a comparative vocabulary. The
vocabulary as it is here presented was prepared from the
original working cards, of which there were several
thousand with vocabulary items already entered from one
or more dialects.

In preparing the final manuscript for publication I
have adhered to the format Hans seems to have envisaged,
the main outlines of which were reasonably clear; and,
rightly or wrongly, I have resisted all inclination to
tamper with his text, even where I could be certain that

he would sooner or later have had second thoughts (the
gloss "alligator," for example) or where I could myself
have supplied what he would surely have added at some
later stage (such as certain Proto-Bantu starred forms.)
Remembering the exacting standards he set himself in all
his scholarly work I cannot pretend that he would have
approved wholeheartedly of what is published here. Never-
theless, I believe that my decision to restrict changes
largely to matters of arrangement and to minor emendations
of the text was correct. These are, after all, field
notes; nothing more is claimed for them. They are none-
theless valuable, since they provide much-needed data on a
most interesting group of languages for which we have had
practically no documentation until now.

A note is, no doubt, required on the typographical
conventions followed throughout the work. Nowhere among
his papers could I find any explicit statement by Hans
which identified the values of his symbols. But it is a
fairly safe assumption that he continued to use the
notational practices to which he had been long accustomed,
so that, to all intents and purposes, the tables he
published in 1959 ("Subsystem Typologies and Areal Ling-
uistics," <u>Anthropological</u> <u>Linguistics</u>, VII [October 1959],
32-34), with some minor additions and amendments, still
apply. These are as follows:

Stops:	p	kp	t		k	
voiced:	b	gb	d		g	
implosive:	ɓ		δ			
Fricatives:	ɬ		s			h
voiced:	β; v		z		γ; γ̃	
Nasals:	m	ŋ	n; nn	ñ	ŋ	
Liquids:			r	l; ll		
Semivowels:	w; w̃		y			

Vowels: <u>close</u> i   u   <u>open</u>   i   u

             e   o   ɛ   ɔ
               ə   a

Tones: high /´/; mid /¯/; low /`/; rising /ˇ/;
        falling /ˆ/

Length: /vv/; /cc/

Nasalization: / ĩ ɛ̃ ã ɔ̃ . . . w̃ ỹ . . ./

From a half-remembered conversation with Hans at a
time when he was working on his manuscript and from the
internal evidence of the manuscript itself, I am reasonably sure that he used the raised dot (/c·/) as an
indication of length where he heard it but was not sure
of its phonemic status; phonemic length he always marked
by doubling the consonant or vowel. For the rest, when
various definitions are included under other headings in
the glossary, reference is made to those headings in the
following manner: ABUSE   see INSULT. Some cross-
references have been added to those noted by Hans, but
they are not meant to be complete. I have noted only
those suggested by his definitions. Definitions, notes,
examples, and translations have been included where they
were available. Parts of speech are indicated after the
main heading only when there is a chance of confusion, as
in BARGAIN and BAT.

Following the main body of the vocabulary are three
separate sections. The first contains personal pronouns;
the second, numbers; and the third, ethnic groups.

I wish to thank Linda Dooley for her invaluable help
in preparing the manuscript. All of us who were Hans's
friends are indebted to her for the scholarly and devoted
attention she brought to the difficult chore.

Jack Berry

Northwestern University
June 1969

ETHNIC AND GEOGRAPHIC CLASSIFICATIONS

ABUA

    I. Central Abua: Abua (ə̀bú₉n); Okana (ɔ̀kàná; including Efebiri farm settlement in Odual); Ogbema (ògbèmə́)-Egbema (ègbèmə́)[close to Odual]; Otari (ɔ̀tàrʄ̩); Omokwa (ùmʉ́kʉ̀à); Odaga (ɔ̀dágà); Omenama (ʉ́mèlèmâ); Arukwo (ə̀rúkúò); Oghora (òɣòrə́); Omoraka (ɔ̀màrákà)[almost extinct]; Amaleghani (ɛmɛ́làɣán); also: ɔ̀málɛm and ɔ̀mâgbèlè [not on map]

    II. Okpéδèn: (south) Emoh (ɛmū); Iyaki (ɩ̩yàɣ); Ighom (ɩ̩ɣɔm); Eluku (èlóɣ); Egbolom (ègbòlòm); Ogbema-Koku (ògbémə́-kɔ̀ɔkʉ̩)

    III. Ɔɣózɔ̀: (southeast) Ɔɣózɔ̀ [not marked]; Ogonokom (ògònòkôm); Otaba (ɔ̀táβà); Ainyade (àɣ̃ʉ̩ádè); Digiriga (bʄrʄgìdì)

    IV. E̩mʉ́ɣān: (northwest) Okoba (ɔ̀kɔbɔ̂); Emebu (ɩ̩mábù); Obarayi (ɔ̀bàráɣ̃); Emesu (èmésù); Agunughan (ɛgʉ́nʉ̩́ɣān); Aminigboko (ɛmánágbɔ̀kɔ̀)

KUGBO

    Emago (ɛmàgó); Amoroto (àmʉ̩rʉ́tɔ̀); Amurukeni (àmʉ̩rʉ̩kɛnɩ̩); Akani (ɔɣán)

ODUAL

    Emelego (èmèlɛ́ɣó); Adada (ɔ́dà); Okolomade (ɔɣɔlɔmádì) [=ɔ̀mɔ̀rɔmá + ògbèmá]; Ekunuge (èɣúnúɣə̀); Ayun (áɣ̃ú); Amerikpoko (ɛmɛ́rɩ̩kpɔ̀kɔ̀); Olodo (òbŏlŏ); Obedum (obéδúm); Odao (ɔ̀dáɔ̀)[nameless on map]; Ogboloma (ògbólómə́)

KOLO (EO)

Otégùè [speak archaic Ogbia; no map reference];
Ibelebiri (ìbèlèbìrì) [speak archaic Nembe; right bank
of Kolo Creek]; Uruama (òrùmé)[speak archaic Nembe;
left bank of Kolo Creek]; Otuasiga (òtùəségə)[right
bank]; Imiringi (ìmìrìngí)[left bank]; Emeya (ɛmɛỹà)
[Opu, Kala-- two villages]; Elebele (ɛlɛbɛlɛ)[NW of
Emeya]; Kolo (əγòlò)[three villages]

OGBIA (WO)

Òpòmàtòbó [ɔpừmàtừbó](ɔpừmɛ) [SE of Oloibiri];
Àkípèlàị̣ {Akipelai} [S of preceding]; Abobiri (òtúə́bô
[Kolo Creek]; Oloibiri (òtélèy)[Kolo Creek]; Okpiniama
[òkpìñàmá](òtógìdì) [Kolo Creek, NE of Oloibiri];
Àbừlàbìrì (òtə́bùlə̀) [N of Oloibiri]; Akalabagi
[àkàlàɓàgí](òtâkàlàɓàgị̀) [S of following]; Ogidiama
[ògìdàmá](òtə́ə̀dú) [Kolo Creek; N of preceding]; Ewoi
(ɛwóị̣) [SW of following]; Òtúàká [SW of Emeya on Kolo
Creek]; Èlɛ́ɓèlɛ́ [NW of Emeya; see EO]
Otuokpot (òtúòkpòtì)[archaic Ogbia; Ekole Creek];
Otuogori (òtúôgòrì)[Ekole Creek]; Ikasikarama (òtúégùè)
[Ekole Creek]; Alagbafama (ònừéɓùm)[Ekole Creek];
Sangatama (àyákóró)[Ekole Creek]; Od̲obio (òl·ògì)
[Ekole Creek]; Egbedama (òtúédú)[Ekole Creek];
Anyama (àỹáma)(òtúkpésē)[Ekole Creek]
Ab̲ilab̲io (òtúɔ́ɓị̣y)[E of Ekole Creek]; Ologanga
(òlógóγɛ̀)[E of Ekole Creek, S of Abilabio]; Àmàδùgòàmá
(ɔ́kị̣kị̣)[E of Ekole Creek]; Ekpeinbiri (òtékpêỹ)[on
Ekole, W of preceding]; Òkód̲ógú (òkóδí)[W of Ekole];
Ogbomama (ògbòmàmá)[ɛ̀pɛ̀ɓừ] [on Ekole]; Agudama
(Ògòdàmá)[ɛ̀pɛ̀ɓừ] [on Ekole]

A Comparative Vocabulary
of Abuan Dialects

A

ABLE, BE (v)
    A: -rue/-tue   mî kə-túé-nī à pɛɛβ
                                   'I can fly'
    EO: -rue
    Ku: -rue
    Od: -rue/-tue
    WO: în·è (m-)

ABOVE   cf. FLY
    A: áñ̀ụ   also 'on top'
    EO: àgàñ́ụ
    Ku: ðáñ̀ụ
    Od: àñ̀ụ
          -ɛsìñɔ̀m
    WO: àgím̀ụ

ABUSE   see INSULT

ACCEPT   cf. TAKE
    A: aar/-bɔɔr

ACCOMPANY   cf. FOLLOW
    A: -daβ   also 'follow'
          -tụan

    EO: -βor
    Ku: -tμɔn˙ɔm   also 'follow'
    Od: -tμɔnɔm   also 'follow'

ACCUSE
    Ku: -ɓologiom

ADULTERY   cf. PROSTITUTION
    A: òlé ɛ̀mà
    EO: àrɨ̀gɨ̀   'relations without marriage'
           èbŭm   'adultery fee'
    Ku: òδ-ɛ̀mà   also 'prostitution'
    Od: òlè ɛ́má   also 'prostitution'
    WO: ɛ̀δɛ̂mà   'prostitution'
           àsɔ́à̀δìzà   'adultery' cf. WANT; WOMAN

ADVICE (n)
    A: ó-ròmə́   'moral, advice'

ADVISE, COUNSEL (v)
    A: -romə/-tomə   mí ú-rómə́ ñɔ̀dɨ́
                                     'I counselled him'
                                 mí rə̀-tómə́ 'I was advising'

AFRAID   see FEAR

AGAIN, DO; REPEAT
    A: -bɨlɛ   mí úbilɛ́ ə-βóóɣù
                                     'I breathed again'
                                 ɔ̀bɨ́lɛ́ ɔ̀sòβ 'to cut again'
                                 mí ú-bɨ̀lɛ́ à-gɛ́ δɨ́nà βɔ
                                     'I wrote the letter
                                     again'
    EO: -ti   ɛ̀nà tɛ́rú 'he came again'
                                 ɛ̀ná nɛ̀tí nɛ̀δé
                                     'he's eating again'

EO: ~-kə   ὲná nὲkέrú; ὲná nὲtέrú
                              'he's coming again'

Ku: -pətə   àm'ĭpὲtὲ ábĭɣ ĭnà
                              'I saw him again'

                             έpέtέ 'did again'

Od: -tulə~ -luə (oo-)   'do over and over again'

     -min   òdí nέὲmín ὲlé
                              'he ate again'

     -diɣ   ὲzóór dìɣ òlé
                              'we're eating again'

WO: -ɓaram   ὲn áɓārām nὲδé
                              'he's eating again

AGE GRADE   cf. CLUB

   A: ìgbò
   EO: àkíógbò
   Od: òkí   'age group'
   WO: ìtù

AGREE, REPLY, ANSWER (v)

   A: -meerə   also 'answer in affirmative'
        -meerəəm   'approve, believe, agree'
   Ku: -mərə
   Od: -mərə
        -məruom   'agree with'

AGREEMENT   see COVENANT

AIM (v)

   A: -tụɣ   also 'do same again'

ALIVE, BE (v)

   A: -rɔl/-tɔl éyὲ
   EO: -δum   ὲwùδúm 'life'
   Ku: -δìm òmòm   'seem fresh'
        -δim òn'ị̀

Od: -ɗum
WO: ə̀-ɗûm

ALL
A: ýɥ̀mɥ̀
EO: kààkà
Ku: éɓə̀láwǎ 'all of them'
  èɓə̀lə́
Od: óómə́ə́dí
WO: kàkàn àβár 'everything'
  kàkàn ɔ̀n'ị̀ 'all people'

ALLIGATOR
A: ìñàà
EO: ɔ̀ɓə́γ̀ə̀
Ku: óɓə̀γə́γ̀ə̀ also 'stupid man'
Od: ə̀síbírí
WO: ɛ̀wá; ˆzà

ALMOST, NEARLY
EO: ɛ̀kàkárə́síɔ̀

ALSO, TOO
A: kɛ̀n post position
 -aanị 'as well'
    kàkíáánị 'he'll go too'
    kə̀lěáánị 'he'll eat too'
EO: kpá àmị̀ kpá 'I also'
Od: ɛ̀ɛ̀kɔ́
WO: kpá

ALTHOUGH
Ku: èɓə̀lə́ --- èkə́è èɓə̀lə́ òlògìɗɔ́yɔ́ nə́gùrôm,
         èkə́è ịnà éβèlègə́mə̀ àmị̀
         'even though he was
         angry, he greeted me'

ALWAYS
- A: mém mēm mèm   'all the time' cf. TIME
- Ku: kèrékèré óβèl   'all the time, every time'
- Od: ómémên

ANCHOR (n)
- WO: è-lèmìàñ

AND
- A: rò
- kùó   'and then' clause conj.
- EO: nà   also 'with'
- Ku: sà ~ s'-   clause conj.
- n-   'áw̃à nàmì̀ 'you and I'
- sὲkénà   áw̃à sὲkénà àmì̀ 'you and I'
- Od: ná   also 'with'
- WO: nὲ

ANGER   cf. SHARP, HOT (AS PEPPER)
- EO: ὲ-gàm

ANGRY, BE (v)   cf. SHARP, HOT; PAIN, BE IN
- Ku: -gurom   òlògì δámí̀ nègùrôm
       'I'm angry'
- -gam   kógǎm 'don't be angry'
- -guromeni (tr.)   kógùròmèní mòlògì
       'don't be angry'
- WO: -gam   mí̀ nàgám 'I'm annoyed'
      òl˙óg' émìm nàgám
       'I'm angry, annoyed'

ANIMAL   cf. MEAT
- A: ὲnàm; ì̩-   B *-ama, -nama
- EO: ὲn˙àm
- Ku: ὲ-nàm; ì̩-

    Od: ɛ̀-nàm; ɨ̀-
    WO: ɛn·àm; ˆzà

ANNOUNCE
    A: -gbeel   ògbèèlòm ìgbèèl
                                    'town crier, announcer'

ANOTHER
    A: ɔ̄nòn   ɛ́-nòn ésì 'another place'
    EO: òpónə̀
    Ku: ódì
           ~òpə̀n
    Od: ɔ̀nɔ̌n
    WO: ə̀kèré

ANSWER (n)
    Ku: áwɔ̀rǎn
    Od: ɔ̀βàɣàrànà
    WO: ì-δùmòm

ANSWER (v)   cf. AGREE; BELIEVE
    A: -βaɣaranaan/-p---   B *-ɣata-va
           -meɣeron   'answer from distance, echo'
    EO: -δumom   also 'believe'
    Ku: -wɔran
    Od: -βaɣarana/-p
    WO: ə̀-δúmòm   also 'believe'

ANT
    A: ɛ̀-ráɣádá   'large ant'
          ɛ̀-márà   'small ant'
           ìɣéélèèñ   'driver ant'
    EO: ɛ̀βɨ̀
          ò-tùδôm; ì-   'driver ant'
          ɛ̀-rárà   'sugar ant'

Ku: ɛ́ɛβ}; r-
      ò-tùɣùδíòm; ì-   'driver ant'
      ɛdàɣàdàɣ   'black ant'

Od: ɛ̀ɛ̀-β}; }}-
      è-δùùl; }-   'driver ant'
      }-màlàmàl   'sugar ant'

WO: ɛβ}; 'zà
      ìwùlùwúlù   'driver ant'
      àgóñ

ANTELOPE

A: ò-nừɛ̀n; (à)rừ-   'large antelope with white
                          stripe along belly'

EO: ṑròró; ɛ̀

Ku: ɛ̀gbósó; r-

Od: ò-nự̀ɛ̀; }- ~(à)rừ-

WO: ò-ròrô; ɛ̀-

ANTIDOTE

Ku: ò-sá}   also name of a long green
                        non-poisonous snake

ANUS

A: èpóɣ èn}ừm   'hole of buttocks' cf. HOLE

EO: òñ-òmàt}̂n

Ku: ɛ̀ñóɣừma

Od: }̣pòɣ éètù; èpòɣ-; àrà-

WO: òn}òmààt}
      ~ìgírì   (Nembe)

ANYMORE, ANY LONGER (neg.)

A: mừn   mị́ kə́lè mừ́n
                  'I won't eat anymore'
                ɛ̀lɛ́l ị́lô mừ́n
                  'there's no yam anymore'
                òdị́ rə́tù mừ́n   'he's not
                  coming anymore'

Ku: -mú   kólèɣèmú
                                   'don't cry anymore'
                           ìná nòδémŭ
                                     'he's not eating anymore'
                           àm̄ ìgírmŭ   'I'm not
                                     working anymore'

ARISE   see GET UP

ARMPIT
     A: ɔ-páàβ; (à)rá-
     EO: ədè òβágwò
     Od: ì-βàɣàpàáɣ; àrὺ-
     WO: ɔdɛ́ ɔ́βàgwò

ARRIVAL
     A: èsíòm   èsíòm ɔdì̠   'his arrival'
     WO: érū   cf. COME

ARRIVE, REACH A PLACE   cf. REACH
     A: -si   mísì íímì   'it's my turn'
                        mésì ñɔdí̠   'it's his turn'
                        ísí íímì   'it was my turn'
                        íímì kéèsí   'it's not
                                 my turn'

ARROW
     A: ὲ-kpí̠nà; ì̠-
     EO: ὲw̃ɔ̀w̃ɔ̀
     Ku: èkpó ágὺmὺ̠; r-
     Od: ɔ̀ɔ̀-ná; ì̠ì̠-

AS --- AS
     A: dí --- dí   dí ὲkpàr dí ədíɣíìɣ
                            'as hard as a rock'

AS

    A: ídìβɔ̄   δíɣí ídìβɔ̄ mí̱ á-ɓéní̱ bɔ̀ ñínè̀
                                   'do as I told you'

ASH

    A: ɔ̀ɔ̀-rṳ̀; (à)rṳ̀ṳ̀- ??   B *-ɣî̱v̱û, -î̱v̱û
    EO: è ɓú̱rṳ́   pl.
    Ku: ì̱rṳ̀rṳ̀   pl.
    Od: ɔ̀ɔ̀-rṳ̀; ì̱ì̱- ~(à)rṳ̀ṳ̀-
    WO: é ɓú̱rṳ̀   pl.

ASK   **cf.** QUESTION

    A: -puru   B *-pula
    EO: -puru
          -ɓan   'beg, ask for'
    Ku: -purən   'question'
    Od: -puruən
          -gbeel   'ask for'

ASSEMBLY   see MEETING

ATTACH

    A: -zɔla; -jɔla
          -zɔlɔɣi̱an; -j--   'attach several things'

ATTEMPT   see TRY

AWAKE, BE (v)

    Ku: -rṳmṳm   àmì̱ óδì mṳ̀mṳ̀m 'I'm awake'

AXE

    A: (ə̀)-kùbù; (ə̀)sì-kùbù B *-ḵoka, -v̱aɣo
    EO: è sṳ́á   **cf.** HOE
        ~è dɔ̀

Ku: ù̀dò; r-
Od: ə̀-kùbù; (ə̀)sù-
WO: ò-gə̀mê; ì-gə̀mê

B

BABY   cf. CHILD

    A: ɔ̀bɔ́m-ɔ̀ñ

    Ku: ɔ̀-gbàrɔ́ñı̥̀; ı̥̀gbàráw̃îy

    Od: ɔ̀-bàm ɔ̂ñ; ì-bàm áŋɔ̂ñ also 'child'

BABY-TIE

    A: ò-ɣùδúm   ò-ɣùδúm àmì 'my baby-tie'

BACK (n)

    A: ɔ̀-màn; (à)rà-

    EO: àmàn

    Ku: àmàn

    Od: àmàn; àr-

    WO: àmàn; 'zà

BAD   cf. UGLY

    A: -karaβ

          -beeβ   'bad-tasting'

    EO: ɔ̀-kàràβ

    Ku: -karaβ   ɔ̀kàràβɔ́nı̥̀ 'bad man'

                       ɔ̀nı̥̀β égùrôm 'man was bad'

    Od: -karaβ

          ~-βeeβ   ɔ̀lòɣì àmı́ néβèéβ
                         'I'm angry'

                       ɔ̀lòɣì àmı́ téβèéβìní
                         'I'll be angry'

          -pɥɛ   'to make bad'

          ı̥̀kàràβ   'badness, ugliness'

          ~ə̀βèéβ   'badness, ugliness'

    WO: ɔ̀kàràβ; ɛ-

BAG

    A: ɔ̀kùrù   B *-kutu

    EO: àkpà

Ku: ὲkpà
Od: ὲ-ɓà; (à)rὺ-
WO: àkpà

BALE OUT
A: -mooβ
EO: -moβ
Ku: -moβ
Od: -mooβ
WO: ôβù(m-)
     ὲkpóβùέ   'baling dish, plate'

BAMBOO
A: àgàràbà
EO: àlὺgà
Ku: ókpòkò   also 'elephant grass'
Od: òδùm   'bamboo for thatching'
     àlὺgwà; ìgwa   'bamboo pole'
WO: àlὺgà

BANANA
A: ókὺ ñâm   'banana plant'
     (ә)δì-δííl; ì-δííl   'banana fruit'
EO: òsókpó
Ku: úlὲ; r-
Od: ịsákpÿ; (à)r-
WO: ɔ-ɓààmị; ὲ-

BANK (n)
Ku: әgbó   'steep bank'

BARBER (n)
WO: ɔkpàβàm ὲmú   cf. CUT HAIR

BARGAIN (v)

    A: -mereniən

        ~-mereñən

        -muul   'trade in market, buy & sell'

    EO: -mul

        -mulən   'bargain mutually'

    Ku: -mu·lən   'bargain, make counter-
                             offer'

        -mu·l   'name first price, set
                             price'

        -βin   'make counter-offer'

    Od: -muul   'indicate asking price'

        -muulən

        -mərə   'make counter-offer'

    WO: (m)íìl·ù

BARK (n)   cf. SKIN

    A: òjû(òzû)òrèñ

    EO: òβóβò   'skin'

        òβóβórérén

    Ku: ò-βóβó órérén; ì-

    Od: òó-βō; ìí-

    WO: òβóβòrèn

BARRACUDA

    A: òlól

BASKET

    A: è-gúnùm; (ə̀)rú-   B *-γono 'wicker basket for
                                    catching fish'

    EO: èkpóm

    Od: ò-kpààγ; (à)rù̀-

    WO: è-kpôm; Λzə̀

BAT (n)

A:	ɔ̀-gbɔ́m; (à)rɔ̀-	'large bat'
	(à)-táàkpà; (à)sɪ́-	'small bat'
EO:	ɔ̀-gbɔ̌w̃; ɛ̀-	'large bat'
	ópóβɛ̀; ɪ́-	
Ku:	ɔ̀gbɔ́m; r-	
Od:	ɔ̀-gbɔ̌m; ɪ̀-	
WO:	ɔ̀gbɔ́w̃; ɛ̀-	'large bat'
	əpòⁿgì; əpóⁿgízə̀	

BE

A: ó-dì; é-dì

     B *-li

     ìkpókɪ́ édìnɪ́
       'there is money'

     òyê ódìnɪ́ sɪ́ɛ̀n
       'there's someone here'

     mɪ́ ódìnɪ̄ sɪ̄ɛ̀n   'I'm here'

     ó-dìɣáànɪ̄   'was living'

     é-dìɣèn   'it usually is'

     -lo

     negative

     ìkpókɪ́ ɪ́lô
       'there's no money'

     òyê sɪ́ɛ̀n òlô
       'there's no one here'

     mɪ́ sɪ́ɛ̀n ùlô   'I'm not here'

     ɛ̀lɛ́l ɪ́lô   'there is no yam'

     mɪ́ ù-lô   'I was absent'

EO: -loβə

     -lo

     ɛ̀nà kòló kə́rèsì
       'where is he?'

Ku: ó-ɗì

     àmʉ̀m óɗì   'there is water'

     ə̃w̃únòm óɗì
       'there are people'

     ìkpòkì óɗì ǎ
       'is there money?'

     bɔ́

     negative

     ìkpòkɪ́ bɔ̌   'there's no money'

Od: -di   ɛ̀lɛ̀l ódī   'there's yam'
                                     ɨ̀lɛ̀l ídī   'there are yam'
                                     òdɨ́ ódì súō   'he's here'
                                     àmɨ́ ódì súō   'I'm here'
       -lo   negative
                                     ɛ̀lɛ̀l òló   'there's no yam'
                                     ə̀rə́ì ìló   'there are no
                                         people'
WO: -lə   ó-lə (sg.)   ɛ̀n' ólə̄ 'sānà   'he's here'
              í-lə (pl.)   àwʼ ílə̄ 'sānà   'they're here'
       -ba; ó-bā   negative
                                     àw'óʙ ɛ̄sānà   'they're not
                                         here'
                                     ɛ̀n' óʙ' ɛ̄sānà   'he's not here'

BE IN PLACE   see REMAIN

BE PRESENT   cf. REMAIN
    A: -rólááni̯ ésì/-t---
    Od: -rɔlaani̯/-t--
    WO: à-rô

BEAD (n)
    A: èkótā
          ɛ̀-là   'bead, title'
    WO: ɛ̀l·à   plural

BEAN
    A: ɛ̀lɛ́lɛ̀
          ~ ɛ̀kɨ́δɨ̀
    WO: àgwà

BEARD (n)
    A: ɔ̀-lɛ́ɛ̀m; (à)rɛ́-   B *-lelû
    EO: às̤àl ɛ̀ɓɛ́ɓɛ̀ñ
          ~ ɛ̀wɛ̀l

Ku: ìlíɔ̀m
Od: ìlɛ́ɛ̄m   plural
WO: ɛ̀wɛ̀l; -́zà

BEAT   see HIT

BEAT DRUM (v)
A: -ti
EO: -ti
Ku: -ti
Od: -ti
WO: ə̀-tîm
     ò-tìmòm òzè   'drummer'

BEAUTIFUL   cf. GOOD
A: ímà ɔ̀ñànì̩   'beautiful girl'
     ání̩γέ ɛní̩γέ dí   'attained incomparable
                                 beauty'

     ásɛ̀lɛ̀   'pretty' personal name
EO: -nì̩ɛ
     -ni̩ɛmɛn   'make beautiful'
Ku: -ßonomeni   'make beautiful'
WO: ɔ̀ßàì̩

BEAUTY   cf. GOODNESS
EO: ɛ̀-nì̩έ
Ku: ə̀lìßŏn
Od: ɛ̀-nɛ̀γέ   personal name, fem.

BECAUSE
A: lórésìdí
EO: -di   'to do because'
                              m' ídì mə́ kúmə́rū 'I came
                                 because of you'

                              ɛ̀n' ə̀dì ə́m kə̀rú 'he came
                                 because of me'

Ku: èzìnβɔ́   conjunction
   -tʉn   'to do because'
       àm̂ ɪ́tʉ̀n áw̃à ə̀rú 'I came
        because of you'
Od: -tʉan   'to do because, for sake of'
       àm̂ ʉ́tʉ̀án zánà ə̀rǔ ▪I came
        because of you'

BECOME
 A: -teneɣiən cf. PASS
   -ten   short form

BECOME BIG
 WO: ə̀-bô

BED (n)   cf. LIE DOWN
 A: èmɪ́nà; (à)rɪ́- B *-lili
 EO: àgbàdà
 Ku: èmánà
 Od: ɛ̀-mʉ̀ná; (à)rʉ̀-
 WO: àgbàdà ~ àbɛ́dɪ̀

BEDBUG
 A: èè-bìɣɪ́; ìì-
 EO: ɛ̀kpɪ̀rɪ̀
 Od: ɪ̀-záɣ

BEDROOM   cf. ROOM
 EO: ìgúlə̀   'room'
 Ku: ɛ̀βàɪ̀
 WO: ígùlə́   'room'

BEE
 A: (ə̀)ɗɪ́-òwò; (ə̀)sɪ́- B *-ɣuki, -nuki ~-nukî
 EO: àgámà

Ku: ɔ́βµn̥ýn̥ýn; ɟ́-
Od: ɔ̀pɔ̀ɣɔ̀lmììm; ɪ̀-   cf. DRINK; WINE
WO: àgámà; 'zà

BEEHIVE
    Od: əδəβə

BEG   cf. ASK
    A: -lɔm   also 'borrow without obli-
                           gation of repayment'

    EO: -ban
         -lɛɪ̀   'beg forgiveness'
    Ku: -siseñ   cf. PLEASE!
         -lɛɣ   'beg, ask for'
    Od: -gbeel
    WO: à-lɛ́ɪ̀   'beg forgiveness'
         ɛ̀-lɛ̀yâ   'begging forgiveness' (n)

BEGET   see GIVE BIRTH

BEGIN, START
    A: -gbi
         -miiɣ
    EO: -kɛ   'begin to do'
    Ku: -ɓeton
         -kɛ   'begin to do'
    Od: -kɛ
         -gbi
    WO: -kɛ ~-ka   ɛn ák̄ɛ nɜ̀δé 'he began
                              to eat'

BEGINNING (n)
    Od: ɛ̀-kɪ̀á
         è-gbɪ̀ôm

BEHIND   cf. BACK
    A: ɔ́màn
    EO: àmàn
    Ku: ծámàn
    Od: ààmàn
    WO: àmàn

BELIEVE   cf. AGREE, REPLY
    A: -meeraam   also 'agree'
    EO: -ծumom   also 'agree, answer'
    Ku: -mərə
    Od: -məruom   also 'agree'
    WO: ə̀-ծúmòm   also 'answer'
         ì-ծúmómól·ògì   'faith, belief'

BELL
    A: ɛ̀dɛ̀nɛ̀nɛ́ñ
    EO: ìgbɔ́mə́
    Ku: ìgbɔ́mə́
    Od: ò-ɣònògó
         ò-kélé   'gong'
    WO: ìgbɔ́mə́

BELLOWS
    Od: í-kō

BELLY
    EO: èw̃ùn
    Ku: òkūròɣ
    Od: ò-bàràkà; àrʉ̀-   cf. STOMACH; WOMB
    WO: è-w̃ùnù; ì-

BERRY (n)
    A: óólō   'dark red berry'

BESIDE
    EO: ɔɓàm
    WO: əkpókpôm

BETWEEN
    A: ògbò
    EO: ògbò
    Ku: δésə̀δìó
    Od: èsòδìó
    WO: ògbò

BIG
    A: ògbóγ   n.
        íbòòm   'big, large'
    EO: ògbṵ̀; ɛ̀-   ògbṵ̀ ón·ì̱   'big man'
                      ɛ̀gbṵ̀ éw̃únòm   'big men'
    Ku: ò-bṵ̀òm; ì-   n. òbṵ̀òm ótṵ̀ 'big house'
                      òtṵ̀ßɔ́ òbṵ̀òm 'the house
                          is big'
    Od: ògbóγ   èvèl òßɔ́ ògbóγ 'the goat
                          is big'
                      èvèl òßɔ́ ɔ́kàñà 'the goat
                          is big'
    WO: ṵ̀bɛ̀ŋì̱   modif. ṵ̀bɛ́ŋ ònì̱ 'big man'

BIG, LARGE, FAT, BE (v)
    A: ɔ̀-bṵ̀γ   B *-kulu, -nene
        -bṵγɛ   'make big, fatten'
        -ßṵγan; -pṵγan 'to be in excess, too much'
                     ɛ́-pṵ̄γān 'it's too much'
                     əwêßɔ̄ ɔ́pṵ̄γān 'people are
                          too many'
        -deγeγe   'to grow big' humorous
    EO: -gen   òn·ì̱ ßà əgén 'the man
                          is big'
                    əw̃únòm ßə̀ wə̀gén 'the men
                          are big'

Ku: -bṳɣ

Od: -bṳɣ   èvèl òβó àbṳ̆ɣ 'the goat
was big'

èvèl òβò ṳ̀bṳ̆ɣ [ṳ̀gbǒɣ] 'the goat is big'

èvèl òβ'ókàñà 'the goat is big'

ób'évél 'big goat, foolish man'

ògbòɣ ɛ́nâm 'big animal'

WO: -bo   m'èbó ólè̩ 'I'm big'

òvíè̩ é̩bō ōlè̩ 'the cow is big'

ìvízè̩ wé̩bō ĪIè̩ 'the cows are big'

BIGNESS

A: (à)ẟị́-bṳ̀ɣ

EO: ə̀lì-gèn

Od: àlị̀-bṳ̂ɣ

WO: ìbò̩ ~ə̀ẟí-bò̩

BIRD

A: ɛ̀-nṳ́n; ị̀-   B *-ɣunî, -unî, -nunî

EO: ɛ̀nṳ̀r(éẟúm)

Ku: ɛ̀-nṳ́r(éẟúm); ị̀-

Od: ɛ̀-nṳ̆n; ị̀-

WO: ɛ̀n·ụ́rụ́; 'zà

      ~ɛ̀n·ụ́réẟùm

BIRTH

A: (à)ẟị́-màr   cf. FAMILY

      ~ɛ̀-màràñán

Od: ɛ̀-márá

WO: ɛ̀-màrànà

BISCUIT

    A: àkíkí̠á

    EO: ɛ̀k̠ìk̠ì̠à

    Ku: íkíkí̠à

    Od: ík̠ìká

    WO: ɛ̀k̠ìk̠ì̠à

BITE (v)

    A: -lom   B *-luma

    EO: -n·om

    Ku: -ɓoβ

    Od: -nom

           ɘlì-nôm   'act of biting'

    WO: ɘ̀-ɓðβ

           ɘ̀-ɓóβlɘ̀n   [insect]

BITTER

    A: -kiðim   v.   B *-lula, -ya̲va̲

    Ku: ɔ̀ɣèðùmɣéðùm

BITTERLEAF

    A: úk̠ì̠ɔ̀

    EO: ɔ̀lúgbɔ̀   cf. SOAP

          ~ àðírì̠ɔ̀só

          ɘ̀ðíré-ɔ̀só

    Ku: ósɔ̀ tôðù kàbù̠   named after man who intro-
                                 duced it to Kugbo
                                 cf. SOAP

    Od: úk̠ì̠à; àrú̠-

    WO: ɘðíríósɛ́   cf. SOAP

BITTERNESS

    EO: è-ɣèðèm

BLACK

   A: -wil/-bil   v. 'to be black' B *-îlu

                               ògâɓó ɛ́-bìl lí
                                   'goat is black'

                               ògâɓó ɛ́-wíl lī
                                   'goat was black'

                               cf. Nembe bìlé, bìló (v.t.)
                                   'to color, stain, tinge'

           òɗììl   'blackness'

   EO: òzṳzṳ̀à   'blackness'

          -zṳ   'be, become black'

   Ku: òzṳ̀zṳ́á

   Od: -ɓil   èvèl òɓó ə̀ɓĭl
                               'the goat was black'

                               èvèl òɓó òɓìlè
                               'the goat is black'

                             òɓìlí évèl 'black goat'

   WO: ò-zṳ̀zṳ́; ɛ̀   modif.

          -zṳ   v. 'be black'

                               m'àzṹ ólə̀ 'I'm black'

          ɛ́-zṳ̄   'blackness'

BLACKEN

   A: -wile/-bile

   EO: -zṳɛmɛn   v.t.

   Od: -ɓile(mi)

   WO: -zṳɔman   v.t.

BLACKSMITH

   A: òl·ɛ̀mòmòl·ɛ̀m

          ól·ɛ̀mòmòl·ɛ̀m   voc.

   EO: òlɛ̀mmòlɛ̀m   cf. CREATOR

   Ku: òn·ị̀ ólɛ̌m

          ~òlɛ̀mólɛ̌m

          ~òlɛ̀mǎ

    Od: ɔ̀-l·ɛ̀má; ̱ɪ̀-
    WO: ɔ́n·ɪ̱̀ ɔ̀n·ɛ̀m

BLADDER
    EO: ɔ̀tù-ə́mínɔ̀m
    Ku: ɔ̀ɓɔ̀m ə́mínɔ̀m
    Od: ɔ̀tù ə̀mónɔ̀m   cf. URINE

BLESS, THANK
    A: -sɛβ   ú-sɛ̀βìlmì 'thank, bless me'
                         mɪ̱́ ú-sɛ́βñɔ̀dɪ̱́
                            'I thanked him'

        -su ógèñ ɔ̀nṵ̀   'to bless'
        (à)ɗɪ̱́-sɛβ   n. 'blessing' personal name

BLINDNESS
    A: ɛ̀mɪ̱́ìn ètèn

BLOOD
    A: ɪ̱̀-ɓààl   *-lopa, -γalî
    EO: àzàrà
    Ku: á·sɪ̱̀
    Od: ɪ̱̀ɓààl
          ~àzàrà
    WO: àsɪ̱̀ (A)
          ìgwóɓù (O)

BLOOD-BOND   see COVENANT

BLOW (v)
    A: -βulə/-pulə   B *-pûla, -pepa, -puṅga
                        'blow with mouth'
        -γuγ/-kuγ   'blow as wind'
    EO: -pue   'with mouth'
        -ku·   'as wind'

Ku: -puɣe   'as wind' or 'with mouth'
Od: -pulo   'with mouth'
     ɔ-βi̥β/-pi̥β   'as wind'
WO: ðβùlò (m-)   'with mouth'

BLUNT

A: ə́βùlə̀   B *-tûpa
EO: -ɓulom   v.i.
     -ɓulemen   v.t. 'make blunt'
     ò-ɓùlòmɓùlóm   modif. as in 'blunt knife'
Ku: -ɓulomeni   v.t. 'to blunt'
     òɓùlòmɓúlòm   modif.
     èɓùlòm   n. 'bluntness'
WO: -ɓólòm   v.i. 'be, become blunt'
     -ɓolomən   v.t. 'make blunt'
     ò-ɓòlòmɓólòm; ì-   modif.
     ì-ɓòlóm   n. 'bluntness'

BOARD BOAT, TO (v)   cf. ENTER
A: - δiɣ óɣúùɣ
EO: -δi   'enter'
Ku: -δiɣ
Od: -δìɣ òɣúùɣ
WO: ə̀-δî òwù

BOAT

A: ò-ɣùùɣ; (ə̀)rù-   also 'canoe'
                             B *-ombo, -ato, -ɣato
EO: òwù
Ku: ò-ɣùɣ; ə̀rù-
Od: ò-ɣùùɣ; (ə̀)rù-
WO: òwù

BODY

A: (ə̀)-lòòr; (ə̀)sì-   B *-mîmba, -utu, -vili

    EO: əlùzú
    Ku: ózù; r-   cf. SKIN
    Od: ə-lòòr; ərə̀-
    WO: òɓú; ì-   cf. SKIN

BOIL (n)

    A: òfúkū
    EO: èɓòɓólə̀
    Ku: èɓòɓə́lə́
    Od: ɔ̀-zừγừ
    WO: òtòñ

BOIL, COOK (v.t.)

    A: -sa
             -saaγi   á-sááγì áá 'cook big
                               quantity and ate' [sic]
    EO: -sa   'cook'
             -suemen   'warm up'
    Ku: -sa
    Od: -sa   ị̀sáán éɓíə̀n 'cooked food'
    WO: à-kásị̀
             ɛ̀-kásànà   'something boiled'

BOIL (v.i.)

    A: -βul/-pul   also 'cook'
                              B *-pupuma, -pûla
    EO: -βul   'be boiling'
    Ku: -βul
    Od: -βul/-pul
    WO: ə̀-βúlù

BONE

    A: òɔ̀-kpɔ̀; (à)rɔ̀ɔ̀-   B *-kûpa
    EO: ɔ̀kpɔ̀lɔ́kpɔ̀
    Ku: ɔ́-kpɔ́kpɔ̀; ị́-

Od: ɔ̀ɔ̀-kpɔ̀;]̀]̀-
WO: ìgbɛ́; ^zɚ̀

BOOK (n)
A: (à)ðíñá   cf. LEAF
EO: ɚ̀ðírí ~ àdíàn
Ku: ɚ̀ðìrè
Od: ɔ̀-βrɛ̀ɛ̀r
WO: ɚ̀ðírí

BORROW, LEND
A: aalɛ/-bɔɔlɛ   B *-ɣalîma
                                mí kàbɔ́ɔ́lɛ́ íkpɔ̀kì
                                    'I'll borrow money'
                                mí kàbɔ́ɔ́lɛ́ ñɔ̀dí íkpɔ̀kì
                                    'I'll borrow/lend him
                                    money'
                                mí kàbɔ́ɔ́lɛ́ íkpɔ̀kì ðíɣááɣ ɔ̀dì
                                    'I'll borrow money from
                                    him'
                                mí u̯à"àlɛ́ ñɔ̀dí ðíná
                                    'I lent him a book'
                                mí ràbɔ́ɔ́lɛ́ ñɔ̀dí ðíná
                                    'I'm lending him a book'
                                    'I'm borrowing a book
                                    from him'
Ku: -wɔlɔnì   'borrow'
     -wɔlɔnìan   'lend'
Od: -ɓɔɔlì   'borrow'
     -ɓɔɔlìan   'lend'

BOTTLE (n)
A: ɛ̀ɛ̀kù
     (à)-kárámá; (à)sí-
          (àmì)   'glass bottle'
EO: ɔ̀lɔ̀lɔ̀
Ku: ìkárámá

    Od: à-kárámà
    WO: òlòlò

BOTTOM
    A: ɛ́nɪ̰̀ṳm   cf. BUTTOCK
    EO: ə̀dè
    Ku: èkpúkù
    Od: ə̀dè   'bottom, ground'
         ə̀zìn   'bottom'
    WO: ɔ̀dɛ̰̀

BOUNCE, THROW UP AND DOWN
    WO: -teɓele   cf. CONVERSE

BOUNDARY
    Ku: ɔ̀-gbàkɪ́

BOW (n)
    A: (à)-kṵ̀mṵ̀ɣ; (à)sɪ̰̀-
    EO: àgbànɪ̰̀à
    Ku: àgṵ̀mṵ̀; r-
    Od: à-ɣṵ̀nṵ́; (à)sṵ̀-
    WO: àgbànà; -̰zà

BOW [OF BOAT] (n)
    A: ɛ̀sɔ́β óɣúùɣ   cf. TAIL
    EO: ɔ̀sɔ̀β òwú
    Ku: ɔ̀sɔ̀β óɣùɣ
    Od: ɛ̀-sɔ̀β
    WO: ɔ̀sɔ̀βówù

BOX (n)
    A: ígbē
    EO: ìɓékù

```
Ku:  ìgbǎ
Od:  è-ɓìnə̀; (ə̀)rì-
WO:  ígbèkú
```

BOX (v)   cf. HIT

```
A:   -gi̱ß
EO:  -kuloɣən
     òɓólə́                      'boxing'
Od:  -kpɔl
     -kpɔlɔɣan                  'box one another'
WO:  àyi̱ß-òɓòlò
```

BOY

```
EO:  ò̃(òlóɓírì);               cf. MALE
     àw̃i̱y ìlóɓírì
```

BRAIN

```
A:   é-pùl; (ə́)rú-             B *-vo̠ńgo
EO:  èßùl                       pl.
Ku:  èßùl ɛmú
Od:  i̱lɛ̀lɛ̀mú                   pl.  cf. YAM
WO:  òkpótó
```

BRANCH (n)

```
A:   ò-kâl; (à)si̱-
EO:  ɛ̀ɣ(à)òrérén
Ku:  òɣà òrérén; ì-
Od:  òò-ɣà; i̱i̱-
WO:  ɛ̀ɣórèn [<ɛ̀ɣá]
```

BREADFRUIT

```
A:   ɛ̀-l·él·ɛ̀
```

BREAK (v)

A:	-wun/-bun	v.t.	'break something long'
	-ɓom	v.t.	-ɓomǝǝn 'smash, shatter'
	-ɓiɣ	v.t.	'break small piece off'
	-ɓomoɣiǝn	v.t.	'break into pieces'
	-wunaan/-bunaan	v.i.	'break something long, e.g. stick'
	-ɓomaan	v.i.	'shatter, such as eggs, pots'
EO:	-w̃in	v.t.	
	-w̃inǝ	v.i.	also 'snap'
Ku:	-w̃in	v.t.	'snap'
	-ɓom	v.t.	'shatter, crack'
	-w̃iniǝn	v.i.	also 'snap'
	-ɓomǝn	v.i.	'shatter'
Od:	-ɓun	v.t.	'break, as stick'
	-ɓomǝǝn	v.i.	
WO:	ə̀-w̃ínì	v.t.	'break, as wood'
	ə̀-ŋôm	v.t.	'break, as pot'

BREAST   cf. MILK

    A: (à)-mámām; (à)rá-

    EO: àmàmǎm

    Ku: àmàmám

    Od: àmàám; àr-

    WO: àmámám; 'zà

BREATH (n)

    A: (ə̀)ðí-ɓóɣù; (ə̀)sí-   B *-aɣa, -ɣaɣa

    EO: èfə̀fə́

    Ku: ìpóɣù

    Od: ìpòòɣù

    WO: ɛ̀bà

BREATHE (v)
    A: -ßooɣu/-pooɣu
    EO: -fə
    Ku: -ßoɣu̱
    Od: -ßooɣu/-pooɣu
    WO: ôßə̀(m-)

BRIDE-PRICE
    Ku: è-ròɣ   ògùnán·ị̀ 'big marriage feast'

BRIDGE (n)
    A: (à)-ɓágá; (à)sị́-
    EO: ògbònògì
    Ku: àwáfụ̀
    Od: ɔ́ɔ́-dà; (à)ràá-
    WO: àwáfụ̀   cf. English 'wharf'

BRING   cf. TAKE; COME
    A: -siɣε...-ru
          -miteɣom   'come out with..., bring out'
    EO: -ßin...-ru
    Ku: -ßin...-ru
    Od: -ßin...-ru   'take...come'
    WO: ə̀-ßí ə̀-rù   'take come'

BROOM
    A: ɔ̀zànị̀
    EO: ɔ̀ßị́ßị̄
    Ku: àzị̀ɣàzị̀ɣà
          ɔ̀ßị́ßị̀   'short broom'
    Od: ɔ́ßị̄ñ; (à)rị́- ;
            ɔ́-ßīñ
         à-zàràzàrà   'broom made from palm'
         ò-ɓéròm   'anything used in sweeping'

WO: òwòlòmòtù   cf. SWEEP
~ ɛ̀sɛ́kílàm̀

BUILD
A: -lɔɣ   B *-ɣaka, -ɣeṅga, -tuṅga
-ja~za
EO: -gim   cf. PIN; PIERCE; STAB
Ku: -lo
Od: -ɓoɣ
WO: è-gîm   also 'pin, pierce'
ò-gìmòm òtù   'builder of houses'

BULLET
A: èkpó áláágbà   cf. GUN
EO: è-kpâvà; ì-
Ku: èkpò ávà
Od: èkpàlàágbà
WO: èkpáàvà

BULL FROG
Ku: ùgbógù̀

BUNDLE (n)
A: òkól
EO: òkŏn
Ku: òkŏn
Od: ò-kŏn
WO: òɣòrògì̀

BURIAL   cf. BURY
Ku: èmèδ̀ì
Od: èmèδí

BURN (v)

A: -le   v.i. òtú βɔ̄ rè̩lé
                                    'the house is burning'

      -mor (oo-)   v.i.

      -sṳ...ánî̩àn   v.t.

EO: -n·ṳ   v.i.

      -n·ṳɛmɛn   v.t.

Ku: -n·ṳ   v.i.

      -βṳgi̩   v.t.

      -βṳgi̩ɔm   v.t. 'to burn...with'

Od: -lì (àni̩ân)   v.i.

      -nṳ   v.i. 'to burn small item'

      -sṳ (àni̩ân)   v.t. ɔ̀δìòβó náásṳ̀
                                    'the day is hot'

                                    í̩sṳ̀ ámṳ̩ṳ̀m 'hot water'

      -sṳɛmi̩ (ɔɔ-)   v.t. 'to heat liquids or
                                     food in pot'

WO: à-yɔ̂   v.i.

      à-yɔ́màn   v.t.

BURY

A: -δi   B *-k̲ila ɛ́δí̩ə̀ lóór á·mì̩
                                    'bury myself'

EO: -δiˠ

      ∼δiʔ

Ku: -δi

Od: -δi

WO: ə̀-δî

BUSH, FOREST

A: è-δúm

      ɛ̀-kpṳ́à; (à)rṳ̀-   'deep, never cultivated'

EO: èδùm   'bush'

      ɔ̀gbá   'high forest'

    Ku: è-ðúm

        ɛɣàná

    Od: è-ðǔm; (ə̀)rù-

    WO: èðúm

BUSH COW

    EO: èrìmə̀

    Ku: èrúmə̀

    Od: ə̀-mùzí; (ə̀)sù-

    WO: òkpókóró; ì-...(zə̀)

BUSH PIG

    A: (ə̀)-mújí

    EO: òɓùtòn·ụ̀

    Ku: ègbə́rə́wèl

    Od: ə̀-mùzí; (ə̀)sù-

    WO: óɓútòn·ụ̀

BUT (conj.)

    Ku: yə́ə̀

BUTCHER (n)

    Od: òzèmị̀nàm   cf. KILL; ANIMAL

BUTCHER (v)

    A: -kañan

    EO: -ɣɔzɔn

    Ku: -kañɔɣ

    Od: -kañɔɣ

    WO: ôkòsòn (m-)

BUTTERFLY

    A: òɓìlíɓə̀

    EO: òɓòríɓò

Ku: óɓòríɓò
Od: àmɛ̀mɛ́ɓ
WO: òɓòríɓò

BUTTOCK
    A: ɛ́-nḭ̀ṳ̀m; (à)rḭ́-   cf. BOTTOM
    EO: ìkpókí   pl.
    Ku: èsìn
    Od: àmàn éētū
         èètù
    WO: ìkpókí   pl.

BUTTON (n)
    A: èzùòm
    EO: òzù ə̀rúə́
    Ku: òzìɓ
    Od: ò-zìm
    WO: òzúə́rùə̀   'nut/shell of shirt'

BUY
    A: -ko/-γo   B *-γula
        -soɓ   'buy liquid (wine, oil, salt,
                            kerosene) in limited
                            quantities'
        -l·ol   'buy oil'
    EO: -γo
    Ku: -γo
    Od: -γo/-ko
    WO: ə̀-γô

BUYER
    Ku: ò-γòmə̆

C

CALABASH

    A: ò-tè; (ə̀)rè-

    EO: ègbèlè

    Ku: áfà; r-

    Od: àfà; (à)r-

    WO: àɓàɓà; ꜜ-zà

CALL (v)   cf. GREET

    A: -maɣ

    EO: -ɓelegi

    Ku: -ɓelegi

    Od: -ɓeleɣi/-peleɣi

    WO: ə̀-wə̂

CAMWOOD

    A: ìgbìlə̀

    EO: ə̀dòló

    Ku: ə̀dòlǒ

    Od: ì-gbùlə̀

    WO: ìsélé

CANEROPE, CLIMBING ROPE

    A: (ə̀)-lóòɣ; (ə̀)sí-   cf. ROPE

    EO: ìwôɓ   'rope for climbing'

          àlɩ̀zè   'canerope'

    Ku: ìwóɓ

    Od: ə̀lɩ́óɓ; əsíóɓ

    WO: òɗìɗì   'canerope'

          ɔ̀gá   'rope for climbing palms'

CANNON   cf. English 'cruiser'

    A: òkùrúsì

    EO: ə̀kùrúsì

Ku: ə̀kùrúsə̀
Od: ò-kúrùsù; (ə̀)rù-
WO: íkùrúsì

CANOE   see BOAT

CANOE-POLE
   EO: ò̠tî̠r
   Od: ò-sóbíòm
   WO: ə̀sú

CANOE SEAT   cf. PULL
   A: òδúròm
   EO: ə̀lùdùm
   Ku: ə̀lùdúm óγùγ
   Od: ə̀-lùdŭm
       ə̀-lùdùm óγúúγ
   WO: ə̀δúrówù

CAPE [OF LAND]
   EO: ə̀tókì

CAREFULLY, PROPERLY, TO DO (v)
   A: àmáár   á-máár á-bý̠γ 'got fat
                properly, good and fat'

      máár   'be careful, learn'
             máár ə̀-δíγí 'do it
              carefully'

      -maar   'to be careful, do properly'

CARRY (v)
   A: -tool/-rool
   EO: -βam
   Ku: -βam
   Od: -rool/-tool

Od:	òtòòl dòòl	n. 'carrier'
WO:	à-ßâm	
	ɔ̀-ßàm	'load, act of carrying'

CARRY CHILD (v)

A:	-lɔɣ -kàbá	'carry on back without cloth'
	-kàbá	'carry on back with feet astraddle'
	-gbana	'tie on back with cloth'
	-ßaara/-paara	'carry at side'
EO:	-ben	'carry on back'
	-bebe	'carry on side'
Ku:	-kpɔ	'carry on back'
	-bebe	'carry on side'
Od:	-kpa	'carry on back'
	-kpoɣ	'carry on side'
WO:	à-bábà	'carry on back'
	ə̀-mómòr	'carry on side'

CARRYING POLE

A:	ɔ̀fɛ̀gúmà	'for palmfruit'
EO:	ìpìó	'for palmfruit'
Ku:	òdólòmə̀~òdólmə̀	'for palmfruit' also 'head pad'
Od:	ìgbérə̀	'for palmfruit'
WO:	ɔ̀kómŏm	

CARVE WOOD

A:	-ka	
	ɔ̀kààm àmàkà	n. 'carver'
EO:	-ka	
Ku:	-ka	
Od:	-ka	
WO:	à-kâ	

CASE [AT LAW]
    A: (ɛ́)ðíɣítòn
    EO: ɔ̀kpɛ̀
    Ku: ɔ̀kpɛ̀
    Od: ɔ̀-kpɛ̀
    WO: ɛ̀ɓɛ̀rɛ̀

CASSAVA
    A: á-pị́tàkà; (à)rị́-
    EO: àðị́ɔ̀bɔ̀
    Ku: ɔ̀byárụ̀; ì-
    Od: ɛ̀-l·ɛ̀ɛ́bɔ̀; ị̀-
    WO: ɛ́p(ị́)tākà; 'zà

CAT
    A: ɛ̀-pùsí; (ɛ̀)sí-
        ~ pósị̀
    EO: ɔ̀lɔ̀gbó   cf. Yoruba ɔ̀lógbò
    Ku: àbôñ; r-
    Od: ɔ̀-fùgùrù; ì-
    WO: ɛ̀légbèsíɛ̀; 'zɛ̀

CATAPULT (n)   cf. English 'rubber'
    Ku: àvá árɔ́bà
    WO: àrɔ́bà

CATCH (v)   cf. HOLD
    A: -siβ
    EO: -su
    WO: -su

CEILING   see ROOF

CERTAIN, BE (v)
    Od: -kar   àmį̀ tákărìnį́ àmį̀į̀nân zòdí
                                     'I'll definitely meet
                                     him'

CHAIN (n)
    A: ìzìmè
    EO: ègórógóró
    Ku: ìgòrógòrò
    Od: ə̀-gbìrígbìrì; (ə̀)rì-
    WO: ìgbírígbírí

CHAIR (n)
    A: à-gàdà; (a)sį́-
    EO: òkóbò
    Ku: ìkásį̀
    WO: òbákù

CHALK (n)
    A: ámɛ̄lɛ̄β ~ ámį̄lį̄β   'white chalk'
           údə̀   'red chalk'

CHALLENGE (v)
    A: -pa   mį́ úpá ñɔ̀dį́ į́nų́ɣ 'I chal-
                                   lenged him to wrestle'

CHAMELEON
    A: òò-nə̀ə̀ɣ; (ə̀)rə̀ə̀-
    EO: àkpátɛnàñ
    Ku: àkpótɛnàį̀; r-
    Od: ò-nə̀ə̀ɣ; į̀-
    WO: àkpátɛnàį̀; ``zà

CHANGE (v)
    A: -ŋme

EO:	-mogonə	v.t.
	-tibirə	v.i.
Ku:	-w̃e	v.t.
	-w̃egiən	v.i.
Od:	-ŋue ~ -ŋe	v.t.
	-ŋiən	v.i.
WO:	ógùə̀n (m-)	v.t.
	ógùə̀nə̀ (m-)	v.i.

CHARM (n)

Ku:	ɛ̀gbà	'protective charm'
	ə̀mə̀gò	'charm to ensure opponent's weakness'
	ə̀gòròdí	'a more powerful charm to ensure other's weakness'

CHEAP   cf. SOFT

A:	ə̀dùɣ ðíɣí	
EO:	òɓùr	
Ku:	òɓùɓùrə̀n	
Od:	~duɣ	ùkpê̂ɓó àláðìó 'cloth is not expensive'
WO:	ò̩gù̩gú̩r ə̂ɓ̀ù̀ə̀	

CHEAT, DECEIVE

A:	-gbeɣeðiom	
	íìgbèɣèðìóm	'cheating'
	-bi	'deceive' rə̀-bíə́nā̄n 'is deceiving himself'

CHECKERED, BE (v)

A:	-ki̩ri̩ɓa	cf. CUT

CHEEK

A:	ò-kpó; (ə̀)rò-

EO: àɓàgá   also 'jaw'
Od: à-gbá; àrà-
WO: ə̀kɔ̀; ˗́zə̀

CHEST
A: è-kpól·óɣì; (ə̀)ró-
EO: ìkpúkpólògì
Ku: èkpə́kpə̀ɣ
Od: èé-kū; ə̀rùú-
WO: íkpòkŏm (A); ˗́zə̀
     ìkpòkòmə̂ (O)

CHEW   see EAT

CHEWSTICK
A: ɔ̀ɣóóɣ
EO: ɔ̀ɣŏ
Ku: ɔ̀ɣóɣ
Od: ɔ̀-ɣóóɣ; ḭ̀-
WO: ɔ̀ɣó

CHICKEN   cf. BIRD
A: (à)-kínìɣ (-kɛ́nɛ̀ɣ);
        (à)sḭ́-
EO: ɛ̀nṳ̀r ɛ́mà
Ku: ɔ̀ñɛ̀nṳ́r; àw̃ḭ̀yḭ̀nṳ́r
Od: (à)-kɛ̀nɛ́ɣ; (à)sḭ̀-
WO: ɔ̀ñɛ́n·ṳ́rṳ́; àw̃íɛ́n·ṳ́rṳ́

CHIEF (n)   see KING

CHILD
A: ɔ̀ñ; ám̂-   also 'son'
     mómò   'small child' personal name,
                                 if child is expected
                                 to die

A: ò-ɓèl ôñ   'first-born, either sex'
      ò-kpán·á   'first-born male'
      ò-kpáñàn   'first-born female'
      óñdí ósóβōm ðḭ́màr 'last-born' 'child which
                               cuts child-bearing'

EO: òñḭ̀   also 'son'
Ku: óñḭ̀; áw̃ḭ̂y   also 'son'
Od: òñ; àŋòñ ~ àŋṵ̀ñ also 'son'
      òkpàn·á   'first-born, either sex'
      òkpònôñ   'first-born male'
      òkpònóñánḭ̀   'first-born female'
      òñ ósòβ òòlá   'last-born' 'child that
                               cuts womb'

WO: òñ; àw̃ḭ̀   also 'son'
      àðḭ́z' óñ   'daughter'
      óñ ónòβìrì; àw̃ḭ́
         ínòβìrì   'boy'
      òkpánà   'first-born'
      òkpán ôñ   'first son'

CHIN
   A: ɛ́ɛ́wɛ̀; (à)rɛ́ɛ́-
   EO: èɓèɓéñ
   Ku: èɓéɓèγ
   Od: èɛ́-vɛ̄; àràá-
   WO: èðɛ́ðèñ; ‐za

CHOOSE
   A: -γim/-kim
   EO: -sɔn
   Ku: -sɔn
   WO: à-sɛ́lɛ̀
       ɛ̀sɛ̀lɛ̀   n. 'choice'

CHOP   see CUT

CIRCUMCIZE
    A: -δun   applies to male or female
    EO: òwùr óδùl
          òδùl   'circumcision'
    Ku: -tìpó [<ò-tì ìpó]   cf. BEAT DRUM [-ti]
    Od: -δun
    WO: ə̀-tîpò (-ti)
          ò-tìòmìpó   'circumcizer'
          òtípò   'circumcision'

CIVET
    A: à-n·ɔ̀; (à)sɪ̀-

CLAM
    Ku: é-gbə̆; r<u>e</u>

CLASS   see GROUP

CLAW (n)
    A: ɛ̀-ráàβ; (à)rá-   also 'fingernail'
    EO: ɛ̀wàβ
    Ku: ɛ̀wàβ; r-
    Od: àrààβ; (à)r-   also 'fingernail'
    WO: ɛ̀wàβ

CLEAN
    A: -buroγ   v. 'to clean by rubbing'
          -ɓaal   cf. WHITE v.i.
                                      òlóɣí ámɪ̀ áɓààllɪ̄ 'I'm
                                          happy, my mind is clean'
                                      òlóɣí ámɪ̀ ɔ̀ɓáàl
                                          'I'm unhappy'

EO: -ɓalaɓal   cf. WHITE
Ku: -ɓul   v.t.
    -ɓalaɓal   ɔɓàlaɓâl úkpè 'clean cloth'
    -ɓal   úkpè βɔ́ áɓăl 'cloth was
                         clean'
    ɛɓàɓàlà   'cleanliness'
Od: -ɓaal   cf. WHITE
    ɔɓààl òlóɣì   'happiness'
                     òlòɣì àmɪ́ náɓàál 'I'm happy'

WO: ɔɓàɓăl

CLEAR BUSH (v)   cf. SLASH
  A: -sɪ̣
  EO: -sɪ̣
  Ku: -sɪ̣
  Od: -sɪ̣
  WO: ə̀-sî

CLIMB, GO UP
  A: -sɪ̣ñ
       -sɪ̣ñɔm   'climb with...'
                       mɪ́ ụ̀sɪ̀ñɔ́m óδìɣ 'I climbed
                          with a rope'
  EO: -βun   cf. LAND (v)
  Ku: -sɪ̣n
  Od: -sɪ̣ñ
       ɔsɪ̀ñ mɛ́sɪ̀ñ   n. 'climber'
  WO: ə̀-βúnù   cf. LAND (v)
       é-βùnú   'climbing, going up'

CLING TO, HOLD ON TO WITH HAND
  A: -kpaβ

CLITORIS
  EO: ɔkàlkàl

    Ku: ɔ́ñăm

    Od: ɛ̀-γàr; (à)rà-

    WO: ɛ̀γàr

CLOSE (v)

A:	-puγi/-βuγi	
EO:	-kpegi	'close box, etc.'
	-gugu	'close door'
	-ɓulugi	'close bottle'
Ku:	-kpegi	kpègí mɔ̀nṳ̀ 'shut your mouth'
	-gugi	'close door'
	-nani̧	'close eyes'
Od:	-γuuγi/-kuuγi	'close door'
	-kpereγi	'close cover'
	-ɓuluγi	'close stopper'
	-γuuγiom	'close door when someone is inside'
WO:	îgùgù (m-)	'close door'

CLOTH

A:	ù-kpê; (ə̀)rú-	also 'clothing'
	í̧mà ə̀rúkpé	'fine clothing'
EO:	ìkpé	
Ku:	úkpè; ə̀rúkpê	
Od:	ù-kpé; (ə̀)rù-	
WO:	íkpè	
	íbùɛ̀ðɔ̀	'clothing' cf. DRESS
	ə̀rùə̀	also 'clothing'

CLOUD

A:	òkù-ə́ðí̧ò	
Od:	ɔ̀-βṳ̀rṳ̀bṳ̀ṳ̀r; ì-	also 'fog'
WO:	òγêγè; ì-	

CLUB, SOCIETY   cf. AGE GRADE
    A: ò-gbò
    EO: ògbò
    Ku: ògbò
    Od: ògbò
    WO: ògbò

COAL
    A: ìì-ɣù   'charcoal'
          ìì-ɓù   'hot coal'
    EO: ɛŋànàŋàn   'charcoal'
    Ku: èɓùɓù àñâ   'charcoal'
    Od: èè-ɓù; ìì-   also 'charcoal'
    WO: ɛ̃ɣánálɛpɛ̀

COCK (n)   cf. BIRD
    A: òléɓìrì àḳìṇìɣ   ògèlè àḳíṇìɣ 'cock's comb'
    EO: òlòɓìr-ɛ́nụ́r
    Ku: ò-lóɓírí ɛ́nụ́r; ì-..ị̀-
    WO: ònóɓìrì ɛ̀n·ụ̀rụ̀
          ~ òkpókpòrókpò

COCONUT
    A: òzíɓ ə́ɓèkèñ; òjíɓ...
    EO: òkòkòdíə́
    Ku: òzìɓ ə́ɓèkéì   'coconut palm'
          ~òtù ózìɓ
    Od: ò-zìm; ì-   also 'seed of palmfruit'
    WO: òkòkòdíə́   also 'coconut palm'

COCOYAM
    A: òkòlò   àδịná òkòlò 'cocoyam leaf,
                                      very tender'
    EO: òkòlò

Ku: òkòlò
Od: ʉ̀-ɓòkò; (à)rà-
WO: òkɪ́ɗè̀

COFFIN   cf. BOX; CORPSE

A: ígbé òɗìm
EO: ìɓékù égúə́dè
Ku: ìgbé égwə́dè [égúə́dè]
Od: èɓìnə
WO: ígbèkú íwòn·ì̩

COLD

A: áàβɔ̀ɔ̀m

     -βɔɔm/-pɔɔm   v. 'be cold'
                                 ə̀lóór ámì̩ ɛ́ɛ̀βɔ̀ɔ̀mnɪ̄
                                     'I feel cold'

     (à)ɗɪ́ɪ̀βɔ̀ɔ̀m   'coldness'
EO: -ɓoɣom   v.i. 'become, be cold'
     -ɓoɣomen   v.t. 'make cold'
     òɓòɣòmɓóɣóm   modif.
     è-ɓòɣòm   'coldness' also 'dull
                                     person'
Ku: -ɓòkum   v. 'be cold'
                                 èɓòɓókùm ámʉ̩m 'cold water'
                                 àmʉ̩mmó éɓòkûm 'water
                                     was cold'

     -ɓòkumeni   v. 'make cold'
     èɓòkùm   n. 'cold'
     òkíríkè̀   n. òkíríkè̀ nè̀ɗìɣí àmì̩
                                     'I feel cold'
Od: -ɓokoom   v. 'be, become cold'
                                 ə̀lòòródɪ́ nə́ə̀ɓókòòm 'his
                                     baby is cold'
                                 ùútè̀ nə́sɪ̆βàmì̩ 'I feel cold'
WO: ɔ̀-ɗòɗóɔ́; è̀-   modif.

WO: -ɗɔ (ɛ́ɛ̀-) (m-)   v.i. 'be, become cold'
     ɛ́ɛ̀-ɗɔman(m)   v.t. 'to make cold, cool'
     ɛ̀-ɗɔ̀ɗɔ́   'coldness'

COMB (n)
   A: ɔ̀záránààm
   EO: ɔ̀sàlàmá
   Ku: ɔ́z̃ṳlṵ́ɓáḭ
   Od: ɔ̀-sàlâm; ḭ-
   WO: ɔ̀sàlàmà

COMB (v)
   A: -zarḭɔn
   EO: -sal
   Ku: -sal   'comb someone'
        -sala   'comb oneself'
   Od: -sala
   WO: à-sálà
        à-sál èmù   'to comb hair'

COME
   A: -tu/-ru
   EO: -ru
   Ku: -ru
   Od: -ru/-tu
   WO: ə̀-rû
        tḭé   imperative

COMPANION (n)
   A: ɔ̀ñ-ɔ́ɔ̀gbɔ̀; ḭ̀ḭ̀-gbɔ̀   cf. CLUB [ɔ̀gbɔ̀]

COMPLAIN
   Ku: -w̃ɛnḭ   ɔ̀nḭ̀ ḭ́w̃ɛ̀nḭ́ 'complainer'

COMPLETE (v)   cf. FINISH
   A: -muneni
   EO: -liemen
        -madan   'finish'
   Ku: -man
        -leɣən   'be complete'
        -leɣemeni   'to complete something'
   Od: -gbeβe   'supply missing remainder'

COMPLEXION [SKIN]
   A: δì-jû   cf. SKIN

COMPOUND [RESIDENCE] (n)
   A: èɣùn   cf. WOMB
   Ku: əpòló
   Od: ò-ɣóól ótù; (ə)rə-   cf. HOUSE
   WO: əpóló

CONCEIVE
   A: -mor (oo-)   cf. BURN
   EO: -momor
   Ku: -mumor   also 'be aflame'
        ɔsʉ̀sʉ̀   'first three months of
                            pregnancy'
   Od: -mor (oo-)
   WO: êmùr (m-)
        émùr èw̃ùnù   'conception'

CONGEAL
   A: -niir   v.i.
        -niire   v.t.
   EO: -kpomen   v.t.
        -kpo   v.i.
   Ku: -kpo

Od: -kpo   v.i.
WO: ə̀-kpê̂n   v.i.
     ə̀-kpə́nə̀mə̀n   v.t.

CONTINUE TO... (v)
   A: -ɣiom/-kiom   mí úlénī rə̀kíóm •I
                                 continued to eat'
   Ku: -gɨ̀ɔm   gìré mâgɨ̀óm 'continue
                                 working'
       kə-   'again'? gìré kə̀gírə̀
                                 'continue working'
                             ɨ̀ná nə̀ké́lèɣè 'he's crying
                                 again'
                             ɨ̀ná nə̀ké́ðè 'he's eating
                                 again'
   WO: -ya~-yə   suffix ɛ̀n ólə̀yə́ nə̀ðé 'he's
                                 still eating'
                             ɛn árōyanɨ̀ ə̀ðé 'he was
                                 still eating'
                             gìréyè̀ 'to continue working'
                             dò̀nɛ́yè̀ 'keep walking'

CONTRIBUTE
   A: -soɣ
   EO: -tuo
   Ku: -tuə
   Od: -soɣ
   WO: ôtù̀ò(m-)   'take up collection,
                                 contribute'
       ó-tū̄ō   'contribution, collection'

CONVERSATION (n)
   A: ɔ̀ɣàà𝛽
   WO: ètéɓél' ón·ʉ̀

CONVERSE (v)
    A: -ɣaaβan/-kaaβan   'converse with'
              mí úɣààβán rɔ̀dí
                 'I talked with him'
              mí ràwá ɔ́ɣààβàn ràn·â 'I
                 want to talk with you'
    WO: ə̀-téβèl(è) ɔ̀n·ṳ̀   'converse casually'
                            cf. BOUNCE

COOK (n)   cf. BOIL, COOK
    A: ɔ̀sààm ị̀sâ
    Ku: ɔ̀sàmèδ ì ə̀n; r-
    Od: ɔ̀sàm èδ ì ə̀n; ị̀sàr èδ ì ə̀n

CORNER (n)
    A: ɛ̀kṳ̀lɛ̀ñ
    EO: ɛ̀kṳ̂l
        àkákà   'side'
    Ku: ɛ̀kɔ̀l
        àká   'corner, hidden place'
    Od: ɛ̀-kṳ̀l
    WO: ìkórótù   'outside corner of house'
        ə̀kpɔ̀kpɔ̀m   'corner, side'

CORPSE
    A: ɔ̀-δìm; ì-   ìδím kə̀yɔ̀ɔ̀r 'our ancestors,
                            family dead'
                      ɔ̀màɣ íδìm 'to invoke
                            ancestors'
    EO: èguə́dè
    Ku: èguə́dè   cf. EARTH
    Od: ɔ̀-δìm; ì-
    WO: íwɔ̀n·ì; íwə̆w̃ùnɔ̀m   'dead person' cf. DIE
        èguə́dè   'corpse'

CORRECT   see RIGHT

COST (n)

    A: ɛ́mú ìkpòkì   cf. BEAD; MONEY

    EO: ə̀ɓùə̀

    Ku: ə̀ɓùə̀

    Od: ə̀-ɓùə̀

    WO: ə̀ɓùə̀

COST (vi)

    Od: -l·a   'cost'

           -leñ   'be worth'

                       àl·á mə́ɗìòβ ə̀séléní
                           'it costs 10/-'

COTTONWOOD TREE

    EO: ɔ̀ɓàl órérén

    WO: ìmùmù

COUGH (n)

    A: ɔ̀-kɔ́nὲ(ὲ)ñ; (à)rɔ́-   'whooping cough, TB'

    EO: ɔ̀kɔ̀nɔ̀n

    Ku: ɔ̀kɔ̀nɔ̀n

    Od: ɔ̀kɔ̀nɔ̀

COUNCIL   see MEETING

COUNSEL (v)   see ADVISE

COUNT (v)   cf. MARRY

    A: -gbi   'think, reckon'

           -aal/-fal

    EO: -wal

    Ku: -wal

    Od: -ɓal

    WO: à-wâl

COVENANT, AGREEMENT, BLOOD ALLIANCE
 A: ì-yɔ̀   also 'oath of special friendship'
 EO: ɛ̀zɔ̀   'blood alliance'
 Ku: ìzɔ̀   'blood-friendship'
   ómɔ̀lɔ̀l   'blood brother, intimate friend'
   ómɔ̀lɔ̀l ízɔ́ ō 'remember the oath!'
 Od: òtùlɔ̀nʉ́
 WO: ɛ̀zɔ̀

COVER (v)
 A: -kpereɣi
 EO: -kpegi
 Ku: -kpegi   'nothing inside'
   -kpegiom   'something alive inside'
 Od: -kpeeɣi   'with lid'
   -zuom   'with cloth'
   -ẟi   'with earth, bury'
   òkpèrèɣìòm   n. 'cover'
 WO: íβùgòm (m-)
   ì-βùgòmɛ̂   n. 'cover'

COW (n)
 A: (à)-n·àm; (à)sḭ̀-
 EO: àn·ám
 Ku: ánàm; r-
 Od: àn·àm; (à)r-
 WO: ò-ví; ì-

CO-WIFE
 A: òyóbòβ   also 'mate'
 EO: òyóbə̀
 Ku: òyóbə̆

Od: òzóbòβə́

WO: ə̀γôbə́

COWRIE

EO: òkóɓə̀

Ku: ò-kóɓə̀; ì-

Od: ìkòɓə́

WO: òkóɓə̀

èkpókòɓə̀; ìkpíkòɓə̀

CRAB

A: (ə̀)δì-kóróròβ; (ə̀)sì-

EO: ə̀líkòrò

Ku: ə̀δì-kórò; àsì-   'fresh water crab'

è-lù   'land crab'

Od: ə̀δì-kòróγ; ə̀sì-

WO: ò-kóòtò; ì-

CRACK (v)

A: -γɛn/-kɛn   'crack, crush palmkernels'

EO: -ŋɛn

Ku: -kpɔl

Od: -ɓom(oo-)   'to crush, flatten' cf. HIT

-βum/-pum   'crush flat'

-bum(oo-)   'to flatten by beating'

WO: ə̀-ŋôm

ɛ̂ŋìnì̩(m-)   'crack nuts'

CRAWL (v)

A: -γùγòl/-kùγol

EO: -kpuluγu

Ku: -kpuloγu

Od: -ɓoorə   'as child'

WO: ə̀-kpúùlù   'as baby'

CRAYFISH
    A: ɔ̀gɨ̀rɨ̀gɨ̀rɨ̀   cf. CRICKET
    EO: ɔ̀-zɔ̀l; ὲ-
           ɔ̀gàgà   'prawn'
    Ku: àlɨ̀-zɔ̀l; ɨ̀-   also 'prawn'
    WO: ὲtàtá (A)
           ὲtὲkú (O)

CREATOR
    EO: ɔ̀l·έm   cf. BLACKSMITH
         ɔ̀n·έm
         ɔ̀nὲnὲmá
         ɔ̀lὲm mɔ̀lὲm   'blacksmith'

CREEK
    A: ɔ̀βμ́ ɔ́βɨ̃
    EO: ìyì
    Ku: ùyɔ̀
    WO: àdμ́ɔ́βɨ̀   'small river'
         ìyì   'for fishing only'

CRICKET [ANIMAL]
    A: àà-gɨ̀rɨ̀; (à)rɨ́ɨ̀-   cf. CRAYFISH
    EO: ὲgέnέné
    Ku: έgὲnέnέn
    WO: ὲgέnέné

CROCODILE
    A: é-ɣōl; (ə̀)ró-
    EO: ə̀sὲgì
    Ku: àgbɔ̀gɨ̀rɨ̀
    Od: ὲnàm ɔ̀βɨ̃   'river animal'
    WO: ə̀sὲgì; ˋzə̀

CROSS [RIVER, ETC.] (v)

    A: -ɓɛ(ɛ)ñ   ɛ́ɓɛ́ñɔ̀m ɔ̀βḭ̀ñ 'on other side of river, across river'

    EO: -ɓɛñ

    Ku: -ɓɛi̯

           -ɓɛ̀i̯yɛ́ni̯   'to take across'

    Od: -ɓɛñ

    WO: à-ɓɛ̂ñ

CROWD (n)

    A: i̯bàdi̯ ɛ́wè

    EO: ɔ̀lɔ̀ ə̀w̃únɔ̀m

    Ku: ɔ̀l·ɔ̀ɣ ə̀w̃únɔ̀m

    Od: èɣú   no pl.

    WO: ɔ̀lə́w̃únɔ̀m

           [ɔ̀lɔ́]

CRY (v)

    A: -moɣi

           èmɔ̀ɣì   'cry of animal, shedding tears of human'

    EO: -l·eɣe   'weep'

    Ku: -leɣe   ɔ̀lèɣèmèδí 'cry-baby'

    Od: -leɣe

           èδí   'act of crying'

    WO: óɔ̀lɔ̀(m-)

           è-δí   'act of weeping'

CURE (v)

    A: -δíɣí ɔ̀ɔ̀ɣɔ̀   'to treat, make medicine'

    EO: -koko

    Ku: -koko

    Od: -ko (oo)   'cure other'

           -kuə (oo)   'cure self'

    WO: à-gbâl   'maintain'
         -wo   v.t. 'heal'

CURSE (v)
    A: -su ɔ́kàràβ ɔ́nʊ̀   'curse'
         -roñon   'make adverse comment'
    EO: -rogi
    Ku: -γaδị
         -gurugi   'curse someone, invoking
                             ancestors'

         -gurugiən   'curse oneself, invoking
                             ancestors'

    Od: -γɔr/-kɔr
         àlị-γɔ́r   n. 'curse'
    WO: àñɔ́n·ʊ̀   also 'wish bad luck'
         ɔ̂gɔ̀l   'abuse'

CUT (v)   cf. FELL
    A: -soβ
         -kịrịβ   'cut into small pieces'
                            cf. CHECKERED
         -kịrịβa   'to be checkered'
         -ben   also 'chop; hit with matchet'
         -benoγ   'cut repeatedly'
    EO: -soβ
         -gu   'fell tree'
         -γɔzɔm   'cut up whole animal'
         -pol   'chop wood'
    Ku: -soβ   'cut, buy small quantity
                                of liquid'

         -gbodo   'cut into small pieces'
    Od: -soβ   'cut horizontal thing: wood,
                                meat, rope'

         -gbo   'cut palmfruit'
         -bul   'cut grass, vegetation'

Od:	-ben	'cut something alive'
	-mɛɛɣ	'with razor or sharp grass, cut throat'
	-vɛlɛ	'slice'
	-δun	'circumcize'
	-ɓu	'cut open (abdomen, exposing intestines); harvest tubers'
WO:	ə̀-sôβ	'cut into pieces'
	ə̀-gbódò	'cut down'
	ə̀-gbódògì	'chop' repeated action
	ə̀-sóβògì	'chop' repeated action'
	à-kpâβ	'cut hair'

D

DANCE (n)

    A: ìɓà

    Ku: ìgbà

    WO: ὲ-gbà

DANCE (v)

    A: -γεr/-kεr

    EO: -γεr

    Ku: -γεr

    Od: -γεr/-kεr

    WO: à-δá ὲgbà
           [έ]

        ɔ̀-δàm ὲgbà   'dancer'

DARK, BECOME

    A: -γul/-kul   cf. NIGHT

                      ə̀-δúγùl rè-kúl 'night is
                         falling'

    Ku: -gul   ə̀δìɔ̀ ɛ́gŭl 'night fell'

DARKNESS

    A: ùfìrì

    EO: àzìm

        ~àzìmə̀δìɔ̀

    Ku: ə̀δíázìm

    Od: ùfìrì

        ~ɔ̀kìnìm

    WO: ɔ̀zù̀δìɔ̀

        ~ ɔ̀kìnìkìnì

DASH [PRESENT]   cf. GIVE

    A: -ŋaanì   v.

    Ku: ὲnὲγĕ   n.

DAY
    A: (ə́)-δíò; (ə̀)sí-   'as opposed to night;
                                      daylight'

         (ə̀)-δúɣūlūtù; (ə̀)sí- 'time unit'

    EO: èrə̀δìó

    Ku: əδəmə; r-   əδə̀mə̀ əδə̀mə̀ 'day after day'
                              kèrékèré əδə́mə̀ 'every day'

    Od: ə̀-δìò; (ə̀)rì-   'day, weather, daytime'
         ə̀-δùmə̀; (ə̀)rù-   'period of time'

    WO: ə̀δìò; ˆˋzə̀
         ò-gbέrâ   'daylight'

DAY AFTER TOMORROW
    A: òmán ìɓùè   cf. BACK
    EO: àmélégèn nə́rú   cf. COME
    Ku: ə̀mélègyèn nə́rú   cf. COME
    Od: àmáàδìé

DAY BEFORE YESTERDAY
    A: òmán ìδùe   cf. BACK
    EO: ə̀mélégèn ə́tén   cf. PASS
    Ku: àmélègyèn ə́tén   cf. PASS; BACK
    Od: àmáàδùé
    WO: ə̀mélègènə̀

DEAF
    A: -ɓaaɣaβ   v. 'be deaf'
    EO: ààɓà
    Ku: òɓàɣáɓàɣ
         -ɓaɣ   'be deaf'
         àɓàɣ   'deafness'

DEAR, EXPENSIVE
    A: áman δíɣí
         ~ áman íkpòkì

EO: ɔ̂kpàr   cf. HARD, STRONG
~ə̀ɓ̀ùə̀

Ku: ɔ̀δìɣ ə́ɓúə̀

Od: -la   ɛ̀nám àlă 'the meat was dear'
ɛ̀nàm ų́láálá 'expensive meat'

WO: ɔ̀kpàkpár ə̂ɓùə̀

DEATH
A: ə̂-δùùɣ; (ə̀)sì-
EO: ə̀δù
Ku: ɔ̀mùɣ   cf. DIE
Od: ɔ·ɣɔ
WO: ə̀δù

DEBT
A: ɔ̀mų́ɣ
EO: ɔ̀mų́
Ku: ɔ̀mų́ɣ
Od: ɔ̀-mų́ɣ
WO: ɔ̀mų́

DEBTOR
Ku: ɔ̀δìɣ mɔ̀mų́ɣ
Od: ɔ̀lèmɔ̀mų́ɣ

DECEIVE   see TRICK; CHEAT

DECREASE (v)
A: -ɣome/-kome   v.t.
EO: -kị̀rị̀mɛn   v.t.
Ku: -kɛrɛmɛnị̀
Od: -kiemi   v.t. cf. SMALL
WO: ɛ́kị̀rɔ̀màn(m-)   v.t. also 'look down on,
                                        belittle'

DEEP

    A: -kɛl   v.i.

          -kɛlɛ   v.t. 'deepen'

    EO: -kuδum   v.i.

          òkùδùmkúδúm; ì-   modif.

          -kuδumen   v.t. 'deepen'

    Ku: -kuδum   v.i. òkùδùmkúδùm óβị̂y
                                               'deep river'

                                   òβị̂y nǒ ꞔkùδûm 'this river
                                               is deep'

          -kuδumeni   v.t. 'deepen'

    Od: -kuδum

    WO: ò-gùgúᵷβ; ὲ-   modif.

          -gμβ (móò-)   v.i.

          óògùβòman(m-)   v.t. 'deepen'

DEFECATE

    A: -nị̇ (ɔɔ-?)

    EO: -n·ị̂

    Od: -nị̇ (ɔɔ-)

    WO: a-n·ị̂

          ó-n·ị̇án   'act of defecating'

DEFORMITY

    A: ὲὲγá

          òδíγ έέγā   'be deformed'

    WO: ὲγá

DEMOLISH

    A: -ler   cf. FELL

    EO: -gbogon   [house]

    Ku: -ɓogion   [house]

    Od: -ler   [house] cf. FELL

    WO: ôkò(m-)

DENY

    Ku: -kwa

DEPTH

    A: (à)δɨ́-kɛ̀l   cf. DEEP

    EO: è-kùδùm

    Ku: è-kùδùm

    WO: ɔ́-gṵ̄β

DESCEND, GO DOWN

    A: -soor   also 'assemble'

                        əδɨ́ɣɨ́ βɔ̄ mé-sòòr 'the
                          market has assembled
                          (started)'

          -kuruβ   'descend from height'

    EO: -sor

    Ku: -sor

    Od: -soor

    WO: ə̀-sôr

          é-sōr   'descent, going down'

DESIRABLE, NEEDED, BE (v)

    A: -βṵ/-pṵ   àmṵ́úm rṵ́βṵ̀ ɨ́ɨ́mɪ̀ 'I'm
                       thirsty'

                       àmṵ́úm ràpṵ́ ñɔ̀dɪ̰́ ▪he's
                       thirsty'

DEW

    A: ì-kóróɣór

    EO: ìkòròɣór

    Ku: ìkòróɣòr

    Od: òɣòròɣôr

    WO: òtítə̀   Nembe?

DIE (v)

    A: -muɣ   é-múɣù 'they died'
                                              (things collectively)

    EO: -mu

    Ku: -muɣ

    Od: -βɔ/-pɔ   (person)

           -muɣ   (trees, plants)

    WO: íù ~ íẁ (m-)

DIFFERENT

    A: kɩ̀ró ɛ̀lɛ̀l   'a different yam'

    EO: ɔ̀púnágwɔ̀

    Ku: ɔ̀w̃ègyɛ̀n

    Od: -koronuən

DIG (v)

    A: -guβ

    EO: -gbo

           ~-mugu

    Ku: -gbo

           -ɓu

    Od: -guβ   'dig well'

           -gbo   'dig, not deep'

    WO: îgɩ̀(m-)

DIP WATER

    A: -δu   'dip water out'

DIRT

    A: ɩ̀-sâ   n.

           ɔ̀-δíɣɛ́ɛ́nɩ̀r   'dirty'

           -δíɣ ɩ́sà   'dirty' ə̀δíwɔ̀βɔ́ éδīɣ ɩ́sâ
                                             'the rat is dirty'

           ɔ̀gbə́ə́nə́m-gbə́ə́nə̀m   'old and dirty'

EO: -bu̥du̥   'dirty'

Ku: ìnìnòr

     -dɔti̥   úkpè βɔ́ nâ·dɔ́ti̥ 'cloth is dirty'

     -dɔti̥mɛni̥   'make dirty'

Od: ɛ̀ɛ̀ni̥r

DISCUSS

WO: ɛ̂ɓɛ̀rɛ̀(m)   cf. CASE

     ɛ̀ɓɛ̀rɛ̀   'discussion, dispute'

DISHONEST, FALSE

Ku: ɔ̀-βi̥γíβi̥γ

DISSOLVE

A: -gbɔɔmi̥   v.t.

    -gbɔ   v.i.

EO: -gbɔdɔ   v.i.

    -gbɔdɔmɛn   v.t.

Od: -vɔ

WO: ɛ̂mɛ̀(m-)   v.i.

    ɛ̂mɛ̀màn (m-)   v.t.

DISTANCE (n)

Od: è-gbɛ̌ñ   cf. FAR

DIVE (v)

A: -δiin

EO: -δin

Ku: -δin

Od: -δiin

WO: ə̀-δíni̥

    ɔ̀-δìni̥   n. 'submerging, diving'

DIVIDE (v)

    A: -di

    EO: -rụgị

         ~-rụgụ

    Ku: -rụgị̀

         -za   'distribute drink by pouring'

    Od: - δị

         ὲ-δị̂m   n. 'division'

    WO: ὲ̂gὲ (m-)

         ὲ̂gὲmà   'distribute shares'

         ὲ́ὲgàrụ̀gụ̀   n. 'division'

         ὲ́ὲgὲmà   n. 'distribution, division (math)'

DIZZINESS

    WO: ὲβérə̄δíen   cf. EYE

DO

    A: -δiɣi

    EO: -δi

    Ku: -δiɣi

         -gir   'to do work'

    Od: -δiɣi

         ù-δíɣí   'deed' fem. name

    WO: à-kέnὲ

         -giri   'to work'

         ὲ́-kὲnέ   'activity, behavior'

DO ACCORDINGLY

    A: -tụụ̃ɣ   mị́ útụ́ụ́ɣnī ə̄δíɣí 'I did accordingly'

DO FOR SAKE OF...

    A: -tụ   mị́ ụ́-tụ́ ñínə̀ kú ə̀rú 'I came because of you'

Ku: -tṵn   àm' ítṵn ā̃w̃à ə̀rú 'I came
                   because of you'

Od: -tṵan   àm' ṵ́tṵan zòdí ə̀rú 'I came
                   because of him'

DOCTOR
A: ò-yî̃l; (ə̀)rí-
Ku: ò-wî̃l; ə̀rù-
Od: ò-zî̃l; (ə̀)rì-
WO: òwí̃lì; ì-

DOG
A: (ə̀)ɣòòɣ; (ə̀)sùòɣ
EO: ìsíə̀
Ku: ə̀-ɓòɣò; ə̀sì-ɓòɣò
Od: ə̀-ɣòòɣ; ə̀sì-ɣòɣò
WO: ə́óɓò; ə̀sìɓò ~ ə̀óɓôzə̀

DOOR
A: è-ɣúúɣ; (ə̀)rú-
EO: è-gŭ; ì-
Ku: ànṵ́ótù; r-   cf. MOUTH
Od: è-gùúɣ; (ə̀)rù-
WO: ègú; ì-

DOVE
EO: kúkù
     ~ òmòdí
Ku: òkúrósè̀gè̀; r-
WO: ə̀kúkū̄; ⁻zə̀

DRAGONFLY
A: (ə̀)δḭ́-pàràrâñ
EO: èmóδ̀ìm

Ku: ɛ̀mʉ́óẟ ì̀m   cf. HEAD; CORPSE

WO: ò̀bè̀mú   lit. 'big head'

DRAUGHTS [GAME]

A: ɛ́bì̀lɛ̀

EO: ɛ̀pɛ̀lɛ̀

Ku: ɛ̀pɛ̀lɛ̀   also 'tricking someone into
                       trouble'

WO: ɛ̀pɛ̀lɛ̀

DRAW WATER

A: -kpámʉ̀ʉ̀m   'draw from well (only)'

     -ẟúámʉ́ʉ̀m   'draw from well or container'

EO: -ẟu

Ku: -ẟu

Od: -kor

WO: ɜ̀-ẟû

DREAM

A: (à)màlà; (à)rà-   n.

     -mala ámálà   v.

EO: àmàlà   n.

     -mala   v.

Ku: àmàlà; r-   n.

Od: àràmàlà   n.

     -mala   v.

WO: àmàlà   n.

     à-málà   v.

DRESS (v)

A: -lɔγa   'put on clothing'

     -ŋmenə·n   ɛ́ménɜ̄ɜ̄n ì̠lɔ́ í̠tāyā 'he
                           dressed for hunting'

                        -mènɜ̀ɜ̀nì̠lɔ́ ɛ́yáàl 'to dress
                           for feast'

EO: - δ ì ɛ́   ɔ́ δ ɔ̀
Ku: -burə
Od: -burə   'dress oneself'
       -bur   'dress someone'
WO: ɔ̂δɔ̀(m-)   'dress oneself'
       δδɔ̀màn(m-)   'dress someone'

DRIFT (v)
EO: -tama   'be adrift'
Ku: -tama   'be, go adrift'
Od: -tama
WO: à-têñ   'go adrift'

DRINK (v)
A: -Pṵγɔl
EO: -δa
Ku: -δa
Od: -βṵγɔl/-pṵγɔl   ɔ́pɔ́γɔ́ míìm ▪wine drinker,
                                 drinker'
WO: à-βṵ́ɔ̀

DRIVE AWAY, PURSUE
A: -poroγ/-βoroγ
       -tum   'to drive away'
EO: -βiriγən
Ku: -ze   'drive away'
       -βiriγən   'pursue'
Od: -βiriγən/-piriγən
WO: ɔ̀-βírìγɔ̀n

DROP (v)
Od: -tuɓeen

DROWN (v)
A: -ɓi   v.i.

Ku: -βụγụδị   v.t.
    -βụγụδịan   v.i.
    -δa   'drown'
Od: -gụɓa   v.i.
    -zụβ   v.t.   'drown someone'

DRUM (n)   cf. TOMTOM
  A: ɔ̀-kàmà; (à)rà-
  EO: ɔ̀zè
  Ku: ɔ̀-kụ̀mà; àrụ̀-
      àdrɔ̂m   'kerosene drum'
  Od: ɔ̀-kụ̀mà; ị̀- ~ (à)rụ̀-
  WO: ɔ̀-zè; ì-

DRUMBEAT
  Ku: ə̀mɛ́tĭ   cf. BEAT DRUM

DRUNKARD
  WO: ɔ̀βụ̀ɔ̀mə̀mì   cf. DRINK; WINE

DRY THINGS (n)
  A: ị̀-βɛ̀rɛ̀βɛ̀r

DRY (v)
  A: -γaraγar/-karaγar   v.i. 'become dry, dry up'
      -ɓụr (v.t.)   mị́ ákàràγàrrị́ 'I'm dry'
                           mị́ ụ́γàràγárrị̄ 'I was dry'
                           kɛ́ɛ̀γàràγár 'it hasn't
                             become dry'
                           ə̀δíɓòkúβɔ̄ mɛ̄kārāγàr 'the
                             lizard has become dry'
  EO: ɔ̀-γáγáràn; ɛ̀-   modif. n.
      -γaγara   v.i. 'become dry'
      -ɓụr   v.t.

EO:	-tar	'to spread for drying'
	ò-γàγàrà	n. 'dryness'
Ku:	-γaγara	v.i. 'be dry'
		ìγáγàràn íγóγò 'dry grass'
		òγóγòβó náγáγàrà 'grass is dry'
	-ɓu̱r	v.t. 'dry, as fish, meat'
	-γaγaramɛni̱	v.t. 'make dry'
	ὲ-γáγárà	n. 'dryness'
Od:	-γara (ɔɒ-)	v.i. 'dry, dry up, as cloth'
	-karaγan (ɔɒ-)	v.i. 'dry, as leaf'
	-γor/-kor	v.i. 'dry, as pond'
	-ɓu̱r	v.t.
	-γarami̱ (ɔɒ-)	v.t. 'make dry'
	àlì̱-ì̱γárá	n. 'dryness'
WO:	-γara	v.i. 'be, become dry'
	ò-γàràγâr; ὲ-	modif.
	à-γáràγàrà	v.i. 'dry up'
	ên·ὲ(m-)	v.t. 'dry, as fish, meat'
	-γaraman	v.t. 'make dry'
	ò-γáγàrà	n. 'dryness'

DRY SEASON

EO:	ògbè̱γózòn
Ku:	è̱kózò̱γ
Od:	ò-n·óōr; (è̱)rù-

DUCK (n)

A:	àki̱ní̱γ ə̀βèkèñ	cf. CHICKEN
EO:	ὲkɛ́n-ə̀βèkêñ	
Ku:	ὲkɛ́nɛ́ ə̀βèkéì	
Od:	àbàdàféni̱	Kalabari?
	àkὲnɛ́γ ə̀βèkêñ	
WO:	ὲn·ú̱r éβèké	

DUIKER
    EO: èzò
    WO: èzò

DUMB PERSON
    Ku: émùɛ́

DUST (n)
    A: ò-βúɣ
    EO: ɛ̀βʉ́ɔ̀m
    Ku: ò-βûɣ
    Od: è-βŭɣ; ì-
    WO: àdɔ̀tĭ

DWARF, DEFORMED PERSON
    A: ɛ̀-kʉ̀ɣà

DWELL, STAY, LIVE IN
    A: -ruɣ/-tuɣ
    Ku: -ruɣ
    Od: -ruɣ/-tuɣ

DWELLING   see HOUSE

E

EACH

    A: ò-yêyèyè   'each person'

           óñòñòñ   'each child'

    Ku: ódì ɪ́sɛ̌   'each of them, one by one'

EAGLE

    A: ùgè

    EO: ìgò

    Ku: ùgò

    Od: ùgò; (è)r-

           àkpúgò   'young eagle'

    WO: ìgò

EAR

    A: (é)-ɓérì; (é)ré-   Ijo?

    EO: ètò

    Ku: éɓérī; r-

    Od: èɓèrì; èrèɓèrì

    WO: ètò; (-)'zè

EARRING

    A: éɓérísʉ̀à   cf. EAR

    EO: ègôl

    Ku: ìgólì   cf. English 'gold'

    Od: èɓèrìsʉ̀à

    WO: ègôl

EARTH

    A: èdè   'earth, land'

    EO: èdè   'earth, ground'

    Ku: èdè

           ègbòlòm   'land, dry land'

                           nickname of Amoroto

Od: ə̀dὲ; (ə̀)r-   'earth, land'
WO: ə̀dὲ   'earth, land'
     ə̀dὲdə̀   'the planet earth'

EAST
  A: ὲmítὲnὸm   cf. GO OUT

EASY, BE (v)
  Od: -ɓur   ὸɗìɣìὸβó nə́ə̀ɓûr 'the work
                          is easy'
                       ὸɗìɣìὸβó ə̀ɓŭr 'the work
                          was easy'
                       ὸɓùrə̀n óɗìɣì 'easy work'

EAT, CHEW
  A: -le   'eat'
       ìlὲ   'act of eating, feast'
       -ɣooɣ/-kooɣ   'eat palmfruit'
       aañ/-ba   'eat, chew meat, fish, eggs'
       -raal/-taal   'chew sugar cane, yam, etc.'
  EO: - δe   'eat fruit'
       -wa   'eat meat'
       -lài̧   'lick'
       -kὸ   'eat palmfruit, scrape'
       -rar   'chew'
  Ku: -δe   àbàr óδὲ 'something to eat'
       ə̀bŭm   'something to eat'
       -ɓùrugi   'make appetite'
       -ràɣàlà   'chew'
       -wà   'chew meat'
       -ɣὸɣ   'chew palmfruit'
  Od: -le   'eat in general, not meat'
       -ɣooɣ/-kooɣ   'eat palmfruit'
       -ɓa   'eat, chew meat'
       -raal/-taal   'chew palmkernel'

WO:	ə̀-ðé-βàr	'eat something (general)'
	-wa	'eat meat, fish'
	à-râr; -rar	'chew, eat pepper, sugarcane'
	-ko(móò-)	'scrape, eat palmfruit'
	-kpʊɔl	'gnaw'
	-βi̱(mɔɔ-)	'eat soup with spoon'
	ò-ðé	'act of eating'

EBB (v)

A:	-keleɣéèl	cf. GO HOME
EO:	-yel	lit. 'go home'
Ku:	-yel	
Od:	-ɣeel/-keel	also 'go back'
	ì-kèèlə́	n. 'ebb-tide' cf. GO HOME
WO:	ôwừ	
	ówáámừ	n. 'ebb-tide'

EDGE (n)

| A: | ògbòm |

EGG

A:	è-ɣèlè; (ə̀)rè-
EO:	àgá
	àg-ɛnú̱r
Ku:	àgà; r-
Od:	ɔ̀-gá; ì̱-
WO:	àgɛ́n·u̱ru̱; ´zà

EGRET

| A: | éèlè |

ELBOW

EO:	ɛ̀kálám ágwɔ̀
Ku:	ɛ̀kálàm ágwɔ̀

Od: ὲkpúlómávὸ
WO: ὲkólómàgwὸ

ELEPHANT
A: ɔ́ɔ́-mà; (à)rų́ų́-
EO: ų̀b-ὲn·àm
Ku: óbɛ́nàm; r-   cf. ANIMAL
Od: ų̀bàkὲnɛ́γ; į̀bàsį̀kὲnɛ́γ cf. CHICKEN
WO: ų̀bὲnàm   lit. 'big animal'

ELEPHANT GRASS
EO: ὲkéré
Od: ì-kpù
WO: ókpôkὸ

EMBRACE (v)
Ku: -ɓelən   ɔ́ñā tú ὸɓɛ́lɛ́n 'child, come
                          to my arms!'

EMPTY
A: óóβō   àδį́γááγ àmį̀ édì óóβō
                          'my hand is empty'
EO: ὸfórófo   modif. 'empty, emptiness'
    -foforomen   v.t.
WO: ὸ-fórófὸ; ì-

END (n)
A: éékùnὲ̀
EO: ὲkùkúnὲ̀
Ku: ὲkùkún·ɛ́   δékúkúnɛ́ 'at the end'
Od: ὲ-kúnúγí; ì-
WO: ὲkúnùmɛ̂

ENDURE

    A: -kparam   also 'try'

    EO: -n·e   'endure, suffer'

           -gam   'suffer pain'

           -n·é pòβ   'suffer hunger'

           -δígbìr   'suffer from neglect'

           -yε   'be in need without help'

    Ku: -n·e

    Od: -γurụγiɔm/-kụrụγiɔm

    WO: în·èβàr(O)(m-)

           în·èmə̀ (m-)

           în·è (m-)   'suppress pain'

ENEMY

    EO: ɔn·ị́ ámásúàn

    Ku: ɔn·ị̀ ɔ̀lóγị́án ə́δíèn

    Od: ɔ̀lɔ̀γδìèn; ị̀-

    WO: ɔ́n·ị̀ ὲkpụ̀kpụ̀

ENTER

    A: -δiγ

    EO: -δi^h

           ~-δi·

    Ku: -δiγ

           -δiγom   (when door closes after one)

    Od: -δiγ

    WO: ə̀-δî

           é-δī   'act of entering, entrance, entry'

ENTERTAIN

    A: -kɔ́ ígònì   'show hospitality, give food and drink'

                                  mɔ́ ụ́kɔ́ ñị́nɔ̀ ìgònì 'said one took care of him'

EO: -kḭɔm   cf. FEED

Ku: -kḭɔm   'entertain guest with food
                                   and drink'

     -βeβeleβom   'show hospitality'

Od: ɔ̀-kɔ̀ ógònì

WO: à-kḭɔ̀m   'show hospitality'

     ɛ̀kḭɔ̀má   n. 'entertainment'

ENTRANCE [OF DWELLING]
  A: (ə̀)δḭ́-bō̄; (ə̀)sḭ́-bō̄

ENVY (n)
  Ku: è-gbɔ̀gbɔ̀lɔ̀gì

EQUAL, BE (v)
  A: -leñ (oo-?)

EQUAL TO, WORTH, BE (v)
  A: -man   mḭ́ ámān(bɔ̀) δḭ́óβ ásḭ́à 'I'm
                         ten years old'
                      ámán δḭ̀òβ ə̀sélénì 'it
                         costs 10/-'
                      ámán ìkɔ̀ 'how much is it?'

ERRAND (n)
  A: (ə̀)-dôm   'errand, job'
      ò-rèlè ə́dòm   'to run errands'
      ɛ̀lɔ́ ōrōm   'whatever errand to do'
      ə̀bú-télé dòm á Jésùs 'Christ's disciples'

ERROR, FAULT
  A: ɔ̀pḭ̀ɔ̀màn

ESCAPE (v)   cf. GO AWAY
  A: -sumə

EO: -γil -δ̪ua   'run away'
Ku: -mizən
WO: îzə̀(m-)   used of animal, something
                         trapped

     ə̀yílìzə̀   used of human

EVENING
A: (ə̀)-dùlè
EO: ə̀dílè
     ~ èrə̀δìó
Ku: ə̀dúlə̀
Od: ùdùlè; (ə̀)r-
WO: ə̀dìlè

EVERYONE
A: ýỳmə̀wè (óòm'ə̀wè)   cf. ALL
     tò rótò rò òyè   'every person'
     òyé ōyē òyè   'every person'
                           δíóδīōδìò 'every day'
                           mémmēmmèm 'always'
EO: kààkòn·ì̤
     ~kààkə̀w̃únòm
Ku: kə̀rékə̀rònì̤
Od: ó·mə́ré̤ì
WO: kàkànòn·ì   'all people'

EVERYTHING
A: ýỳm-àràràr (oom?)   cf. ALL
EO: kààkìbú
Ku: kə̀rékə̄rābār
Od: óómɔkpó
WO: kàkànàβár   cf. ALL

EXPENSIVE   see DEAR

EXTEND, REACH (v.i.)
    A: -siemi

EXTINGUISH
    A: - δime(ánɨ̀àn, ɔ́tɔ̀zɪ̀)
          -δim   'become extinguished'
                                        cf. CORPSE, FAMILY DEAD

EYE   cf. SEED
    A: èkp-é-δíèn; (ə̀)rí-
    EO: ə̀δìèn
    Ku: ə́-δíèn; ə̀sí-
    Od: ə̀-δìèn; ə̀rì-
    WO: ə̀δìèn; ⸱zə̀

F

FACE (n)

A: (ə́)-ɣísìɣ~(ə́)-rísìɣ;
      (ə́)sí-

EO: -ə́wísì; ə̀r-

Ku: ə̀mìsìɣ; r-

Od: ə̀ɣìsìɣ; ə̀sùmùsìɣ

WO: ə́wúsì (A)

      èrésì (O)

FAECES

A: (à)-rị̀ịr; (à)rị̀-

EO: àtị̀n

Ku: àbtị̀n

Od: ə̀-rèèr; ə̀rè-

WO: àbtị̀

FAINT (v)

A: -ɣaarụ/-kaarụ

EO: -fụm

Ku: -fụmụ

Od: -ɣɔrɔm/-kɔrɔm

WO: à-fụ̂m

FALL (v)

A: -meel

      -meelom   'to fall on' 'to lose case'

      -loβom   'fall on (rain)'

      kpàị   ideoph.? 'fell, dropped'

      -βum/-pum   'fall on'

      ə̀ðíɣítón méβûm ñínə̀ 'you've lost the case (court)'

EO: -men

Ku: -mel

       -meleə   'fall on'   òrèrén ə́mèlèmə́ 'mì̦
                              'a tree fell on me'

Od: -meel

       -meelom   'to fall on'

       -kpetəən   'to stumble, trip over'

       èmèèl   n. 'fall'

WO: êl·ì (m-)

FALSE   see DISHONEST

FAMILY

   A: èɣùnótû   cf. WOMB

   EO: ɔ̀màr

        èw̃ùn   'stomach'

        àmàr ɛ́n· àm   'animal kingdom'

        àmàr ìn·ə́   'the fish (collectively)'

   Ku: ɔ̀ɣôl   'extended family'

   Od: ɔ̀tù

        ɔ̀tɔ̀...   'house of...'

   WO: ɔ̀màr   'family, including ancestors'

        àmàr   àmár ə́w̃únɔ̀m 'family of man'

        èw̃ún' ótù   'family'

        ɔ̀tù   'house, immediate family'

        ɔ̀már ótù   'extended family'

        ɛ̀wɛ̀dɛ̀   'fathers, ancestors'

        ɔ̀ɓə́n ɔ̀màr   'head of family'

FAMINE

   A: ì̦gbàkúrɔ̀

FAN (v)

   Ku: ɔ̀-fúgùmɔ̀

FAR

    A: -kɛl   v. cf. DEEP
          kɛ̀pɛ́
    EO: è-gbèñ
    Ku: -gbeñ   v.
          égbèñ   n.
    Od: -gbeñ   'far, distant'

FARM (n)

    A: ò-zò(~jò); ì-
          -ɓeɓójò   v. 'to farm' cf. PLANT
          òɓèɓòm ójò   'farmer'
    EO: ə̀dè   cf. EARTH
          ~òδì
    Ku: ó-sị̀; àrɛ́-
          -fɛgụ   v. 'to farm, wind'
    Od: ò-δìγì; (ə̀)rì-
    WO: ə̀dè; ˋzə̀   cf. EARTH

FAT

    A: ɛ̀-nụ̀ụ̀m
          -bụγ   v. 'be fat' cf. BIG
    EO: ɛ̀nụ̀m   n.
          ə̀lìgèn   adj.
    Ku: ɛ̀nụ̀m
          ɔ̀nụ̀nụ̀màn
    Od: ɛ̀nụ̀ụ̀m   n.
    WO: àmɛ̀lɛ̀ñ   n.

FATHER

    A: ɔ̀dɛ̀; àbụ̀rụ̀-
          / ádɛ̀ ~ dɛ́dɛ̀   voc.
    EO: ɔ̀-wɛ̀dɛ̀; ɛ̀-
          áádà   voc.

Ku: ɔ̀wɛ̀dɛ̀; r-
     àádà   voc.

Od: ɔ̀dɛ̀; àbʉ̀rʉ̀dɛ̀
     ádà   voc.

WO: ɔ̀wɛ̀dɛ̀

FATHOM (n)

EO: ə̀kùɓɔ̀

Ku: ə̀kùɓú   'distance between out-
                               stretched hands'

     ɔ̀gbáàgwɔ̀   'distance from armpit to
                               finger'

WO: ə̀kúbú

FATIGUE

A: (à)δɟ́-βɛ̄r   cf. TIRED

EO: ɔ̀βɛ̀r

Od: àlɟ̀-βɛ̂r

WO: ə́gbē̄β ə̄m̀   'I'm tired'

FAULT   see ERROR

FEAR

A: ə̀rúùgù   n.
     ə̀rúùgù -siβ...   v.i. 'fear catch...,
                                  be afraid'
                               ə̀rúùgù rúsìβ ímì 'I'm afraid'

     -γiilaan/-kiilaan   cf. RUN v. mɟ́ ràkíílaàn
                                  ñɔ̀dɟ́ 'I fear him'

EO: -tete   v.

Ku: ə̀rù-gúgù   n. ə̀rùgúgù nè̀δìγí àmɟ̀
                                  'I'm afraid'

     -γil   v. cf. RUN

Od: -γiil ə̀rúùgù   v.

WO: è̀tɛ̀tə̀   n.
     ềtɛ̀tɛ̀ (m-)   v.t.
     ~ềtɛ̀tə̀   v.t.

FEAST (n)
    A: ὲ-yààl   also personal name
    EO: έ-yàl   also fem. name
    Ku: ὲ-yàl   also fem. name
        ɔ-lálí   also masc. name
    WO: ὲ-yàl   also fem. name

FEATHER
    A: (ὲ) δú-βúúβ; (ὲ)sú-
         ~(ὲ)δú-γúúγ; (ὲ)sú-
    EO: àtàm έnúr
    Ku: àtâm; r-
    Od: ὲlù-βúúβ; ὲsù-
    WO: ὲlḁlέn·úrṵ; ′zà

FEED (v)
    A: -ŋɔ́έδíὲn [ɔ̀ŋέδíὲn]   'give food'
    EO: ɔ̀ñɔ̀δé   'feed'
        ɔ̀ñɔ̀mâm   'feed at breast'
        -kḭɔm   'give food to stranger'
    Ku: -nìγə έδíὲn   'feed children, animals'
        -kḭɔm   'feed visitors, humans'
    Od: -nɔγ' έδíə̀n   cf. GIVE
    WO: à-gbâl
        ὲ-gbàlâ   n. 'feeding'

FELL (v)
    A: -ler   cf. CUT
    Ku: -gu   'fell tree'
    Od: -ler
    WO: ə̀-gû (ɔ̀rὲn)   'fell tree'

FEMALE
    A: ànḭr

EO: ɔ̀yà
Ku: ɔ̀yà
Od: ɔ̀zà
WO: àδìzà

FENCE (n)
   A: óɣōñ
   Ku: ɔ̀kpàɣ
   Od: ì̩-kɔ̀   'fence of sticks and bamboo'

FESTIVAL
   Od: ɛ̀-zààl   fem. personal name

FEVER
   A: ò-síβí̩ñ; (ə̀)rí-
   EO: ìɓógí
     ~òkógóròt   Harmattan òkògòró nə́sù ə́m
                    'I have a fever'
   Ku: àmù̩m ɔ̀βì̩y
   Od: ɔ́ɔ́lɛ̄   ɔ́ɔ́lɛ̀ nə̂δíɣ zòdí 'he has
                    fever'
   WO: ìɓógí   Nembe ìɓógí nə̀sú ə̀m "I
                    have a fever, feel cold'

FEW
   A: i̩bam
     ~ikomə
   EO: -kì̩r
     ɛ̀-kàkárà
   Ku: ɔ̀ñ-èkékə̀rɛ̄

FIGHT (n)
   A: èléβìrì   cf. MALE
     èèɣìòm   'manner of fight'

Ku: èl·óβìrì
      í-nìnŏm   'severe fighting'
Od: èlèβîr

FIGHT (v)
A: -éγí éléβìrì
     èèγì ~ èèγì   'to fight'
                    mí úèγí ròdí 'I fought
                      with him'
EO: -we
Ku: -we
Od: -βe
     -βezuən   'fight one another'
WO: ə̀-wê   cf. WRESTLING
     ə̀-wê ɛγ̃àm   'fight battle'

FILE (n)
Ku: ígbígífàrì̧

FILL (v)
A: -mujeδi   'fill up'
       z
     -muzə   'fill'
       j
EO: -mizoδi ~ -mizoδom v.t.
Ku: -muzoγoδi
Od: -βule/-pule
WO: ûzòlòmə̀n(m-)

FILTER   see STRAIN

FIN   cf. BREAST
EO: àmàgàn   'sharp fins'
Ku: àmàmám   'lateral, pectoral fin'
Od: ì̧-γèrèγèr   pl. 'fish fins'
WO: ə̀lélín·ə̀

FINE, BE (v)   cf. HEALTHY
    Ku: -βon   βòné mòlògì 'enjoy yourself'
                                òlògì δámį̀ nòβónnǒ 'I'm sad'

FINGER
    A: (à)-γúnų́γ; (à)sų́nų́γ
    EO: ὲkpàlį́ ágwò; ὲkpàsį́... cf. TOE
    Ku: àδὲ-γáγ àgwò; àsὲ...
    Od: àγų̀nų́ ávō̄; àsų̀nų́...
    WO: ὲkpásálàgwò

FINGERNAIL   see CLAW

FINISH (v)
    A: -mineen (v.i.)   mémínèèn 'it's finished
                                   (story)'

         -madan (v.t.)   ímìnéènní 'it was finished'
                                ímínèèm 'it was not
                                   finished'

    EO: -muneñ ~ -mineñ
    Ku: -man
         -muniən   v.i.
    Od: -man   v.t.
         -muneen   v.i.
    WO: ínùèñmὲn   v.t.
         ínùèñ (m-)   v.i.   'get finished'

FIRE (n)
    A: (á)-nį́àn; (á)sį́-
    EO: àñà
    Ku: àñà
    Od: ànį̀àn; (à)r-
    WO: àlὲpὲ; ´^zà   cf. FIREWOOD

FIREFLY   cf. STAR
    A: έέ-nààn

EO: ɛ̀n·ànâñ
Od: ɛ̀-náñ
WO: ɛ̀nànâñ

FIREWOOD

A: ị̀-pɛ̀; sg. (à)ɗị̀-pɛ̀
EO: àlɛ̀pɛ̀
Ku: ị̀pɛ̀
Od: àlị̀-pɛ̀; ị̀-
WO: àlɛ̀pɛ̀   cf. FIRE

FISH

A: è-n·ə̂; ì-   n.
     -ɗá ín·ə̀   v. 'fish, angle'
     òkóñóm ákò̀nị̀   n. 'fisherman'
     (à)ɗị́-ɓaβ   'fish-hook'
                                    'fish spear' see SPEAR
     àkò̀nị̀   n. 'fishing'
     ò̀ò̀-nụ̀; (à)rụ̀ụ̀   'fishpond'
     (à)ɗị́-ɣɛ́ɛ̀l   'fishtrap'
EO: ìn·ə́   n.
     -tɔɓɔgị̀   v. 'angle'
     ò̀gìmìn·ə́   'fisherman'
     ~ ò̀kwèmìn·ə́   'fisherman'
     àlụ̀kpàβ   'fish-hook'
     ò̀kpó   'fishpond'
     è̀ŋìnì   'very large fishpond'
     ə́lúkê   'fishtrap'
     ɛ̀ɣɛ̀lɛ̀ɣêl   'fishtrap'
     ò̀súsū ~ ò̀súɣúsūɣū   'fishtrap'
Ku: én·ə̀; í-   n.
     -gị̀ ò̀gbó   v. 'cast net'
     -gị̀ ékò̀   v. 'use framed net'
     tò̀rụ̀sàrà   v. 'fish with hook'
     -ɗa   v. 'fish with rod'

Ku:	-kpɔgị̣	v. 'fish with line while absent'
	ɔ̀zɛ̀mín·ə́	cf. KILL 'fisherman'
	àmụ̀kpáβ	'fish-hook'
	ɛ̀-tôn	'fishtrap, set by women'
Od:	è-n·ə́; ì-	n.
	-δa	v. 'fish, angle'
	ɔ̀zɛ̀mín·ə̀; ị̀-	'fisherman' cf. KILL
	à-mụ̀kpáβ	'fish-hook'
	ì-zìə́	n. 'fishing'
	ə̀-ɣìní; (ə̀)sì- ~ ə̀sìní	'fishpond'
	ɔ̀ɔ̀-tà	'fish weir made of bamboo'
	è-kùɣè	'fishtrap'
	ɛ̀-ɣɛ́ɛ̄l	'fishtrap'
	ɔ̀-ɣɛ̀	'fishtrap damming up river'
WO:	én·ə̀; í-	n.
	à-rɔ̂β àtụ̀kpàβ	v. 'put hook in water'
	-girin·ə	v. 'fish (in general)'
	ɔ̀gìrɔ̀m ín·ə̀	'fisherman'
	àδụ́kpáβ ~ àsụ́kpáβ	'fish-hook'
	ɛ̀kụ̀	'fishing, cutting through the creek'
	èɣɔ̀	'fishpond'
	ɛ̀ɣɛ́lɛ̀(ɣɛ̀lɛ̀)	'woven fishtrap'
	àw̃àị̀	'very large fishtrap'
	ɔ̀kwálɛ̀	'fishtrap, has elastic bamboo'

FIT, SUIT (v)		cf. PAY
A:	-kpɛ	ɛ́kpɛ̀ní lɔ̄ mị̄ kə̀lɛ̀ ɛ̀δìèn 'it's necessary that I eat'
		àsɔ̀màβɔ̄ ụ̀kpɛ̀nị̄ līmì 'the shirt fits me'
EO:	-δikən	
Od:	-kpɛ	v.i. used of clothing
	-nɛɣị̣ɔm	v.i. of peg in hole, etc.

WO: ə̀-δíkə̀n

FIX, SET, APPOINT
A: -gu   ò-gú ə́δíò 'to appoint a day'
Ku: -guən   'set a date' ə̀δə̀mə̀ wúgúə́nβɔ̌
                                     'the appointed day'

      ògúə̄n   'act of fixing date'

FLAG (n)
A: àlàgbà
EO: ìkp-ówù   'canoe cloth'
Ku: úkpè óɣúɣ   'canoe cloth'
Od: àlàgbà
WO: ìkpòwù   cf. CLOTH; BOAT

FLAY   see SKIN (v)

FLEA
A: ɛ̀sǘ ə̀ɣòòɣ   cf. DOG
EO: è̃w̃ə̀m
Ku: èwə̀β; r-
Od: ị̀-zǎɣ
WO: ìwə̀β; ᷘ-zə̀

FLOAT (v)
A: -βooβ/-pooβ
EO: -foñ
Ku: -βoβ
Od: -βooβ/-pooβ
WO: ə̀-fôñ

FLOG   see HIT

FLOOD SEASON
A: (ə̀)δíɣò   also 'flood'

A: èɣélé érù   'coming of flood'
   èɣélé ékèèl   'departure of flood'
   (two ceremonies performed by Òɣòré village, Abua)
EO: ə̀δíò̝
Ku: ə̀δíɣò
Od: ə̀-δìɣò; (ə̀)rə̀-
WO: òlógə̝́δíò̝

FLOW (v)
 A: -kil
   -δikḷá   used of tide
   -kiliɣíìl   used of tide
 EO: -δi   'enter, as tide'
   -tama   used of river
 Ku: -βaɣ   'flow as tide'
   -gbɔ   'flow as river'
 Od: -gbor   'flow as river'
   -δiɣ   'flow, enter, as tide'
 WO: ə̀-kílì   'flow as river'
   ə̀-δî   'flow as tide' cf. ENTER

FLOWER   see FRUIT

FLY (n)
 A: ɛ̀-βị́; ị̀-
 EO: ɛ̀gị̀
 Ku: ɛ̀gị̀; ị̀-
 Od: ɛ̀-gị̀; ị̀-
 WO: ɛ̀gị̀; `zà

FLY (v)
 A: -βɛɛβ/-pɛɛβ
 EO: -βul
 Ku: -βɛβ
 Od: -βɛɛβ/-pɛɛβ

WO: ə̀-βúlù
    ó-βùlú   'flight' é-βùlóβù 'smart-
                                        ness, maneuvering body
                                        as in flight'

FOAM (n)
    A: ò̄βə̀
    EO: òfòkòfòkò
    Ku: óβóβò
    Od: òβə̀
    WO: òfúkò

FOG
    A: óòtụ̀
    EO: òmụ̀mụ̀tôr
    WO: òkòŋgòrò   'mist of Harmattan'

FOLD (v)
    A: -kpo
    EO: -kpaβ
    Ku: -ɓaragị
    Od: -kpal
        -kpṳl   'fold once'
        -kpṳlṳɣị   'fold several times'
    WO: à-kpôl

FOLLOW   cf. ACCOMPANY
    A: -tṳan   also 'accompany'
        -daβ   ụ́-dàβ íímị 'follow me'
        -tum   'be next'
    EO: -βoronom
    Ku: -tṳɔn·ɔm
    WO: ə̀-βə́rə̀n

FOOD
    A: è-ðìèn; (ə̀)rìì-
    EO: èðìə̀

Ku: éɗíə̀n; r-
Od: è-ɗìə̀n; (ə̀)rì-
WO: éɗíə̀

FOOT
    Ku: ɛ̀ɓáɓā ə̀wèl   cf. LEG

FOREHEAD
    A: èlór
    EO: ègbódó
    Ku: ègbòdó
    Od: è-gbòdó; (ə̀)rə̀-
    WO: òkòdì

FOREST   see BUSH

FORGE (v)   cf. BLACKSMITH
    EO: -lɛm   also 'create'
    Ku: -suɣíkò
    Od: -lɛm   'to do blacksmithing'
         -suɣíkō   'work bellows'
    WO: à-nɛ̂m

FORGET
    A: -bulə/-wulə
    EO: -weletə
    Ku: -weletən
    Od: -ɓulo
    WO: ə̀-βôl·ògì

FORGIVE   cf. PASS
    WO: -βì ə̀tènèmə̀n   'take and pass over'
         ò-tènèmə̀n   'forgiveness'

FORK (n)
    WO: à-gbófị̀

FREE
    EO: ɔ̀-bènémúágwɔ̀   'to be manumitted'

FRIEND   cf. AGREEMENT
    A: ɔ̀yá-ɣɨ̀rɨ̀; (à)rɨ̀-ɣɨ̀rɨ́
    EO: ɔ̀-gbágɔ̀; ɛ̀-
            ɛ́wɔ̀   'blood-ally'
    Ku: ə̀tɔ̀lɔ̀ɣə̀n; r-
    Od: ɔ̀-bɔ̀lɔ̌l; àbʉ̀rʉ̀-
    WO: è-βɛ́rɛ́nɛ́dɔ̌n; ì-   cf. FOLLOW
            ɔ́gɔ̀   'special friend, ally'

FROG
    A: ɔ̀-ɓàl; (à)rà- ~(à)sɨ́-
    EO: ɔ̀gʉ̀m   'bull frog'
            àkɔ̀rɔ̀kɔ́rɔ̀   'green frog'
            ànɨ́ àpɛ̀tɨ́pɛ̀   'brown, soft-skinned frog'
            àyɔ́ʉ́   'tree frog'
    Ku: ɔ́βúɔ̀m
            ɔ́-gwɔ̀m; ɨ́-
    Od: ɔ̀-gáām; ɨ̀-
    WO: ɔ́-wɔ̀; ɛ́-   cf. TOAD
            ɔ́gʉ̀m

FRONT
    A: -ɣísìɣ
    EO: èðɨ́ɛ́
    Ku: ðéðɨ́ɛ́   cf. EYE
    Od: ə̀ɣìsìɣ
    WO: éðìɛ́

FRUIT
    A: éé-mūmə̄; (ə̀)rúú-
    EO: ìmúmə̀   also 'flower'
    Ku: ɔ̀-tù(ɔ̀rérén); ì-
    Od: ì-múúmə́   also 'flower'
    WO: ímùmù ɔ̀rèn; ímùmù ìrèn

FRY (v)
    A: -gbaɣaδị
    WO: ɔ̂fàràị̀ (m-)

FUFU
    A: èɣúménèèn ɛ̀lɛ̀1   cf. POUND
    EO: àkpʉ́kɔ̀rɔ̀   'fermented cassava'
    Ku: àkpókɔ̀rɔ̀
    Od: ìɣùmáàn
    WO: ɔ̀kpʉ́kɔ̀rɔ̀

FULL
    A: -muzə ~ -mujə   'be, become full' cf. FILL
    EO: -mìzɔ̀   v. 'be full'
        ɔ̀-mìzɔ̀mízɔ̀   modif.
        ɔ̀-mìzɔ̀   n. 'fullness'
    Ku: -mùzɔ̀   v. 'be full'
                       ɔ̀mùzɔ̀múzɔ̀ àfà 'full calabash'
                       àfàβɔ́ nə́múzɔ̀ 'calabash is
                         full'
    Od: -muzə   v. 'be full'
        èβùlíɔ̀m   n.
    WO: (m)íì-zo   v.i. 'be, become full'
        îzɔ̀nɔ̀   n. 'full measure'

FUR
    A: (ə̀)δú-βúúβ   cf. FEATHER
    EO: àtàmà
        àtàm-ɛ́nàm
    Ku: ìpúr
    WO: àtámà

FUTILE
    Ku: ị̀kpɔ́   'in vain, unsuccessfully,
                          for nothing'

G

GAIN (n)

  A: à-sṹ (àmɪ̀)

GALL

  A: è-l·û; (ə̀)rú-
  EO: ànṹn
  Ku: ə̀nòn
  WO: ə̀nòn

GAME   see PLAY (n)

GATHER (v)

  A: -kpomoɣiən   v.i.

       -sɔn   also 'pick up' ɔ̀dɪ́ rà-sɔ́n í-pɛ̀ 'he's gathering firewood'

       -kpomoɣi (oo-)
       -koroɣi (oo-)

  EO: -kokoδi   v.t.

       -kokoδiən   v.i.

  Ku: -kokoδi   v.t.

       -kokoδiən   v.i.

  Od: -koβoɣi (oo-)   v.t.

       -kpo   v.t.   'gather fruit, berries'

       -koβoɣiən (oo-)   v.i.

  WO: ə̀-kókòδìə̀n   v.i.

       í-kōkōδīə̀n   'unexpected, emergency meeting'

       ə̀-kókòδì   v.t. also 'collect'

GECKO

  A: ò-kòrìòm òtù
  EO: òkòδùm òtù
  Ku: òkòδùmótù

Od: òkè̀rè̀mòtù
WO: òkòδùm òtù

GET UP, ARISE
   A: -ɓetenu   mí ú-ɓētēnú 'I got up'
   Od: -ɓetunu   also 'wake up'

GHOST, SPIRIT
   A: è-rù; (è̀)rù-
   EO: ègù-ə́dè   also 'dead person'
   Ku: ègùə́dè   'dead person'
       èrù   'evil spirit'
       ɛ̀-mu̞γ   'spirit'
   Od: ɛ̀-mù̞γ; (à)rù̞- 'soul'
   WO: ɛ̀-mù̞β   'spirit, soul'
       íwô̂n·ì̞
       ~ àtámár égúə̂dè

GIFT, PRESENT
   Od: ɛ̀-nòγó ~ ì̞-   cf. GIVE

GILLS   cf. FISH
   A: ì̞tákù̞ én·è̀
   EO: à̀ɓàgá
       ~àsì̞àl èmú-ín·è̀
   Ku: àsì̞γàl én·è̀
   Od: ì̞-nàγànàγ

GIN   cf. WINE
   A: àkánèmè   locally brewed
     ~ káí̞káí̞   locally brewed
     ~ ááɓā̄β   locally brewed
     è̀zínì̞
     ~ àkámèrè

    EO: ὲzín
    Od: àzínì

GIRL   cf. MAIDEN

    A: ɔ̀ñ-ánì; (à)ŋáñàan   ñánì àmì 'my daughter'
                                    (address)

                                         ɔ̀ñánì àmì 'my daughter'
                                       (praise, compliment)

    EO: ὲñànì; àw̃ìñân
    Ku: ɔ̀ñánì; àw̃íñàn
    Od: ɔ̀ñànì; àsùmùñáān
    WO: àδízóñ; àwáràw̃ì

GIVE

    A: -ŋɔ   ú-ŋɔ̀ 'give me (less polite)'
        -ŋaanì   'to give as gift, dash'
                           ú-ŋàànì 'please give me'

    EO: -ña
    Ku: -niɣə
    Od: -nɔɣɔ
    WO: à-ñέ̂

GIVE BIRTH, BEGET   cf. FAMILY

    A: -mar   also 'have child' (of man
                                  or woman)

    EO: -mar   also 'have children'
    Ku: -mar
        -ɓolóruɔ̀m   'get additional child'
    Od: -mar
    WO: à-márì

  GO

    A: -kì/-ɣì
        -ɣì(m)ɔm/-kì(m)ɔm   'to go by...' mì úɣìmóm
                                    óɣùùɣ 'I went by canoe'

    EO: -gì

Ku: -gḛ

Od: -γḛ/-kḛ

        -ɓɔl   'to go in specific manner'

                     àm'ụ́ɓɔl tə́vèl 'I went on foot, trekked'

WO: à-gî̟

        ɛ́-gī̟   'act of going'

GO AWAY   cf. ESCAPE

  A: -ɓụa

  EO: -δụa

  Ku: -δụa   also 'heal' [int]

  Od: -δụa   also 'escape'

        -sumə   'run far away'

  WO: à-δụ́à

GO BACK   see RETURN

GO HOME

  A: -γeel/-keel

        -γeelom   'go home with'

                    mḭ́ ụ́-sḭ̀γɛ́ ñɔ̀dḭ́ ə̀-γéélóm 'I took him home with me'

                    mḭ́ ú-γèèlóm ñɔ̀dḭ́ 'I went home with him'

  EO: -yel

  Ku: -yel

  Od: -γeel/-keel

  WO: ḭ́lṵ̀ə̀ (m-)

GO OUT, COME OUT

  A: -mite   also 'happen'

                    ə́-mḭ́ténōm 'went out with...'

                    ééγē kú ḭ̀-mḭ̀tè 'what happened'

GO OUT

A: -βun/-pun   'come out of, as water, hole'

                          ə̀-δíγí βɔ̄ rè-βùnùγù 'the
                             market is breaking up'

                          ə́-βún ú-mɯ̀ɯ̀m 'he came out
                             of the water'

      pún   'come out!'

EO: -mite

Ku: -mite

      -mutiom   'take outside, go to place
                             of work'

                          (ìnà) nə́mútíɔ̀m 'he's gone
                             to work'

      -βun   'come out of canoe, leave
                             canoe, go up'

Od: -mute

WO: íìtè (m-)

GO ROUND

A: -γironom/-kironom

EO: -ko   also 'fence'

Ku: -gir   also 'work'

Od: -kìn ɔ̀kítǒn

WO: ə̀-gírì   cf. WORK (v)

GO THROUGH

A: -ɓuγ   'go under and out other side'

                          ə́γííl ə́ɓúγ ótúβɔ̄ 'he ran
                             through the house'

GOAT

A: ɔ̀-gâ; ì-
      è-kpé; (ə̀)rè-   'he-goat'

EO: èwèl
      èkpé   'he-goat'

Ku: è-wèl; ì-
      èkpé; r-   'he-goat'

Od: è-vèl; ì-
     è-kpé; (ə̀)rə̀-   'he-goat'

WO: è-wèl; ì-wèl
     è-kpé; ì-   'he-goat'
     ɛ̀zɛ́   'she-goat'

GOD

A: àkɛ́   (creator)
     ɛ̀nàan   (Christian preference)

EO: ə̀zìbə̀

Ku: ə̀zìbə̀

Od: ɛ̀nàan   also 'luck'

WO: ə̀zìbə̀

GONG

A: ò-gélè   -kool ógèlè 'hit gong'
              -kər ógèlè 'ring gong'

Ku: ò-kélè

GOOD

A: -nị̀γɛ   v. 'be good'
              ɛ́nị̀γènị́à 'all right--'
                 (warning)
              ɛ̀nị́γɛ́ 'beautiful'
              ị́-nị́γὲ 'it's not good'
              ə̀lóór ámị̀ ị́nị́γὲ 'I'm sick'
              ə̀lóór á·mị̀ rὲtól ɛ́nị́γὲ
                 'I'm getting sick'

EO: -nị̀ɛ   v. 'good, beautiful'
     ò-ɓèɓí; ì-   n. 'goodness, beauty'
                 cf. BEAUTY

Ku: -ɓèɓí   v. also 'pure'
     ò̀ɓéɓì   n.
     -ɓon   èɗìɛ̀nɓɔ́ éɓŏn 'food was good'

Od: -nɛγɛ   ə̀lòòr àmị́ óóɓì 'I'm well'
     ~(-ooɓi)

Od: əlòòr àmí náànɛ̀ɣɛ́ 'I'm
         well, I've recovered'

  -nɛɣɛmi̱ v.t. 'make good'
  ɛ̀nɛ̀ɣɛ́ 'goodness, beauty'
  ~ əlì-íɓì   cf. BEAUTY

WO: ɔ̀ɓêɓ; ì-

  -ɓai̱ 'be, become, good, pretty'
  -ɓai̱man 'make pretty'
  ɛ̀-ɓáí̱mán ól·ɔ̀gì 'joy, joyfulness'
  mí̱ nàɓáí̱mán ôl·ɔ̀gì
         'I'm joyful'

  ɔ-ɓài̱ n. 'goodness, beauty'
  ò-ɓêɓ 'goodness, beauty' fem. name

GORILLA
  A: é-mèlékɛ̀; (ə̀)ré-
  EO: ɛ̀télé
      ~ ɛ̀kpu̱làgwɔ̀
  Ku: ə̀télé
  Od: è-mèléké; (ə̀)rə̀-
  WO: èl·é; ì-

GOWN see ROBE

GRANDCHILD
  EO: ɔ̀ñ-ə́kɔ̀

GRANDPARENT
  EO: ɔ̀kéñ-ɔ́wɛ̀dɛ̀
      ɔ̀kéñ-ɔ́w̃ìn
  Ku: ɔ̀wɛ̀d'áku̱ 'grandfather'
      ɔ̃̀w̃ènì áku̱ 'grandmother'
  Od: ɔ̀di̱àkɔ́ 'grandfather'
      ònììnàkɔ́ 'grandmother'

GRASS
    A: àr-ɔ́ɔ̀ɣɔ̀   cf. MEDICINE
    EO: àsɔ́ɣɔ̀
    Ku: ɔ̀-ɣɔ́ɣɔ̀; ị̀-
    Od: ị̀ị́ɣɔ̀
    WO: ɔ̀-ɣɔ́ɣɔ̀; ɛ̀- ~ àsị́ɔ̀
                        ~ àdị̀ɔ̀

GRASSCUTTER [RAT]
    A: éè-bìú; (ə̀)ríì-
    EO: ògbòmə́
    Ku: ə̀kírì
    Od: ə̀-kìrì; (ə̀)sì-
    WO: ìkìrìkìrì

GRASSHOPPER
    A: ə̀ɣóóɣ ə́bên   'Ibo dog'

GRATE (v)
    A: -ɣɔl/-kɔl
    EO: -fɔkɔ
    WO: ɔ̂fɔ̀(m-)

GRAVE (n)
    A: ɔ̀-ɗì; (ə̀)rì-
    EO: ɔ̀ɗì
    Ku: àñ̀ụ̀ óɗì
    Od: ɔ̀ɔ̀gù
    WO: ɔ̀ɗì   'burial, grave' cf. BURY

GRAY HAIR
    A: àsùɔ́l
    EO: àsɔ̀n
    Ku: àsɔ̀n

    Od: àn·ɔ̀ñ
    WO: àrɔ̀n(ɨ̀)

GREASE (n)
    WO: ɛ̀gɨ̀rízɨ̀

GREET, SALUTE   cf. CALL
    A: -maɣ
    EO: -βelegom
    Ku: -βel·egəmə
    Od: -βeleɣiən/-peleɣiən
    WO: ə̀-wɛ́nə̀n
          ìwə̀nə̀n   n. 'greeting'

GRIND (v)   cf. WHET
    EO: -gbɛ
    Ku: -gbɛ
    Od: -gbɛ
    WO: ɛ̂gbɛ̀(m-)

GRIP (v)
    A: dìm   ideophone? mɨ́ dìm 'I
                               gripped'

GROAN
    -kụ̀β   v.
    ɨ̀-kụ̀β   n. 'groans, moans'

GROUNDNUTS
    A: àpàpá
    EO: àpápá
    Ku: àpàpà
    Od: àpàpá
    WO: ápàpá; ´-zà

GROUP, TRIBE, SPECIES, CLASS   cf. FAMILY
    A: ɔ̀-màr   ɔ̀màr ɔ́wὲ 'world of living'

                                   ɔ̀màr íɓîn 'world of the dead'

                                   ɔ̀màr ɨ́nàm 'group of animals,
                                       species of...'

GROW (vi)
    A: -βoβ/-poβ   ɔ̀réñβō rὲpóβ 'the tree is
                                       growing'

    Ku: -ɗìɣ ὲmú   'grow up, become head'

          -ruβe   'mature (of plantain, raffia
                                       palm)'

GUEST
    A: óó-rúèn; (ɘ̀)rúú
    EO: ìsùlòmɘ̀
    Ku: ísólómɘ̀; r-

          ɔ̀-rorúə; ì-   'outsider who has settled
                                       in village'

    Od: ìsɔ̀lɔ̀mɘ̀n   sing./pl.
    WO: ìsɔ̀lɔ̀mɘ̀

GUINEA FOWL
    A: έέ-sàràɣʉ̀
    EO: ɔ̀kɘ̀nɘ̀zὲ
    Od: ɔ̀-zàkʉ́rʉ̀rʉ̀; (à)rɨ̀-

GULP DOWN
    A: gbà kóòɣ...bìm   'gulped... down'

GUN (n)
    A: (à)láàgbà
    EO: àvà
    Ku: àvà
    Od: à-làágbā; àsɨ̀-
    WO: àvà

GUNPOWDER
    A: ópɔ̀lì̤
    EO: ɔ̀rṳ̀rṳ̀
    Ku: èrɔ̀rɔ̀ ávà
    Od: ɔ̀ɔ̀rṳ̀
    WO: ɔ̀rṳ̀rṳ̀

GUNSHOT
    A: (à)ɓì̤-àɓâ àlààgbà   'talk of gun'

GUT [INTESTINE]
    A: ɔ̀ɔ̀-lá; ì̤ì̤-
    EO: ìgùnùgùn   pl.
    Ku: ɔ̀ɔ̀-l·à; ì̤ì̤-
    Od: ɔ̀-là; ì̤-
    WO: ìgùnùgù   pl.

H

HAIR

    A: (á)ᵭí-láàl ~ -láị;
             (á)sí-

    EO: àsịál (èmú)   'head hair'
         àsịal ᵊlúzù   'body hair'
         ~ àtàm ᵊlúzù
    Ku: àsɛ̀ɣàl
         i·púr   'body hair'
    Od: àsí-lāān
    WO: àsịàl

HALF

    A: ᵊbìn ésè ịyàl ᵊsìbìn 'part of two parts'
         ékùlᵊ   'half'
    EO: èkúᵭī   (anything that has length)
    Ku: átụ̀gyán
         ~ ᵊpàᵭị̀
    WO: êgáwàlàgwᵊ   'this and that side'

HAMMER (n)

    EO: ìkólɓágú
    Ku: ìkólíɓágú
    WO: ìkólóɓágí

HAND (n)

    A: (à)ᵭí-ɣááɣ; (à)rí-
             ~(à)rá-
    EO: àgwᵊ
    Ku: à-gwᵊ; àrụ̀-
    Od: àvᵊ; àr-
    WO: àgwᵊ; ´zà

HANG (vt)

A: -sin   'hang living things, kill
                                        by hanging'

Ku: -sineni   'hang person to kill'
        -kɛrị

        -sin   'set noose, strangling trap'

        -tekele   v.i. 'hang'

        -kɛðịan   'hang, rest on'

HAPPY   see CLEAN

HARD   cf. STRONG

A: -kpar   v. 'be hard'

        -kparamị   v.t. 'harden'

        (à)ðị́-kpàr   n. 'hardness'

EO: -kpar   also 'strong'

        ɔ̀kpàràkpàr; ɛ̀-   adj.

        -kparamɛn   v.t. 'harden'

        àlị̀-kpàr   n. 'hardness'

Ku: ɔ̀kpàràkpár   also 'strong'

        -kparamɛnị   v.t. 'harden'

        àlù̀kpár   n. 'hardness'

Od: -kpar

        -kparamị   v.t. 'harden'

        àlị̀-kpâr   n. 'hardness'

WO: -kpar   v.i. 'be, become hard,
                                        strong'

        ɔ̀kpàkpár; ɛ̀-   modif.

        -kparaman   v.t. 'harden'

        ɛ̀-kpàr   n. 'hardness'

HARMATTAN

A: òkògòrò

Ku: òkògòrò

Od: òkògòrò
WO: òkòŋgòrò

HARPOON [FOR MANATEE]
WO: ɔ̀sɔ́ɓə̄δê̄ɓ

HARVEST (v)
Ku: -ñɛr   'reap poor harvest'
     -ɓogion   'reap good harvest'
WO: -gi(íì)(m-)   'to dig up'
     -kμ   'harvest by plucking'

HAT
A: è-ɣóòñ; (ə̀)ró-
EO: èɣóí
Ku: èɣóì; r-
Od: è-ɣóñ; (ə̀)rə̀-
WO: è-ɣóì; ì-

HATCH (v)
A: -ɓom éɣélè   v.t.
EO: -kɛkɛ
Ku: -kɛkɛ
WO: ɛ́kɛ̀kɛ̀[m-]

HATE (v)
A: -kiə
EO: -sμa
Ku: -l·ɔɣ ə̀δìên
Od: -lɔɣ ə̀δíèn
WO: à-sμ́à
     ɛ̀-sμ̀ànàn   'hatred'

HAVE, OBTAIN
    A: -mɔɔɣ
    EO: -ɓenə   'have, own'
          -βin   'obtain'
    Ku: -w̃unə   cf. REACH
    Od: -tɛñ   also 'reach' cf. REACH
    WO: ə̀-ɓə́nə̀

HAWK
    A: áà-kpɔ̀; (à)rɔ́ɔ̀-
    EO: ɔ̀kpɔ̀kpɔ̀
    Ku: ɔ̀kpʉ̀kpɔ̀ɣ
          ɔ̀tɔ̀gɔ̀; ótógô; r-
    Od: ʉ̀-dɔ̀kɔ̀; ị̀-   'large hawk'
          ààkpɔ̀ɣ; (à)r-
    WO: àkpɔ̀kpɔ̀; ˋzà

HEAD (n)
    A: ɛ̀-mʉ́; (à)rʉ́-
    EO: -èmù; ə̀r-
    Ku: ɛ̀mʉ́
    Od: ɛ̀-mʉ́; (à)rʉ̀-
    WO: èmú; ìmú(zə̀)

HEADTIE
    A: ɔ̀káɣàm ɛ̀mu
          ~ àlɔ́kɔ̀
    EO: ɔ̀kpénémú
    Ku: ɔ̀kpíə̀n ɛ́mʉ́
    Od: ɔ̀-kàɣâm
    WO: ɔ̀βɔ́rɔ́gɔ́mémù

HEAL   see also CURE
    A: -ɣeel/-keel   v.i. 'go' èsì βɔ́ rèkéél
                                 'the wound is healing'

A: -ɣeelemi/-keelemi   v.t. 'make go'
EO: -ɗųɛmɛn   v.t.
     -ɗųa   v.i. 'go away, heal'
Ku: -gbam   v.t.
WO: ə̀-wô   v.t.

HEALTHY, WELL, BE (v)
A: -moon   ə̀lóór á·mì̧ émòònnī̧ 'I'm well'
                ɔ̀dí̧ rə̀móón 'he's getting
                    well'
    òmòòn ə́lóòr   n. 'health, well-being'
EO: -ɗìkə̀n   'be well' ə̀lùzùɗə́m ɔ̀ɗíkə̀nɗɔ̌
                    'I'm not well'
                mì̧ nə́ɗùm 'I'm alive, well,
                    all right'
Ku: -βon   ózù ɗámí̧ ə́βɔ̌n 'my body is
                    well'
                ɔ̀βéβì ə̀ɣùɗŭm 'good health'
                ɔ̀lɔ̀gì ɗámí̧ nə̀βɔ̌n 'I'm happy'

HEAP UP
A: -kpol

HEAR
A: -naɣan
EO: -muon
Ku: -mɔɣɔn
Od: -mɔɣɔn
WO: ô-ɣɔ̀n (m-)
     ô·ɣɔ̀nèsì   'hearing something'

HEART
A: è-kpɔ̀m; (ə̀)ró-
EO: èkpɔ̀lógì

    Ku: èkpól·ògì
    Od: è-kpòlóɣī; ̀ə̀rə̀-
    WO: èkpól·ògì
          òl·ógékpò   'inner heart, mind'

HEAT, WARMTH (n)
    Ku: ɛ̀pɛ̀pɛ̀ ̀ə̀rúzù   ɛ̀pɛ̀pɛ̀ ̀ə̀rúzù nə̀ðìɣí àmì̠
                                    'I feel hot'

    Od: ò-βòlo   òβòló nə́síβ àmì̠ 'I feel hot'
    WO: è-gbóɓú   'body heat'
                                 ègbóɓú nə̀sú ə̀m 'I feel hot'

HEAVY
    A: -mɔr   v. 'be heavy'
          (à)-ðí-mɔ̀r   n. 'heaviness'
    EO: -mɔmɔr
          ɛ̀-mɔ̀mɔ̀r   n. 'heaviness'
    Ku: ɛ́-mṳ́mō̄r   n.
    Od: -mɔr   ə̀kòòlβó náámɔ̀r   'the load
                                    is heavy'
          -mɔrɔmì̠   'make heavy'
          ɛ̀-mɔ̀r   'heaviness'

HEEL (n)
    A: éé-ɣìm; (ə̀)ríí-
    EO: ìgíg-ə́wèl
    Ku: ègígì (ə́wèl)
    WO: ɛ̀ɓélêm ə̀lìkè

HELP (v)
    A: -lɔɣɔnaan...ðíɣaaɣ   ṳ́-lòɣònà̀àn 'put in for me,
                                    fix for me'
    EO: -lɔ ágwò
    Ku: -lɔɣ ágwò

```
Od:   -lɔɣ ávò          lóɣ àvò nóɣó  'help me'
      -ɓar              'help with work, support'
                        ɓǎr zààmì  'help me'
      -βɛl/-pɛl         pɛ̌l zààmì  'help me'
      ɔ̀pɛ̀là            n.  'helper'
WO:   à-lágwò           cf. HAND
      [< à-ló àgwò]
```

HERE

```
A:    síɛ̀n
EO:   ì̤sɛ́n
Ku:   í̤sɛ̌n            'this place'
      ènén             'here'
                       tùè ménén  'come here'
Od:   èsúō
WO:   ɛ̀sánà
```

HIDE (v)

```
A:    aaɣi̤/-bɔɔɣi̤        v.t.
      aaɣi̤an/-bɔɔɣi̤an    v.i.
EO:   -wɔgi̤              v.t.
      -wɔgɔna            v.i.
Ku:   -w̃ɔgi̤             v.t.
      -w̃ɔgana           v.i.
Od:   -ɓɔki̤             v.t.
      -ɓɔki̤a            v.i.
WO:   ɔ̂wɔ̀gi̤ (m-)        v.t.
      ɔ̂wɔ̀gà (m-)        v.i.
```

HIGH TIDE

```
Od:   ì-δìké
WO:   òδíáámṳ̀
```

HILL

    A: è-ɓúm

           è-gúm; (ə̀)rú-   'anthill'

    EO: è-gùgúm; ì-

    Ku: è-gùgúm; ə̀rú-~ ə̀sú-

    Od: è̀-gŭm; (ə̀)rùù-

    WO: égùgŭm; í-

HIP

    A: ò-l·ò; ì- ~(ə̀)rò-

    Ku: èkpòl; r-

    Od: ò-mìnúòm; ì-

HIPPOPOTAMUS

    A: ɔ́ɔ́màmụ̀ụ̀m   cf. ELEPHANT

    EO: ò-tòɓò; ì-

    Od: òtóɓòl; r-

    WO: ò-tòɓò; ì-

HIT, BEAT (v)

    A: -gụr   'hit with stick'

           -kul   'butt, crash as car' cf. CUT

           -gị̀ß   'beat' B *-γomba, -koma,
                                       -kuva, -mena, -menya,
                                       -puta (-punta), -piγa,
                                       -panda

           -kußoγ   'to beat several times'

           -kpetəən   'to hit against with foot'

           -gụrɔγ   'flog'

    EO: -ßum   'hit with stick'

           -gor   'hit with hand'

           -gorou   'hit with hand, repeatedly'

           -yị̀ß   'beat with whip, flog'

           -gụr   'flog'

EO:	-gu	'beat with matchet'
	-kul	'box, butt, hit with car'
	-kulən	'hit each other, butt (as with cars)'
	-δul	'strong beat weak' or 'many beat one'
	-ɓal	'slap, hit with flat of matchet'
Ku:	-gʉr	'hit'
	-gʉrɔγ	'flog with cane'
	-ɓoroγ	'flog with stick, large stick'
	-ɓaβ	'slap'
	-δul	'beat'
Od:	-ɓor	'hit with hand'
	-kulən	'butt, as animals'
	-kulom	'hit with car'
	-ben	'hit with matchet'
	-δul	'beat with stick'
	-gʉr	'flog with rod, whip; hit one stroke'
	-gʉrɔγ	'flog'
WO:	à-yɩ̀β	'flog'
	à-gʉ́sɩ̀	'hit with matchet'
	-ɓalɛ	'slap'
	ə̀-δîβ	'strike'
	ɔ́ɓàl (m-)	'slap'
	íkùlù	'crack head'
	íkùlə̀n	'to butt with head'
	ó-δîβ	'act of striking'
	-mʉ	'flog, beat up'
	ɛ̀-mʉ́à	'act of beating, flogging'

HOBBLE (v)
    Od: -βaδɪ̯/-paδɪ̯

HOE (n)
A: ɛ̀-sʊ́à; (à)rʊ́-
EO: ɛ̀súá áw̃án·ì   'women's hoe'
Ku: ɛ̀-sʊ́à; àrʊ̀-
Od: ɛ̀-sʊ̀á; (à)rʊ̀-
WO: ɛ̀sʊ́à; `zà

HOE (v)
A: -kɔr/-ɣɔr
EO: -n·am
Ku: -gu
Od: -kaị
WO: ə̀-kpô
        ə̀-gûñ

HOLD (v)   cf. CATCH
A: -βam/-pam   also 'catch'
Ku: -siβ   'take hold of'
Od: -βam/-pam

HOLD BREATH
WO: ə̀-sé-rè̃ ɛ̀bà

HOLE
A: è-póɣ; (ə̀)ró-
EO: ɔ̀yɔ̀l
Ku: óyɔ̂l; r-
Od: è-pŏɣ; (ə̀)rə̀-
WO: ò-gùgù; ì-

HOME   see HOUSE

HOME, AT [CHEZ]
    A: káámì
          kódì
          kéyòòr
          kéñìnə̀
          kábìdì
          kóñánìβɔ   'the girl's house'
          kábùóñánìβɔ   'the girl's people's house'
          képélēñ   'monkey's house, chez...'

HONEY
    A: ɛnúúm ə́ðíòwò   cf. FAT
    EO: àmɛ́w̃
    Ku: àmɛ̂w̃
    Od: à-mɛ́m
    WO: àmɛ́w̃

HOOK ONTO...
    A: -kɔm
          -kɔman   'put arms around each other,
                               embrace'
                            ɔ̀-kɔ̀m ə́síɣítòn-óséérè
                               'cause trouble'

HORN
    A: ɔ̀-βáàl; (à)rá-
    EO: ɛ̀kà̀
    Ku: ɔ̀-βâl; ì̀-
    Od: ɔ̀-βáál; (à)rà-
    WO: ɛ̀kɛ́nàm; -zà

HORNBILL
    EO: ɔ̀βúβū̄
    Ku: àpípíà

Od: àlòpá; àsʊ̀pá   'smaller hornbill'
    óóβʊ̀; (à)r-
WO: àkámá

HORSE
A: á-sʊ̀; (à)rʊ́-
    ò-yá àsʊ̀; ị̀-yá àrʊ̀sʊ̀ 'mare'
EO: àsʊ́
Ku: ósʊ̀; r-
Od: ásʊ̀; (à)r-
WO: àsú; ´zà

HOT (AS PEPPER)   see SHARP

HOT
A: -ɣɔlɔɣɔl/
    -kɔlɔɣɔl (ɔɔ-)   'warm'
    ñòmñòmñòm   'nice and warm'
    ɛɣɔlɔɣɔl   'warmth'
    ə̀lóór ámị̀ rὲkólóɣól
       'I feel warm'
    -ɣɔlɔmị(ɔɔ-)   'to warm, as food'
EO: ə̀lùzú δə́m nə́sù   'I feel hot'
Ku: ɔ̀sị̀sɔ̀sị́sɔ̀   àsị́sɔ̀ mə́δə́mà 'a hot day'
    ὲsị́sɔ̀ (n)
WO: ò-zùzú   modif. cf. SHARP
    -zu   v.i.
    -zuomən   'make hot, heat, warm'

HOUSE
A: ò-tù; (ə̀)rù-
    ò-tó   'house of...' òtó kə́yòòr
       'our house, our family'
      òtó kámákʊ̀rʊ̀ 'children of
        Amakuru (Abuan village
        name)'

EO: ó-tû; í-
Ku: ò-tù; èrù-
Od: ò-tù; (ə̀)rù-
     òtə̀...   'house of...'
WO: ò-tù; ì-

HOW?
   A: ìkə̀
   EO: èkə̀
   Ku: èkə̂
   Od: ɛ̀kɔ̀
   WO: àkà

HOW MANY?
   A: ìkín·ɛ̀ ~ ìkə́ ìn·ɛ̀
   EO: ɛ̀n·ị̂
   Ku: ìnị̂ ~ ènê
   Od: ìnì̠
        ~ èènè   also 'how much?'
   WO: ìn·íì

HUNCHBACK
   EO: ɛ̀kpụ̀ ámàn
   Ku: èɓùámàn   cf. HILL; BACK

HUNGER
   A: ò-kɔ̂ñ; (à)rɔ́- (rare) mị́ rə̀múɣ ɔ́kɔ̀ñ 'I'm dying
                                  of hunger'
                            ɔ̀kɔ̂ñ rúsìɓíími̠ 'I'm hungry'
   EO: èpòβ   èpóβ nə́sù ə́m 'I'm hungry'
   Ku: ɔ̀kɔ́ị̠   ɔ̀kɔ́ị̠ nə̀ɗìɣí àmì̠ 'I'm
                            hungry, hunger is doing
                            me'
   Od: ɔ̀kɔ́ñ   ɔ̀kɔ́ñ nə́sĭβ àmì̠ 'I'm hungry'
                            cf. SEIZE

Od: àmɪ̀ nápɔ̀ mɔ́kɔ̆ñ   'I'm dying
                                     of hunger'
WO: èpɔ̃̀β   èpɔ́β nɛ̀sú ɘ̀m   'I'm hungry'
                                  cf. CATCH

HUNT
A: -taya   v.
      ɔ̀ñ-ɪ́tāyā̄; àbʉ̀-   n.   'hunter'
EO: -kue   v.   'fish'
      -teñ   v.   'shoot'
      ɔ̀téñmōtèñ   n.   'hunter'
Ku: ɔ̀tàβá   n.   'hunter' cf. SHOOT
Od: -rele/-tele èðúm   v.   'hunt, walk in bush'
      ɔ̀-tàzǎ; ɪ̀-   n.   'hunter'
WO: ɘ̀-têñ   v.
      ɔ̀tèñ   n.   'hunting'
      ɔ̀n·ɪ́ɔ̀tèñ; ɘ̃̀wúnɔ́mɔ̀tèñ n. 'hunter'
      ~ ɔ̀tèñmɔ̀tèñ

HUSBAND
A: ɔ̀-l·ɔ̀m
EO: ɔ̀w̃ùnɔ̀m
Ku: ɔ̀-wɔ̀lɔ̀m
Od: ɔ̀-l·ɔ̀m; (ɘ̀)bùrù-
WO: ɔ̀w̃ɔ̀nɔ̀m

HYENA
EO: ɛ̀zɪ̀nɛ̀kpɛ̀

I

IDOL, JUJU
    A: èrù

IF
    A: múmmɔ̄ ~ ɛ́γɪ́γlɔ́
    Ku: k-   kɪ́nà ə̀rŭ... 'if he comes...'

                               kámɪ̀βɪ́γ ɪ̀nà... 'if I see him...'

                               kʊ̀bákʊ̀máā...sʊ̀máā 'if... then'

                               náàβɔ̀...sʊ̀máā 'if...were... then' (contrary to fact)

IGNORANCE
    Od: èlóγòm   also 'ignorant person'

IGUANA, MONITOR LIZARD
    A: é-gbēkə̀; (ə̀)ré-   'monitor lizard'
         (à)-βàày; (à)sɪ̀-   'large lizard, iguana?'
    EO: ɔ̀wà
    Ku: ɔ́wàγ
    Od: ə̀bə̀dɪ̀   'iguana'
        ~ àbàày
    WO: ɔ̀wà   'iguana'

IMITATE
    A: -tʉγaam
    EO: -tʉana   'learn'
    Ku: -tʉγan
    Od: -tʉʉγa
    WO: à-tâ

IMMEDIATELY
    EO: ìsɛ́nísɛn

INCREASE (vt)
    A: -bu̧ɣɛ   cf. BIG
    EO: -ɓuñemen
         -gəlemen   'praise, make big'
    Ku: -ɓuyùméní
    Od: -bu̧ɣɛ
    WO: ə̀-ɓúímə̀n
         ə̀-bómə̀n   'enlarge, praise'

INHABITANT OF, PERSON OF
    A: ɔ̀-l·ɔ́   mí ɔ̀l·ɔ́ ə́búə̀n 'I'm an
                                       Abua man'
    Ku: ɔ̀l-   àmì̧ ɔ̀lɛ́mágɔ́ 'I'm from
                                       Emago'

INHERITANCE
    A: èrúə̀
    EO: àδì̧à
    Ku: àδì̧à
    Od: -lì ótù   'to inherit'
         òlèrùtù   'heir'
    WO: àδì̧à

INITIATION (SACRED)
    A: ɔ̀-kɔ̀

IN-LAW
    A: ɔ̀-yɔ́gɔ̀; (à)rɔ̀-   'brother, sister in law'
    EO: ɔ̀yɔ́gɔ̀   'brother, sister in law'
         àŋì̧nì̧nì̧   'in-laws'
    Ku: ɔ̀yɔ́gɔ̀; r-   'in-law, collateral'

Od: ɔ̀zɔ́gō̄; àràzɔ́gō̄   'in-law, collateral'

WO: àwɔ́gɔ̀   'brother, sister in law'

     àw̃ɨ̀nɨ̀nɨ̀   'in-laws, ascending and
descending only'

INNOCENCE

Od: è-lɔ́ɣō̄m   masc. personal name

IN ORDER THAT, SO THAT

A: ɔ́kɔ́rɨ́   contrast: -kɔ̀rɨ̀ 'to wait'

                    mɨ́ ú-kɔ́rɨ́ ñɔ̀dɨ́ 'I awaited
him'

     ídì   mɨ́ ràlɔ́ ìdɨ́ ɔ̀dɨ́ kɜ̀ɓètènù
'I'm shouting so he will
wake'

Ku: màgwɔ́lɜ̄ɜ̄

     ~ ɓɔ̀kàá ~ ɓɔ̀kǎ

INQUIRY   see QUESTION

INSIDE

A: ɔ́lɔ̀ɣì

EO: ɔ̀lɔ̀gì

Ku: δɔ́lɔ̀gì

Od: ɔ́lɔ́ɣì

WO: ɔ̀l·ɔ̀gì; ì-

INSTEAD

A: kpàrɨ̀pɛ́   kpàrɨ̀pɛ́ rō̄ɣēēl 'instead of
going home'

Ku: kpɜ̀lɜ̀mènɨ̀   kpɜ̀lɜ̀mènɨ̀ mɨ̀nà mɔ̀kɔ̀δù ɨ̀nà
ɜ̀ɣìl ɜ̀ɣílɜ̀ àδɨ́á 'instead
of sleeping, he ran away'

     kɔ̀mɜ̀   'instead'

Od: kpɜ̀lɜ̀m

INSULT (v)

A: -gɨ̀laam ~ -tuun(oo-)

EO: -rogi   also 'abuse'

Ku: -rogi

Od: -sụ ɔ̀nṵ́   ɔ̀dɪ́ násụ̃á zàmɪ̀ mɔ̀nṵ̀ 'he's
                                 insulting me'

WO: ɔ̂gɔ̀l (m-)

     ɔ̀-gɔ̀lá   'abuse, act of abusing'

IROKO TREE

Od: àδɪ̀ɔ̀β

IRON

A: ò-kúròn; (ə̀)rú-

EO: òkùròn

Od: ò-kùróγ; (ə̀)rù-

WO: òkúròr

IRONWOOD

A: òγòòγ

EO: òβòm

Ku: àkpɔ́

Od: òγòòγ

WO: òβòm

IS IT?

A: tɔ́mɔ́ mɪ̰́   'is it not I who...?'

ISLAND

A: ȇkpúɔ́gbò

EO: òtòkòlò

Ku: èkpɛ́

WO: òtòkòlò

ITCH (v)

A: -rụβɛ/-tụβɛ   also 'scratch someone'

EO: -rɔβịan

Ku: -kan

WO: à-dṵ̂   v.i.

J

JAUNDICE
    Od: ákɔ̄m

JAW
    A: (à)-lɛ́ɛ́ɣ; (à)sɪ́-
    Ku: àbàkágbà
    WO: àɓágá (O)

JELLYFISH
    A: ə̀ɗúɗú ábàzɪ̀

JOIN (vt)
    A: -tul   'join two things'
    EO: -tulugi
    Ku: -tụlɔm
    Od: -tul   cf. LOVE
    WO: ɔ́kpɔ̀gɔ̀m(m-)

JOKE   see PLAY (v)

JUDGE CASE (v)
    A: -sɔ́β ə̀ɗɪ́ɣítōn   cf. CUT
    EO: -soβ ɔ́kpɛ̀
    Ku: -sɔ̀β ásɛ́
    Od: -soβ àráàkpɛ́
    WO: ə̀-sôβ ɛ̀ɓɛ̀rɛ̀

JUG
    EO: ìzókò
    Ku: àmɔ́gɪ̀   'jug for wine'
    Od: àfà   'jug for wine' also 'cala-
                                     bash'
    WO: ə̀zókò   'wine jug'

JUMP (v)

A: -pel
      -kuruβ
      òpèlòm òpêl   n. 'jumper'
      òpèlòm ị̀kásị̄   'comet'

EO: -pel

Ku: -pel

Od: -pel
      òpèl   n. 'jump'
      òpèlmópèl   n. 'jumper'

WO: ə̀-pêl
      ò-pèl   n. 'jump'
      è-l·é   'high-jumping bar'

K

KEEP

    A: -seere   also 'save'

                                      mí ú-sééré í-kpòkì 'I kept the money'

    Ku: -guri   gùrí 'keep it'

          -koko   'keep for someone, take care of for...'

    Od: -seeri

          -seeriən   'keep in safe-keeping'

KEEP WATCH, KEEP AWAKE   see WAIT

KEROSENE TIN

    A: tínè ìkáràzìnì

    EO: ətín ákàrìzínì

    Ku: ətínì íkàràzínì

    Od: ətín ákàrìzìn

    WO: ətín àkàrìzîn

KEY

    A: ìsábì   Portuguese?

    EO: ɔ̃ñásàbì

    Ku: ìsábì

    Od: ì-sábì

    WO: àsàmbì

KICK (v)

    A: -kuβ   'kick with foot'

KIDNEY

    A: ì-kpíñōm; (ə̀)rí-

    Ku: è-kpíkpìón; ì-

    WO: ìkpò   pl.

KILL (v)
    A: -kiiɣ/-ɣiiɣ
          -zɛ ~ -jɛ   'kill more than one'
    EO: -gi
    Ku: -giɣ
          -zɛ   'kill more than one'
    Od: -ɣiiɣ/-kiiɣ   'kill one thing'
          -zɛ   'kill several things'
          èɣìɣôm   n. 'murder, act of killing'
    WO: ə̀-gíì
          ón·ị̀ ə̀fìnìnìnì   n. 'killer, murderer'
          é-gī̄   n. 'killing'
          ò-gìə̀nə̀n   n. 'killing one another'

KING, CHIEF
    A: ụ̀w-ɛ́ɛ́mā̄; (à)rụ̀wɛ́ɛ́mā̄   'king, paramount chief'
          ɔ̀ɔ́là   'chief, wealthy man'
          ụ̀wɛ́mụ́   'headman, leader'
    EO: ò̀ɓén-ɛ́mà   'king'
          ò̀-làlà; ɛ̀-   'rich person'
    Ku: ɔ̀làlɛ́·mà;
             àrɔ̀làlɛ́·mà   'king, chief'
    Od: ɔ̀ɔ́-lɛ̀má; (à)rụ̀ụ̀-   'king'
          ɔ̀ɔ́-là; (à)rụ̀ụ̀-   'chief, rich man'
    WO: ò̀ɓénèmà; ì-   'king'
          ɔ̀làlà   'rich person, chief'
          ò-ɓénèma   'village headman'
          ò-ɓénòtù   'head of family'

KITE [BIRD]
    A: é-ɣùlè; (ə̀)rú-ɣùlè
    EO: ègúlè
    Od: èɣùlè
    WO: ègúlè

KNEE

    A: éé-kūm; (ə̀)rúú-

    EO: ɛ̀kpɔ́lɔ̀m

    Ku: ɛ̀-kpṹlɔ̀m; àsʉ̀-

    Od: èé-gī; ə̀rìí-

    WO: èδúrûm ə̀lìkè; ìδúrûm

KNEEL

    A: -kpuδiən

    EO: -kpuδiən

    Ku: -kpuδiən

    Od: -gbulumən

    WO: íkpìδìɔ̀n (m-)

KNIFE (n)

    A: ɛ̀-lɛ̀kɛ̀; (à)sḭ̀-
           ~ (à)rɛ̀-

    EO: ɔ̀-gyɛ̀; ɛ̀-

    Ku: ɔ̀gyɛ̀; r-

    Od: à-mʉ̀gɛ̀m; (à)sʉ̀-   'kitchen knife'

    WO: ɔ̀-gyà; ɛ̀-

KNOT, MAKE (v)

    A: -kaγ

KNOW

    A: -leγeri   'know, know how to'

    EO: -δegəri

           -δegiri   'know how to'

    Ku: -loγom   'know, know how to'

    Od: -loγom   'know, know how to'

    WO: éδìgìrì (m-)

           êδìgìrì (m-)   'know how to'

KOLA

    A: è-gbè; (ə̀)rè-
    EO: ègbè
    Ku: ègbè; r-
    Od: ègbè; (ə̀)r-
    WO: ègbě; ʼzə̀

L

LADDER
      A: ógbàdá
      Ku: ègò
      Od: ì-gólí
      WO: íbè̥

LADLE (n)   cf. SPOON
      A: è-kú; (è̥)rú-
      EO: ìgbítē̥
      Ku: òkpé̥kò   also 'big spoon'
      Od: è̥è̥-kpó
      WO: òbè̥gyásí̥   'large spoon'

LAME
      EO: ìkùlè̥   'lameness'
      Ku: ùkùlé̥
      Od: òsùkù
      WO: è̥kpúkù   'to limp'

LAMP
      A: ɔ̀tɔ̀zì̥
      EO: àtų̀kpà
      Ku: àtɔ̀dì̥
      Od: ɔ̀-tɔ̀dì̥; ì̥-
      WO: ɔ̀tų̀kpà

LAND (n)   see EARTH

LAND FROM BOAT (v)   cf. DESCEND
      A: -so·r óɣúùɣ
      EO: -sor
      Ku: -sul
            -βun   'go up, leave canoe'

    Od: -sul
    WO: ə̀-βúnù

LANGUAGE
    A: ɔ̀nṵ́ ɛ́má
    EO: ɔ̀n·ṵ̀ ɛ́mà
    Ku: ɔ̀nṵ̀ɛ́mà; r-
    Od: ɔ̀nṵ̀ɛ̀má
           ɔ̀nɔ̀ɗúə̀l   'Odual language'
    WO: ɔ̀n·úɛ́mà; ɛ̀-

LAST-BORN   see CHILD

LATRINE
    A: ɔ̀sààỳ̰   'public latrine'

LAUGH (v)
    A: -mḭlɔγ
    EO: -mḭlɔṵ
           ~ -mḭlɔw
    Ku: -mɔlɔγ
    Od: -mɔlɔγ
           ḭ̀-mɔ́lɔ̀γ   n.   'laughter'
    WO: ɛ́ɛ̀lɔ̀(m-)
           ɛ̂·là àdḭ̀ɛ̀l   n.   'laughter'
           à-dḭ̀ɛ̀l

LAW
    A: ɔ̀lɔ̀γ
    EO: ɔ̀lɔ́kɔ́
    Ku: ɔ̀lɔ́kɔ́
    Od: ɔ̀-lɔ̀γ
    WO: ɔ̀lɔ́gɔ́   'law, fine' cf. PAY

LAY DOWN (v)

    Od: -mṵnɛɛn   (someone on bed)

LAY EGGS

    A: -lɔɣ éɣélè   cf. PUT

    EO: -mele

    Ku: -mele

    Od: -mele

    WO: êl·è (m-)

LAZY

    A: -gbóɣól·ɛ́r ɛ́gbòɣòl·ɛ̀r 'be lazy'
           èbgòɣòl·ɛ̀r   'laziness'

    EO: -kɔr
           èkɔ́r   'laziness'

    Ku: èbgṵɔ̀r   'laziness'

    Od: -gbṵɔr   'be lazy'
           ɔ̀gbṵɔ̀r mɛ́gbṵɔ̄r   'lazy person'

    WO: èkɔ̀r   'laziness'
           (m)ɛ́ɛ̀-kɔ̀rɛ́kɔ̀r   'be lazy'
           m'ónḭ èkɔ̀r 'I'm a lazy man'

LEAF

    A: (à)ðḭ́ñá; (à)rḭ́ñá

    EO: ə̀t-ò-rérén; ə̀t-ì-

    Ku: ə̀-tò(òrérén);
           r- (ìrérén)
        ~ ò-βɛ̀rɛ̀βɛ̀r

    Od: (ə̀)là-gó; (ə̀)sì-

    WO: ə̀tórén; ə̀tírén

LEAK (v)

    A: -si

    EO: -si

Od: -si
Ku: -si
WO: ə̀-sî

LEARN

A: -tʉ̧ʉ̧ɣa   'learn, study'
     -maar   'learn, know, get to know'
EO: -tʉ̧an·a
Ku: -tʉ̧ɣan   also 'study' àmị̀ nátʉ̧́ɣàn
                          'I've studied it'
Od: -tʉ̧ʉ̧ɣa   also 'study'
     ị̀-tʉ̧̀ʉ̧́ɣá   'act of learning'
WO: à-rʉ̧́à
     ɔ̀-rʉ̧̀àm àβár   'learner'
     àrʉ̧́àβ̀ar   n. 'act of learning'

LEAVE BEHIND
A: -wilɛ/-bilɛ   ʉ́-wìlɛ̀ í·mì 'leave me'

LEECH (n)
EO: áw̃ɛ̀
Ku: ɛ̀rʉ̀m
Od: ɛ̀-rɔ̀ñ; (à)rʉ̀-
WO: ɛ́w̃ɛ̀

LEFT
A: δị̀ɣááɣ èkèñ
EO: èkêl   'left hand'
Ku: ékyèl
Od: èkèñ
WO: ɔ̀kèl

LEG
A: ɔ̀-wɔ̀l; (ə̀)rú-   'human leg'
     (ə̀)δí-kè; (ə̀)sí-   'animal leg'

EO:	ə̀wèl	also 'foot'
Ku:	ə̀-wèl; ə̀síkè	
Od:	ə̀lè-ké; ə̀sì-	also 'foot'
WO:	ə̀lí-kè; ə̀sí-	also 'foot'

LEND   see BORROW

LENGTH

A: (à)ɓárázừ   (a)ɓárázừ 'distance between thumb and index finger (used in selling fish)'

(ə̀)-kúɓú 'arm's length (used in measuring cloth, trees, etc.)'

-dɔñɛ   v. 'lengthen'

EO: è-wéγè

-weγemen ~-weyemen   v.t. 'lengthen'

Ku: é-wèγɛ̌

-weγemeni   v.t. 'lengthen'

Od: àlị̀-dôñ   also 'tallness'

ɛ̀-dôñ   also 'tallness'

ɛ̀dằɓɔ 'length from tip of index or middle finger to tip of thumb'

ɛ́ɓálɛ́kɛ̀ 'length of footprint'

ə̀kừɓừ 'distance between outstretched arms'

ə̀tòbí 'as far as one can see'

-dɔñɛ   v.t. 'lengthen'

~ -dɔñmɛnị̀

WO: í-wèí   also 'tallness'

-weimən   v.t. 'lengthen'

LEOPARD
    A: óó-tììr; (ə̀)ríí-
    EO: àbị́rị̀
        ~ ɔ̀karàβ ɛ̀n·àm   cf. BAD
    Ku: àkɔ̀rɔ̀nɔ̀ma
    WO: àbị́rị̀

LEPROSY
    A: ɛ̀zɛ̂ɣ ɛ̀kpàbị̀a   'Ahoada disease'
          j

LET US
    A: ὐgwâ   ὐgwâ ɔ̀βέε̄β 'let's fly'
                        ὐgwâ ɔ̀lê 'let's eat'

LICK (v)
    A: -lai̧   (with fingers)
    Ku: -lai̧

LIE (n)
    A: ɔ̀-kpὲ   no pl.
                      ɔ̀-gbá ókpὲ 'to tell lies'
                      mị́ ràgbá ókpὲ 'I'm lying'
                      mị́ ràgbáɣán ókpὲ 'I keep
                          telling lies'
           ógbáām ɔ̀kpὲ   n. 'liar, teller of lies'
    EO: ìpésì
    Ku: ìgùnùɣə̀
    Od: ì-bèn   pl. cf. IGBO
    WO: ìl·ù
          àβár ìl·ù

LIE DOWN (v)
    A: -mị̧na
    EO: -selegə

Ku: -manaɣan
Od: -manaɣan   èzòòr ʊ́námàɣàn 'we lay down'
WO: ɛ́ɓɛ̀tɛ̀nà (m-)   'lean back'

LIFE
A: (ə̀)-ɣúɗúm
EO: ə̀wùɗùm
Ku: ə̀ɣùɗúm
Od: ə̀-ɣùɗŭm
WO: ə̀wúɗúm

LIFT (v)
A: -poβe/-βoβe
EO: -ɓeten
Ku: -ɓeton   'lift, begin'
      -βuneni   'raise up'
Od: -βoɣomi/-poɣomi (oo-)
      -ɓeton   also 'make stand'
      -ɓètɔ́n(dòòl)   'lift a load'
WO: à-sâ   also 'carry'
     ~ à-tɛ́lɛ̀mà   Nembe

LIGHT (n)   cf. WHITE
A: (à)ɗɪ́-ɓāāl   also 'light complexion'
EO: ɛ̀ɓàlàɓál
Ku: ɛ̄̀ɓàlàɓâl
Od: ɛ̀-ɓààl   also 'innocence'
WO: ɔ̀gbɛ́râ   'daylight'

LIGHT [WEIGHT]
A: -βooɣ/-pooɣ   v. 'be light'
     (ə̀)ɗɪ́-βooɣ   n. 'lightness'
EO: -βoβoβ
     è-βòβòβ   'lightness'

Ku: -βoβoɣ
Od: -βɛɛβ/-pɛɛβ   cf. FLY

LIGHT FIRE (v)
A: -kpɔɔnị (ánịàn)   'light small fire, as for
                            cooking'
     -gu (ánịàn)   'make big fire'
     -sụ (ɔ́tɔ̀zị̀)   'light lamp'

LIGHTNING   cf. THUNDER
Ku: ɛ́mɛ́mɛ́gɛ́nà

LIGHTNING BUG   cf. STAR
Ku: ɛ̀nànáị̀

LIKE (vt)
Ku: -δìɣ ól·ògì
     -bərə   àmị̀ ɛ́bɛ̀rɛ̀ mɛ̀lɛ̀l 'I like yam'

LIME
A: òlóòmìnì
EO: ìdùkúmɛ̀
Ku: òlómìnì
Od: òl·ómìní; ì-
WO: ègékúmɛ́

LIMP (v)
A: -kpeku   'to limp'
     -gbuluɣu   'to hobble along, limp
                            (derogatory)'
                          òyê βɔ̄ rɛ̀-kpékù 'the man
                            is limping'

LINTEL
A: ɛ̀δíbó ótû   'door lintel'

LION

    EO: àdákà

    Od: ɔ̀-kṳ̀rṳ̀nàmà; (à)rṳ̀-

    WO: àdákà

LIP

    A: ɔ́-dɔ̀rɔ̀nṹ; (à)rɔ̂-   cf. MOUTH

    EO: ɔ̀βóβ ón·ṳ̀

    Ku: ɛ̀dɛ̀dárɛ̀ ónṳ̀

    Od: ɔ̀-dɔ̀rɔ̀nṹ; ị̀- ~ àrị̀

    WO: ɔ̀βóβɔ̀n·ṳ̀; ì-

LISTEN

    A: -naɣan

    EO: -naga

    Ku: -naɣa

    Od: -naɣa

    WO: ə̀-βólə̀n

LITTLE, A, SMALL AMOUNT

    A: ɛ́-nṳ̄m   mị́ úrɛ̀lé ɛ́nṳ̄m 'I walked
                               a little'

        (ɔ́ñ) ɛ́nṳ̄m   mị́ ràβá búə̀n ɛ́nṳ̄m 'I speak
                               a little Abuan'

        ɔ̀-bán   ɔ̀bán ɛ̀lɛ̀l 'small amount
                                 of yam'

    EO: ɛ̀kàkárá   'small amount, size'

                       ɛ̀kàkárá ámṳ́m 'a little water'

        èñùkúnúm   'small number' èñùkúnúm
                                ə̀w̃únòm 'a few people'

    Ku: ɔ̀ñị̀ kị́kàrá   ɔ̀ñị̀ kị́kàr' ə̀w̃únòm 'few
                                 people'

                       ɔ̀ñị̀ kị́kàr' íkpòkì 'little
                               money'

    Od: ɔ̀-bàm; ị̀-   àmị̀ négbēēl mị̀bàm ámṳ́ṳ̄m 'I
                               want a little water'

                       ị̀bàm ə́rə́ī 'few people'

LIVE   see ALIVE, BE

LIVER
    A: (à)-n·ḭ́; (à)sḭ́-
    EO: ɔ̀sármává
         ~ɔ̀sàrmá
    Ku: àɓέlɛɣṵ́óm
    Od: àɓέlέwɔ́; àr-
    WO: ìgèlègì

LIZARD
    A: (ə̀) δí-ɓòkú; (ə̀)sí-
    EO: èkpél-kpē
    Ku: ə̀lù-gbégbèm; ə̀sù-
    Od: ṵ̀kàgárā; (à)r-
    WO: ə̀δìgbè; ˋzə̀

LOAD (n)
    A: (ə̀)-dòòl; (ə̀)sì-
    EO: ɔ̀βàm
    Ku: ə̀δòl; r-
    Od: ə̀-dòòl; (ə̀)rə̀-
    WO: ɔ̀βàm

LOAD (v)
    EO: -sañ
    Ku: -saḭ   'load, as boat'
    Od: -saaḭ
    WO: à-sáḭ

LOBSTER
    A: ɔ̀ɔ̀gà
    EO: ɔ̀-ñə̀ɣólɔ̀; ὲ-
    Ku: ɔ̀gḭ̀gà

Od: ɔ̀ɔ́-gà; ị̀ị̀-   also 'shrimp'
WO: ɔ̀gàgà

LOCK (n)
  A: ìgòdò
  EO: ìgòdò
       ~ àsàbị̀   cf. KEY
  Ku: ìgódó
  Od: ìgòdò

LOCK (v)
  A: -kasị̀   kàsị́ ótừβɔ̄ 'lock the house'
                          mέkásị̀àn 'it's locked'
  EO: -pịkị̀
  Ku: -dụ
  Od: -dụ
  WO: à-pị́kị̀

LOG (n)
  A: é-kừlə́ ɔ̀rèñ

LONG, TALL   cf. TALL
  A: -dɔñ   v.
  EO: ò-wèwèì; ì-   modif.
       -wei   mị̀ nə́wèì 'I'm tall'
       ~-weɣ   Kolo town
                          mị́ nə̀wéì 'I'll be tall'
                          mị́ nə̀wèí 'I'm becoming tall'
  Ku: -weɣ   ɔ̀kàràβ àbár βɔ̀ ə́wĕɣ 'the
                             snake was long'
       òwèwèɣ   n. òwèwéɣ ɔ́káráβ ábá
                             'long snake'
  Od: -dɔñ   ɔ̀rèñ àdɔ̆ñ 'tree was tall'
                          ɔ̀dɔ́ñ óréñ 'tall tree'
  WO: òwèwéí; ì-
       -wei   v.i.

LONG TIME

A:	èbìə̀	n.	
Ku:	òbìə	n.	'long time'
	égbèñ óβèl	n.	'long time'
	ị̀dị́ árɔ		'quite a long time (it was)'
	árɔ́ tótón		'a long time ago; after a while'
	kóbìgèl		'a long time'
Od:	-biə	v.	'to take a long time'
	dòbíə̀δìó 'it hasn't taken long'		

LOOK (v)

A:	-βoγ/-poγ	'look at'
	pòγə̀ə̀ní 'look here; you see'	
	mí ú-βòγə̀ə̀ní óyèβɔ 'I looked at the man'	
	èβòγ	n. 'act of looking'
EO:	-kpon	'look at'
Ku:	-kpon	'look at' àmị́ tĕkpòn áw̃à 'I'll look at you'
		àmị̀ ə́kpŏṇ áw̃à 'I looked for you'
	-kponom	'look after' àm' íkpònŏm ị̀nà 'I took care of him'
		àmị́ tə̀kpónòm áw̃à 'I'll take care of you'
Od:	-non (oo-)	'look after' nònòné lóór ónúmē̱ 'take care of yourself'
	-βəγə/-pəγə	'look at'
		pə̀γə́ lóór ónúmē̱ 'look at yourself'
WO:	ə̀-βô	'look at'
	ə̀-βôm	'look after'
	ə̀-pôñ	'look out for expected thing'

LOSE CASE   see FALL

LOUSE
    A: è-ɣúúɣ; ì-
    EO: ìgù
    Ku: è-gùɣ; r-
    Od: è-gùúɣ; ì-
    WO: è-gú; ì-

LOVE
    A: ɛ́βómóɣḭ́án   n.
         -βɔmɔɣḭan/-pɔmɔɣḭan   v.   also 'become friends'
    EO: -lμan   v.
    Ku: ètùlə̀n   n.
         -tulən   v.
         ɔ̀yṹgà   n. 'lover'
    Od: ètùlə̀n   n.
         -tulən   v.
         ɔ̀-zṹgà   n. 'lover, of opposite sex'
    WO: ɛ̀-lμ̀àn   n.
         ɛ̀-lμ̀ánà   fem. name
         à-lμ̃̀àn   v.
         ɔ̀líə̀nə̀   n. 'lover'

LUNG
    A: (ə̀)-múpúβ;
           (ə̀)sí- ~ (ə̀)rí-
    EO: èfùfú
    Ku: ɛ̀nàm ɔ̀yɛ̂l
    WO: ɔ̀fùrùmɔ̀fú   'fishbladder' Nembe?

M

MADNESS
A: ɛ̀là̀l
    ŋ̀wá-láàl   'madman'
EO: ɛ̀l·àl
Ku: ɛ̀l·àl
Od: ɛ̀w̃ɪ́á
    ɛ̀ráálá
    -w̃ɛ   'to be mad (sick)'
    -raal/-taal   'to be mad (chew)'
                                 òdí nɛ́ðìγì kwɛ́ 'he's doing
                                    like this; he's mad'
WO: ɛ̀l·àl

MAIDEN   cf. GIRL
A: é-sìnɛ́; (ə̀)rí-
Ku: ɔ̀ñánípè; àw̃ɪ́ñànípè
Od: ò-sínɛ́; ì- ~(ə̀)rì-
WO: ɔ̀ñân; àw̃ɪ̀ànà

MAIZE
A: ɔ̀-bɪ̀ààkpà; ɪ̀-
EO: ɔ̀bɪ̀akpà
Ku: ɔ̀bʊ̀kpâ
Od: ɔ̀-bɪ̀àkpà; ɪ̀-
WO: ɔ́kà; ɛ́—zà

MALARIA
EO: àmʊ̀m ɔ̀βɪ̀y
    ákɔ̀m   also 'yellow fever, jaundice'
Ku: ákàm
Od: ákɔ̄m
WO: ìɓógí   'fever'

MAN, MALE
    A: òléβìrì   'male'
         ò-léβír- òñ;
            è-léβír-àŋòñ
    EO: òl·òβírì   'male'
         òn·ị òl·òβìrén   'man'
    Ku: òlóβìrì   'male'
    Od: òlòβîr   'male'
         ò-lòβír-òñ;
            è-lòβír-áŋôñ
    WO: ònóβìrì; ì-

MANATEE
    A: ịmâñ
    EO: ə̀dèm
    Ku: ə̀dèm
    Od: ə̀-dèβ; (ə̀)rə̀-
    WO: ə̀dèβ; ʼzə̀

MANGO
    A: òmị́r
         òmị́r ìɣòòl   'bush mango'
         àβòlò   'seeds of bush mango'
    EO: òmị̀r
         òmị̀r éδúm   'bush mango'
         òkpákpà   'seeds of bush mango'
    Ku: òmị́r
         òmị́r óβèkéì
         òmị́r éδúm   'bush mango'
         ókpàkâ ómír   'seeds of bush mango'
    Od: ò-mị́r; ì-
         òmị̀r éδúm   'bush mango'
         ị́ị́kpā   'seeds of bush mango'

WO: ɔ́kpàkpéɓèké
     ɔ́kpàkpá   'bush mango'
     ɔ́kpàkpá   'seeds of bush mango'

MANGROVE
A: àgálá
EO: àgálá
Ku: àgàlá
Od: à-gàlá; (à)rà-
WO: àgálá

MANILLA   cf. MONEY
A: ɔ̀kpɔ̀kì ə́búə̀n
EO: ó-kpókì; ì-
Ku: ɔ̀kpɔ̀kì ɛmágɔ́
Od: ò-kpòkì ɔ̀ɗúə̀l; ì-
WO: ìkpòkì

MANY
A: ị̀bàdị̀
EO: ə̀ɓùtú   'many, much' (number/quantity)
                        ə̀ɓùt ə́w̃únɔ̀m 'many people'
                        ə̀ɓùt ámy̌m 'much water' (quantity)
     ɔ̀gbỳ   'much' (size) ɔ̀gbỳ ámy̌m 'much water' (size)
                        ɔ̀gbỳ ɛ́lɛ̀l 'big size yam'
Ku: ə́ɗízɔ̀

MARKET
A: (ə̀)-ɗíɣí; (ə̀)sí-
EO: ə̀ɓùə̀   also 'trade'
     ə̀ɗìo ə́ɓúə̀   'market day'
Ku: ə̀ɓùə̀; r-   'buying and selling'
     èsì ə́ɓúə̀   'market, trading place'

Od: ə-δìγí; (ə)rì-
     ə̀δùméδíγí   'market day'
WO: àmákε̄tì

MARKS, TRIBAL
  EO: ὲkánà

MARRY   cf. COUNT
  A: -βin/-pin   masc. actor
                                  ɔ̀dí̧ kúβìn íímì 'he'll marry
                                     me (fem. speaker)'
                                  ɔ̀βɔ́n kúkùβìn íímì 'this one
                                     will surely marry me
                                     (he's my choice)'
       -aal/ bal   fem. actor
                                  ɔ̀dí̧ káàl íímì 'she'll marry
                                     me (masc. speaker)'
       ə̀-pínìə̀n   'marriage'
       aalan   'marry each other'
  EO: -βin   masc.
       -wal   fem.
  Ku: -wal ílòm   fem. actor
       -βin áni̧   masc. actor
  Od: -βin/-pin   masc. actor
       -ɓal   fem. actor
  WO: ə̀-βî   masc. actor
       à-wâl   fem. actor
       -δíìlòm   fem. 'enter into state of
                                     marriage'
       ì-lòm   fem. 'state of being
                                     married'
       ὲ-wàlàm   fem. 'marriage'

MASQUERADE (n)
  A: ɔ̀γú ὲmà
  EO: ìpò   cf. CIRCUMCISION

    Ku: òɣú
    Od: ò-wú; (ə̀)rù-
    WO: ìpó

MASSAGE (v)
    A: -kwɔ   'force out by pressure'
    EO: -zɔm
    Ku: -zʉɔm
    Od: -zʉɔm
    WO: à-gbágbàrà

MAT (n)
    A: éè-tèré; (ə̀)réè-
    EO: èkúnè
    Ku: àtàgàrà; r-
    Od: ɔ̀-tàgàrà; ị̀-
    WO: è-kúnè; ì-

MATCH (n)
    A: (à)fị́nɔ̀kɔ̀rɛ̀
    EO: àkwɛ́rkwɛ́r
    Ku: fị̀nị̀kɔ́rị́má
    WO: àmàsị́sị̀

MATCHET   cf. SWORD
    A: è-lóòl; (ə̀)ró-
    EO: èl·ól ~ èl·êl
    Ku: ògìdì
    Od: èlóōr; (ə̀)r-
    WO: ògìdì

MATURE
    EO: -kpɔ̀   of fruit
    Od: -kpɔ   v.i. 'be mature, old'
    WO: àkpɔ̂   of fruit

MAY [PERMISSIVE]
    A: pél-ə̀   'you may jump'
         kì̧-á   'you may go'
         δíɣí-ə̀   'you may do'
         lé-ə̀   'you may eat'

MEASURE (v)
    A: -tɔ   length or quantity
    EO: -tɔ   quantity or quality
    Ku: -tɔ   length or quantity
    Od: -tɔ
    WO: à-tɔ̂   size or quantity
         ɛ̀-tɔ̀   'measurement, plan'

MEAT   cf. ANIMAL
    A: ɛ̀-nàm; ì̧-
    EO: ɛ̀n·àm
    Ku: ɛ̀nàm
         ə̀bŭm   'meat, fish'
    Od: ɛ̀ɛ̀-nàm; ì̧ì̧-
    WO: ɛ́nàm

MEDICINE   cf. GRASS
    A: ɔ́ɔ̀ɣɔ̀; (à)r-
    EO: ɔ̀ɣɔ́ɣɔ̀; ɛ̀-
    Ku: ɔ̀-ɣɔ́ɣɔ̀; ì̧-
    Od: ɔ̀ɔ́-ɣɔ̀; ì̧í-
    WO: ɔ̀-ɣɔ́ɣɔ̀; ɛ̀-

MEET (v)
    A: -tɛñ   also 'reach'
    EO: -zuən
         -zuənən   'go to see someone'

Ku: -bị̀ɣan   cf. SEE
      -zuən   ị̀nà nàmị̀ ózùə̀n   'he and
                          I met'

Od: -mị̀nan   v.t.   'meet, moving in
                          opposite direction'

      -mị̀ịnan   v.i.

WO: à-têñ   cf. REACH

      ə̀-zúə̀n   'meet unplanned, face to
                          face' also 'go to meet
                          bereaved'

MEETING, COUNCIL, ASSEMBLY
   A: èjúé   -mite ézùè   'to hold caucus'
         z
   WO: ì-ɓìrə̀n   'regular meeting'

MELT
   A: -zaɣanụ (ɔɔ-)   v.i.
          j
        -zàɣàmị̀ (ɔɔ-)   v.t.
          j
   EO: -mɛ   'melt in sun, be thirsty'
                        v.i.   mị́ nàmɛ́ 'I'm thirsty'

        -sanamɛn   v.t.
        -gbɔdɔ ~ -san   v.i.
   Ku: -gbɔdɔmɛnị̀   v.   'melt (oil)'
   Od: -ñan   v.i.
        -ñɛnị̀   v.t.
   WO: à-sân   v.i.
        à-sánàn   v.t.

MERCY
   Ku: ì-gbìrìgbîr

MIDDLE
   A: ògbò
   EO: èsóɓò

Ku: ésə̀δì́ó
Od: ̀ogbò   'center'
     èsò̀δìó   'between two'

MILK (n)   cf. BREAST
A: àmámāām
     ~ à-mí̞lì̞kì̞
EO: àmàmám
Od: àmàám; (à)r-   'breasts'
WO: ə̀mìlíkì

MINNOW
EO: ógò̀ñ
Ku: ò-gò̀ñ   'minnow, small fish'
Od: ègò̀ñ   cf. POOR
WO: ìgbònìɓə̀

MIRROR (n)
A: àtàmà δíkì
EO: àtɛ́mɛ́dígí
Ku: àtàmàδíkí
Od: àtàɓààl ì̞kì̞
WO: àtámáδígí

MISS TARGET   cf. ERROR
A: -pì̞ɔm   'miss in shooting'

MIX (v)
A: -ɓuɣion
EO: -koɓu
Ku: -gwa
Od: -puɣuδi
WO: ə̀-búlùgùmə̀n

MOAN   see GROAN

MONETARY UNITS
   A: (ə̀)-pénì; (ə̀)sí-
        (ə̀)-sélénì; (ə̀)sí-
        (à)-pôm; (à)sí-

MONEY
   A: í-kpòkì
   EO: ìgbògì   modern
        íkpókì   manilla
   Ku: íkpókì
   Od: ò-kpòkì; ì-
   WO: ìgbògì   modern
        ìkpòkì   manilla

MONITOR LIZARD   see IGUANA

MONKEY
   A: ɛ̀-pɛ́lɛ̄ñ; (à)rɛ́-
   EO: ɔ̀ɓừgɔ̀; ɛ̀-
   Od: ɛ̀-pàlá·n; (à)rà-
        ɛ̀nàm áñừ   cf. SKY; ABOVE
   WO: ɔ́-ɓứgɔ̀; ɛ́-

MONTH, MOON
   A: ừw̃áñừ; (à)rứw̃áñừ   'month'
        ừw̃ánừ   'moon'
   EO: àñừ
        ~ òfùmìə̀
   Ku: ùwétírè; r-   'month'
        ùwétírè   'moon'
   Od: ừváñừ; àr-
   WO: àñừ; ʼzà   'month'
        ừwâñừ   'moon'

MOOR BOAT   see TIE

MORNING

    A: (à) δí-róòr   also 'dawn' δíróór èɓāāl
                                 'day is breaking'
                              δíróòr ɓáàδìɓɛ 'that
                                 morning'

    EO: əpìòβ
         ~ògbəpíóβ
    Ku: àδírò; àsírò   kâsírò ~ kâδírò 'since
                                 morning'
         ŋgbàsírò
    Od: ŋ-δìrôγ; (à)rì-
    WO: ɛmɛ̀lɛ̀
         òn·ú ɛmɛ̀lɛ̀   'sunrise'

MORTAR [FOR POUNDING]

    A: ó-dè; (ə̀)ré-
       ~ ó-dò; (ə̀)ró-
    EO: ɛ̀kpá
    Ku: ɛ̀kpá
    Od: ɛ̀-kpá   cf. PLATE
    WO: ɛ̀kpá   cf. PLATE

MOSQUITO

    A: ɛ̀-máám; ì-
    EO: ɛ̀mǎm
    Ku: àlì-mám; ì-
    Od: ɛ̀-kpàbú; ì-
    WO: ɛ̀mám; ^zà

MOTHER

    A: ònììn; ə̀bùr-
         nèné   'mother' personal name
         án·ì ~ n·ín·ì   voc.
         ~ mámà   voc.

EO: ò-w̃ìn; ì-
Ku: òw̃ènì; r-
Od: ònìín; ə̀bùrùnìín
WO: òw̃òn

MOULD (v)

A: -ɓɔl   'pounded yam'
EO: -ɓoloɓol   'mould pot or fufu'
Ku: -ɓoloɓol   'fufu'
Od: -ɓol   'fufu'
     èɓòl   n. 'mould'
     -lɛm   'mould pot' cf. FORGE;
                                BLACKSMITH
WO: ə̀-ɓóɓòl   'mould, shape clay, mud'
     à̃-nɛ̂m   'mould metal or clay pot'

MOUNT (v)

A: -daɣ

MOURN (v)

A: -moɣi óyè   cf. CRY
EO: -kʉn
Ku: -kʉnʉ
     ì̃-kʉ́nʉ̀   n. 'mourning'
Od: -tʉ (ɔɔ-)   -ɗiɣi íʲɪ́tʉ̀ 'set time for
                                mourning'
WO: à-kʉ́nʉ̀
     ɛ̀-kʉ̀nâ   n. 'mourning'

MOUSE   see RAT

MOUTH

A: ónʉ̀; (à)r-
EO: ɔ̀-n·ʉ̀; ɛ̀-   pl. also 'speech'
Ku: ɔ̀nʉ̀; r-

    Od: ɔ̀-nṳ̀; ị̀- ~ àrɔ̀-
    WO: ɔ̀n·ṳ̀; ɛ̀n·ṳ̀ ~ ɛ̀n·ṵ́zà
         ɔ̀nṳ̀ɓɛ́n   'mouth only' 'talkative
                                          (fig.)' masc. name

MOUTH ORGAN   cf. MOUTH
    Ku: ɔ́n·ṳ̀nṳ̀
    WO: ɔ̀nị̀nị̀

MOVE BACK AND FORTH (vt)
    Od: -suɣ

MUCH   see MANY

MUD (n)
    A: ɔ̀-pɔ́sɔ̀
    EO: ɔ̀bị̀bị̀
    Ku: ị̀-dɔ́ɣɔ̀l
    Od: ɔ̀ɔ̀-mị̀; ị̀ị̀-
    WO: ɛ̀tɔ́kɔ́lɔ́

MUD [WALL], TO (v)   cf. THROW
    EO: -roβ
    Ku: -roβ
    Od: -roβ/-toβ ɔ́tṳ̀
    WO: ə̀-rɔ́βɔ̀kì

MUDSKIPPER
    A: ɔ̀ɓɔ̀gì
    EO: ɛ̀kpàrá
    Ku: ɔ̀-ɓègì
    Od: ị̀sàlá
    WO: ɛ̀kpárá

MUDWASP
    A: ɔ́βɔ̀nὲñ
    EO: ɔ̀βṳ̀nṳ̀βṵ̂n
    Ku: ɔ̀gáw̃
    Od: ɔ̀-bṳ̀nṳ̀nṵ́

MURDERER   see KILLER

MURMUR, MUTTER (IN ANGER)(v)
    A: -gum

N

NAIL (n)

A: òɗùɣ
EO: ìgù
Ku: ə̀tùrú
Od: ɔ̀gbɔ́
WO: ə̀túrú

NAIL (v)

A: -kan
EO: -kan
Ku: -dụ
Od: -kan
WO: à-kân   also 'nail together'

NAIL, FINGER   see FINGERNAIL

NAME (n)   cf. EYE

A: (ə́)-ɗíèn; (ə̀)sí-
EO: ə̀ɗìèn
Ku: ə́ɗíèn
Od: ə́-ɗíén; (ə̀)rí-
WO: ə̀ɗìèn

NAME (v)

A: -ɣol/-kol   mí ú-ɣól ñɔ̀dí mɔ́...
                         'I named him...'
                      ú-ɣòl íímì mɔ́
                         'I'm called'
                      ámì̠ ókōl mɔ́...
                         'I'm called...'
                      ɗíén án·à ókɔ̀l ìkə̀
                         'what's your name?'

NARROW

A: -kɔlɔlɔ   v. also 'thin'
      -kɔgɔnɔ   v.
      -kɔgɔnɔmi̱   v.t.
      ɔ́kɔ́gɔ́nɔ̀   n. 'narrowness'
EO: -kpaβa
Ku: -kpori   v. 'make narrow'
      -kpɔ̀rìə̀n   v. 'narrow'
      è-kpɔ̀rìə̀n   n. 'narrowness'
Od: -βiβe/-piβe   'narrow, make narrow'
      -βiβ/-piβ   'be narrow' ɔ̀β̱ìñ ɔ̀β́ɔ́ nə́píβ
                            'the river is getting
                            narrow'

                            ɔ̀β̱ìñ ɔ̀β́ɔ́ nə́ə̀β̱îβ 'the river
                            is narrow'

      ə̀lì- β̱îβ   'narrowness'

NAVEL

A: ò-ɓùn; (ə̀)rú-
EO: ɔ́ɓúlúɓûl
Ku: ɔ́ɓúlúɓûl
Od: ò-ɓùn; (ə̀)rù-
WO: íɓúɓúlû

NEAR

A: étùmə̀n ~ ɛ́tùmə̀n   cf. SIDE
      -tumə̀n   'be near'
      ísùlōm   'it's not near'
EO: ètùə́n
Ku: -tuən
      è-túə̀n   n.
      ð-áká   tŏ ðáká ðámi̱ 'sit by me'
      -tugiom   'to come near'
Od: -tuən
      òtùə̀n   'near, beside'
      ètùə̀n   'nearness'

NEARLY   see ALMOST

NECESSARY
   A: ɛ́-kpènílɔ́ mɪ́ kə̀lè
           eδìen   'it's necessary that I eat'

NECK
   A: ó-rûm; (ɛ́)rú-
   EO: ò-rùm; ì-
   Ku: òrùm; r-
   Od: ò-rùm; ì-
   WO: òrùm; ì- ~ìrúmzə̀

NECKLACE
   A: èkótà òrùm   cf. BEAD; NECK
   EO: òδìδì òrûm   'neck rope'
        ɛ̀lórùm   'neck beads'
   Ku: ìkútá
   Od: ɛ̀-bɛ́   'coral necklace'
        ìlòrûm   [< ìlà 'beads']
   WO: ɛ̀l·órùm   cf. BEADS

NEEDLE (n)
   A: (à)lágá
   EO: àlàgá
   Ku: ànùgá
   Od: à-n·ùgá; (à)sù-
   WO: àlágá

NET
   A: ɔ̀zùgùrù   n.
   EO: ɔ̀gbǒ   n. 'net'
        ɔ̀zùgùrù   'cast net'
        ìbúrú   'net stretched across water'
        ɔ̀gb-áw̃án·ì   'net used by women only'

Ku: ɔ̀gbɔ́   n. 'net'
     ɔ̀gbɔ́ nɔ́róβ   'cast net'
     ɔ̀gbɔ́ ɨ́kʉ̀   'draw net'
     íbùrù   'sticks to which net is
                        attached'
Od: ɔ̀sɛ̀kɨ́   'net tied across water'
     ɔ̀-zʉ̀gʉ̀rʉ̀   'cast net'
WO: ɔ̀gbɔ́   'cast net'
     íbùrù   'trawling net'

NEVER
   A: kékùlɛ́

NEW
   A: òmɔ́ɔ́m
       -fɨafɨa   'new, clean'
   EO: òmòm
   Ku: (ò)mòm   'new, raw'
   Od: òmòòm   òmòòm ùkpé 'new cloth'
        ə̀lì-mɔ́ɔ́m   'newness'

NIGHT
   A: (ə̀)-ɓúɣùl; (ə̀)sí-
   EO: ə̀ɓùgúlə̀
   Ku: ə̀ɓúgə̄lə̀n; r-
   Od: ùɓùgúl; (ə̀)r-
   WO: ə̀ɓúgúlə̀; ˋzə̀

NO
   A: éèyé
   Od: éèñí

NOISE (n)
   A: (à)ɓɨ̀-àbâ

NOON

    EO: àzàñ

    Ku: ètítân

    Od: ṵ̀ṵ̀táñ

NO ONE

    A: kûyé

    EO: ɔ̀n·íbǎ

    Od: ɔ́ɔ́į̀ ɔ̀lɔ́

    WO: ɔ̀n·į̀bǎ   'no person'

NORTH

    EO: òsúə́n   'upper side'

NOSE

    A: ì-jɔ̀n ~ ì-zɔ̀n

    EO: ìzɔ̀n

    Ku: úzɔ̀n; r-

    Od: ìzɔ̀n; ə̀rìzɔ̀n

    WO: ìzɔ̀n; ìzɔ́nzə̀

NOT

    A: kɔ́   mį́ ṵ́-mį́ín ñɔ̀dį́, kɔ́ ɔ̀dɛ̀ ɔ̀dį́ 'I saw him, not his father'

                     ə̀búə̀n kṵ́ kɛ́ɛ̀mà·mį́ 'Abua is not my town'

                     ɔ̀βín kṵ́ kɔ́ɔ̀dɛ̀ à·mį́ 'this is not my father'

                     kɛ́ɛ̀nṵ́ 'it's not a bird'

                     káàmṵ̀ùm à·mį́ 'it's not my water'

                     kɔ́ɔ̀βɔ́n mṵ́ɣṵ̄mɔ̄ ɔ̀pɔ́ 'neither this nor that'

                     káàn·ám 'it's not a cow'

NOTHING   cf. THING
    A: kî̩yaar
    EO: àβárbà
    Ku: àbé̩ràbārɔ̀
    Od: áár òló
    WO: àβárbǎ
          àβár éwèzèn

NOW
    A: égíβɔ̄   'this time'

O

OATH   cf. AGREEMENT

    A: ì̩yɔ̀   'oath of friendship'

                        ɔ̀ðíɣí ɛ́kàràβ   'to swear oath'

    Od: ì̩zɔ̀   'oath, swearing'

    WO: ɛ̀-zɔ̀

OBTAIN   see HAVE

OCCIPUT

    A: ɛ́kō̩l

    EO: ɛ̀kɔ̩̀l

    Ku: ɛ̀kɔ̩̀l

    Od: ɛ́-kō̩l; (à)rá-

    WO: ɛ̀kɔ̩̀l

OCEAN

    A: àbàzi̩

    EO: àbàdi̩

    Ku: àbàdi̩

    Od: à-bàdi̩; (à)rà-

    WO: àbàdi̩

OFTEN

    EO: kàkɛ́ɣí̩rì̩   adv.

    Od: -gbor   v.   'do often, frequently'

                        àmì̩ nɛ́bgòrɣání̩ ámì̩í̩nzòdí

                          'I see him often'

OIL (n)

    A: (à)-mù̩nù̩m   (grease)

    EO: àmù̩nù̩

    Ku: àmù̩nù̩

    Od: àmù̩nù̩

    WO: ámú̩nù̩

OIL CONTAINER
A: ( )pósìrì   'oil cask'
      (à)drɔ̂m àmṵ̀nṵ̀n   'oil drum'
EO: ə̀pôn ámṵ́nṵ̀   'oil drum'
Ku: àgbá ámṵ́nṵ̀m 'oil casket'
Od: ə̀-pònǐ   'keg for oil, casket'
WO: àdrɔ̂m   'oil drum'

OIL PALM
A: ə̀-lè; (ə̀)rè-
EO: ə̀δè
Ku: ə̀δè; r-
Od: ə̀lè; (ə̀)r-
WO: ə̀δ ê; ʼzə̀

OKRA
A: ó-kòrò; (ə̀)ró-
EO: ɔ̀kṵ̀rṵ̀
Ku: ɔ́kṵ̀rṵ̀
Od: ɔ́-kṵ̀rṵ̀; (à)rṵ́-
WO: ɔ́kṵ̀rṵ̀; έ- ˋ(zà)

OLD
A: ògbə̂ñ   ì̩lὲl βɔ́ ògbə̂ñ 'the yams
                        are old'

      (à)δ ḭ̀-kpɔ́   'old age'
EO: òmùgbə̀
Od: -kpɔ   v. 'be old'
                ɔ́ḭ̀ βɔ́ náàkpɔ́ 'the man is
                        old'
                ɔ́ḭ̀βɔ́ àkpɔ́ 'the man was old'
      ùgbə̌·ñī; ì-   'old thing'
      ò-kèñ   'old thing'
WO: îgbòlòm

OLD PERSON

A: ò-kúmòr-òyè;
    è-kúmòr-əwè

    ò-kúmòr-ànịr;
    è-kúmòr-àmàrịr

EO: ò-kéñón·ị;
    ì-kéñ əw̃únòm   masc.

    ò-kéñán·ị;
    ì-kéñ áw̃án·ị

Ku: oke-ɔn·ị; ìkèəw̃únòm

    òké-ànịéβòm; ìkéàw̃ánị

Od: òkéñ óì   'old man'

    ò-kéñ óóị; ì-kéñ
      éréì   'old man'

    ò-ɣùdùànị; ì-ɣùdù
      àráánị

WO: ìgbólómòn·ị;
    ìgbólóm əw̃ùnòm   'old man'

    ìgbólómàδịzà;
    ìgbólóm àwàr   'old woman'

ONION

A: éyō

EO: éyò

Ku: éyòw; r-

Od: éyŏ; (ə)r-

WO: éyò; ˇzə

ONLY

A: bịn   òníīn ɛ̀lɛ̀l bịn 'only one
                           yam'

EO: kụ̀kụ́m   ònín ɛ̀lɛ̀l kụ̀kụ́m 'only one
                           yam'

Ku: kụ̀kụ́m   ònîn ɛ̀lɛ̀l kụ̀kụ́m 'only one
                           yam'

WO: -ɓέn   ònụ̀ɓέn 'mouth only,
                           talkative' masc. name

OPEN (v)

A: -ɣuɣuron   'open door'

        -keɣeron   'open box, lock'

EO: -kperen

        -guron   'open door'

Ku: -kperon

        -guron   'open door'

Od: -ɣuron/kuron   'open door'

        -kpeeron   'uncover'

        -ɓuton   'uncork, unstopper'

        òɓútònòm   n. 'opener'

WO: íβùròn (m-)

OR

A: móɣómó   n·â móɣómó úmòr án·à
                         'you or your brother'

ORANGE

A: óðgìrí

EO: ὲlὲlέńdὲ

Ku: ὲlὲdέdὲ   n.

Od: ὲ-lὲlὲ·zị̀; àrὲ-

WO: égὲ

OTHER, THE

A: ɔ̀βɔ́rὲβɔ́

        nɔ́ɔ́rị̀βɔ́   'the other' nɔ́ɔ́rị̀βɔ́ òyὲβɔ́
                                 'the other man'

        ɔ̀βɔ́dị̀βɔ́; ị̀βέdị̀βɔ́

        mụ̀έrị̀βɔ́

        ðị́έrị̀βɔ́

        ὲβέdị̀βɔ́

        túέrị̀βɔ́

A: búnón ə́wè   'other people'
    búέrìβ5   búέrìβ5 ə́rútùβɔ
                       'other houses'
EO: òβúgè̤
Ku: ùwèδí
Od: ò-pédì; ì-
WO: òdòδə̤̂

OUTSIDE
A: è-rùγ   n.
EO: ègbètírè
Ku: δétìrè
Od: ètèrè
WO: ètìrè

OWE (v)
Od: -le ɔ̀múγ   cf. DEBT

OWN, ONE'S
A: ɔ̀l·á   ɔ̀l·ɔ́dì̤ 'his own'
                       ɔ̀l·ánnà 'your own'
                       ɔ̀l·áábìdì̤ 'their own'
EO: ot-   ót-ə̆m 'mine'
     it-   ít-ăm pl. 'mine'
                      ót-tīōm 'yours'
                      ót-àwá 'theirs'
                      òtù ònón ótə̆m 'this house
                          is mine'
Ku: ol-   òlàmí 'it's mine' 'my own'
     iy-   masc. name
                      ìyàmí 'they're mine'
                      òlòyóm sg. 'yours'
                      ìyòyóm pl. 'yours'
                      òlòyɔ́ sg. 'his'
                      òlìyár sg. 'ours'

Ku: òlàwá   sg. 'theirs'
                                     ị̀yàwá   pl. 'theirs'
Od: V̄1; V̄1 (pl.)   ụ̀lààmị́/ị̀lààmị́ 'mine'
                                     òlònúmə/ìlònúmə̄ 'yours'
                                     òlŏdí/ìlŏdí 'his'
                                     ìlèzóór pl. 'ours'
                                     ìlĕdí pl. 'theirs'

WO: ɔ̀p-ámị̀nị̀
      ɔ̀p-ána
      zừ-áátừm
      zừ-áátà

OWNER (n)
A: ụ̀wá   cf. KING
                                     ụ̀w-ótừ 'head of house,
                                         family'
                                     ụ̀w-ɛmụ́ 'headman'
EO: ò-ɓénémə̀
WO: ò-ɓén...   'owner of...'
                                     òɓén òtừə̀ 'head of family'
                                     òɓén ɛ̀l·ɛ̀là 'owner of yams'
      ò-ɓénə̀   'owner, person in charge'

P

PADDLE (n)

A: ɔ̀-lɔ́m; ì-

EO: ɔ̀ɗɔ̆m

Ku: ɔ̀ɗɔ́m

Od: ɔ̀-lɔ̆m; ì-

WO: ɔ̀ɗɔ́m

PADDLE (v)

A: -zɔɣị

EO: -βa

Ku: -zɔɣụ

Od: -zɔɣị

WO: à-βâ

à-βɔ́ɔ̀ɗɔ̀m   n. 'paddling' cf. PADDLE (n)

PAIN

A: (ɔ̀)ɗí-βìn

-βin/-pin   'be painful' v.

                 rèpín 'it's painful'

                 rèpín ésì àmị̀ 'it's
                   painful for me'

                 òlóɣí á·mị̀ rèpín 'I'm angry'

                 n·â rèpínnī ólógí ámị̀
                   'you're painful to my
                   mind, I'm angry at you'

                 kípín ōlōɣī ānnà 'don't
                   be angry'

EO: -gam   'be in pain, be angry'

                 mị́ nàgám 'I'm angry'

àlị̀-gàm   n. 'painfulness'

PALM OF HAND

A: ɛ̀dà áɗīɣaaɣ

EO: ɛ̀ɓ-agwɔ̀

Ku: ɛɓáɓà àgwɔ̀
Od: ɛ̀-ɓà; (à)ráá-   'palm, sole' 'footprints'
WO: ɛ̀zɛ́rɛ́màgwɔ̀

PALM [USED FOR THATCHING]
Od: òɔ̀-ɗùm; ìì-

PALMFRUIT
A: èkpó ɛ́lê   cf. SEED

PALMKERNEL
A: èkpézíβ
        [j]
EO: ò-zù; ì-
Ku: òzìβ
Od: ékpózìm
WO: ò·zù

PALMWINE
A: ə̀míímí(y)ə̀
EO: ìdè (ə̀mìn)
Ku: ùdè
Od: ə̀-mìlm; ə̀rè-mììm   'bottles of palmwine'
     ìgè ə̀míìm   'non-distilled palmwine'
     ògùmɪ̀ɣɔ́l   'palmwine tapper'
     ɔ̀sàmììm; ɪ̀sàrìmììm   'palmwine distiller'
WO: ìdə́míì

PARE [NAILS]
A: -βɨ(ɔɔ-)/-pɨ
EO: -ba
Ku: -ɓɛl
Od: -ɣo/-ko (oo-)   'pare other's nails'
     -ɣuə/-kuə (oo-)   'pare own nails'
WO: ɛ́ɛ̀bɛ̀ (m-)

PARLOR
    A: ògbótû   'middle of house'
    EO: ìwòl ótù
    Ku: ògbò ~ ògbóòtù
    Od: ògbótū
    WO: òròrò

PARROT
    A: òkóòkó
    EO: òkòlòbị
    Ku: àaβịàl
    Od: ò-kókò; (ə)rə-
    WO: àpòlị́
        ~ òkókòpòlị́

PART (n)
    A: é-bìn; (ə)sì-   'part, portion'
    EO: òpàdị   'part, fraction'
    Ku: òpòδì   'part, portion'
    Od: ò-pàdị   'part, fraction'
        ə-bín   'share'
    WO: òpópòl   'part, fraction'

PARTING, LEAVING HOME (n)
    A: è-γèèl   cf. GO HOME

PASS (v)   cf. ROAD
    A: -ten   rètényén 'they're passing
                    to, becoming'
                 òdị́ ətén éγōl 'he turned
                    into a crocodile'
    EO: -ten
    Ku: -ten
    Od: -ten

Od: -ɓɔl 'pass through'

àm'ṹɓɔ̀l tótù òβó ə̀tĕn 'I passed through the house'

-tṳ (ɔ-) 'pass by side of...'

WO: ə̀-tên

ò-tènèmə̀n 'passing-by, passing-on (to next stage, as in oil manufacture)'

'forgiveness'

PATH see ROAD

PATIENT, BE (v)

Ku: -n·e àmḭ́ tĕn·è 'I'll be patient'

n·ĕ 'be patient!'

PAY (v)

A: -kpɛ also 'to be fitting'

EO: -kpɛ 'pay person or for thing'

Ku: -kpɛ also 'fit'

Od: -kpɛ also 'fit'

WO: ɛ̂kpɛ̀ (m-)

ɛ́-kpɛ̄ 'payment'

ɛ́-kp'ōlōgo 'payment of fine'

è-wèzènə̀ 'free, gratis'

PEACE

A: è-dùɣòm personal name

PECK [AS CHICKENS]

A: -kpoβ

PEEL (v)

A: -ɓɛl 'peel orange, paw-paw'

-mɛɛñ 'peel yams, etc.'

A: -kpoñon   'peel banana, plantain,
                                cassava, orange'
EO: -fo   'peel by hand'
     -kpɔn   'peel with knife'
Ku: -fo   'peel banana'
     -kpɔn   'peel yam, orange'
Od: -kolomi   'peel with knife'
     -kporon   'peel by hand'
WO: ôkpòn (m-)   'peel by hand'
     ôkpòn ózù   'to flay'
     êzɛ̀ (m-)   'peel with knife'

PENIS
   A: ɔ̀-ɣụ́m; (à)rụ́-
   EO: ɔ̀dụ́
   Ku: έɓụ̀tụ̀
   Od: ɔ̀-ɣụ́m; ɨ̀-; àrụ́-
   WO: ɔ́-dụ̀; έ-
        ~ ɛ̀pɛ̀pɛ̀; ´^zà

PEPPER
   A: ó-bɩ̀ə̀n; (ə̀)rɩ́-
        (à)láɣ   'alligator pepper'
   EO: ìdŭ
        àlǎ   'alligator pepper'
   Ku: ùdû   pl. only
        ɔ̀dû; r-
        àlǎɣ   'alligator pepper'
   Od: àlǎɣ; (à)r-
        àlàɣɔ̀δúə̀l   'alligator pepper'
   WO: ɛ̀gàrà; ˋzà
        àlá   'alligator pepper'

PERCH [FISH]
   Ku: ɛ̀wálà
   WO: ìl·ò

PERCH, ALIGHT (v)
    A: -lɛl

PERHAPS
    A: íínī

PERRYWINKLE
    Ku: ɔ̀-sɛ̌m

PERSEVERANCE
    Od: ɛ̀-kpàràm   masc. name

PERSON
    A: ò-yê; (ə̀)wé-   'person, human, man'
    EO: ɔ̀n·ị̀; ə̃̀wúnòm
    Ku: ɔ̀n·ị̀; ə̃̀wúnòm   'person, man'
    Od: ɔ́ɔ́ị̀; ə̀réì
    WO: ɔ̀n·ị̀; ə̃̀wúnòm

PESTLE
    A: è-túbō; (ə̀)rú-
    EO: ɛ̀dǔm
    Ku: ɛ̀dúm
    Od: ɛ̀-dǔm
    WO: ògùmòmề   cf. POUND

PICK OUT
    A: -sɔñɔn   mị́ úsɔ̀ñɔ́n íkpó βɔ̄ 'I picked
                                 out the seeds'

PIERCE (v)
    A: -βuur/-puur   'pierce ear'
          -sụγ   'pierce fish (with implement
                                 in pot'

EO: -roβ   'pierce fish'   also 'throw'
     -βur   'pierce ear'
Ku: -gim   'pierce fish'
     -βur   'pierce ear'
Od: -βuur/-puur   'pierce fish, ear'
WO: ôβòlì(m-)   'pierce ear'
     ə̀-rôβ   'pierce fish'

PIG

A: òβòrópò
EO: òpòríópò
Ku: ópòròpò
Od: ò-βóròpò; (ə̀)rə̀-
WO: òpóríópò

PIGEON

Od: èè-kùmùdé; (ə̀)rùù-

PIN (v)

A: -gìm   'pin, put sticks in ground,
                            stab'
EO: -gim   'pin, fix sticks in ground'
Ku: -gìm   'pin, fix sticks'
Od: -gìm   'pin, fix sticks'
     -gìmoγ   'pin, fix many sticks'
WO: ə̀-gîm   'pin, pierce'
     ə̀-gím òwù   'pin, pierce'

PIT (n)

A: òònì   'pit, hole'
EO: ògùgù
Ku: ògùgwə̀
Od: òò-n·ù; (ə̀)rùù-
WO: ògùgù

PITY (n)
    Ku: ìgbìrìgbîr   òkpòn ìgbírìgbîr 'to look
                                 with pity on...'

PLACE (n)
    A: è-sì; (è)rì-   'place, spot, wound'
         è-kpísí   'general area'
    EO: èsì
    Ku: èsì; r-
    Od: è-sì; (è)rì-
    WO: èsì; ʼzè

PLAIT (v)
    A: -kpa
         -kpɔ   [rope]
    EO: -kpa
    Ku: -kpa   'plait rope, hair'
    Od: -kpa   'plait as hair'
    WO: à-kpâ

PLANK
    A: (à)δу̣́pɔ́
    EO: òkpòkpólòm
    Ku: àδу̣́ɓɔ́
    Od: à-δу̣̀ɓɔ́; (à)sу̣̀
    WO: èkúrú

PLANT (v)
    A: -ɓeβ   'plant tubers'
         -zу̣β   'sowing non-tubers'
    EO: -gbeβ   'plant any kind'
    Ku: -gbeβ   'plant, sow'
    Od: -ɓeβ   'plant tubers, maize'
         -ɓε   'plant bananas, etc.'

WO:	à-nâm	'plant tubers'
	à-sáràgɨ̀	'scatter seed'
	ɔ̀-gbêβ	general term also 'plant seed in holes'

PLANTAIN
A:	ɔ́-kāñ; (à)rá-	'plantain plant'
	(à)δá-kāñ; (à)sá-	'plantain fruit'
	éβúté ɔ́kāñ	'trunk of plantain'
EO:	ɔ̀káɨ́	
Ku:	ɔ́kàɨ́	
	ègúì ɔ́kàɨ́	'bunch of plantains'
	àdɨ́ɣàn	'plantain leaf'
Od:	às̞ɨ̀-nâɣ	'plantain leaf' no sg.
	ɔ̀-káñ; ɨ̀-	
	ɔ̀kpátɨ́àn ɨ́kāñ	'plantain heap'
WO:	ɔ́fɔ̀ñ	

PLASTER (v)
A:	-βɨ̞ɨ̞r	
EO:	-l·ɔ	'plaster wall'
Ku:	-lɔ	'plaster wall'
Od:	-βɨ̞la/-pɨ̞la	
WO:	ɔ́ɔ̀l·ɔ̀(m-)	

PLATE (n)
A:	(à)-gbàgbà; (à)s̞ɨ̀-	'enamel plate'
	ɛ̀kpá	'wooden bowl' cf. MORTAR
EO:	ɛ̀kpá	'wooden plate'
	àpánɛ́fɛ́rɛ́	'enamel plate'
	ɛ̀fɛ́rɛ́	'zinc, china plate'
	ɛ̀bôl	'bowl'
Ku:	ɛ̀fɛ́rɛ́	'enamel plate'
	àbɔ́dɨ̀	'china plate'

Od: ɛ̀-kpá   'wooden bowl'
     à-pànḭ̀   'enamel plate'
     ɛ̀kpɛ́pɛ́rɛ́   'china plate, delicate bowl'
WO: ɛ̀kpá   'wooden plate'
     àpánɛ̀fɛ̀rɛ̀   Nembe 'enamel plate'
     ə̀ðègɛ́fɛ̀rɛ̀   'china plate'

PLATFORM
EO: ìkpò
WO: òkpó   also 'table for offerings'

PLAY
A: -βeγ/-peγ   v. 'to play'
     è-βèγ   n. 'play, game'
     ò-pèγòm è-βèγ   'someone who plays'
EO: -zo   v.
     ə̀lì-zó   n. 'play, game'
Ku: -deγ   v.
     -deγən   v. 'to joke, play with'
     è-dèγ   n. 'play, game'
     òdèγ mèdèγ   n. 'player, time waster'
Od: -geme   v.
     -gemiom   v. 'play with, joke'
                        àm' úgèmé nòdí 'I played
                           with him' (among equals)
                        àm' úgèmìóm zòdí 'I played
                           with him' (with
                           younger person)
     ə̀sə́ə́gémé   n. 'play, game'
WO: ôl·ò(m-)   v.
     òl·ó   n. 'play, game'

PLEASANTNESS   see also SWEETNESS
EO: ə̀lì-ròβ

PLEASE!   cf. PRAY
   A: sésèñ
   Ku: síséñ
   Od: sésén

PLEASE (v)
   A: -ɓɛraan   'please, delight'
                      ɛlɛ́l ɪ́ɓɛ̀ràan ɪ́ɪ́mɪ̀ 'I like yam'
                      ɛlɛ́l ɪ́ɓɛ̀ràan ɪ́ɪmɪ̀ épū ɛ̀nàm 'I prefer yam to meat'
   EO: -ɗɪ̀ólògì
   Od: -ɓaalmɛnɪ̀ òlóɣì   'please, make happy'
        -ɗiɣ   ɪ̀lɛ́l èɗìɣ tólóɣí ámɪ́ 'I like yams'
   WO: ə̀-ɗíɔ̀l·ògì

PLEASURE (n)
   A: ɔ̀-ɓààlólóɣì

PLUCK, PICK (vt)
   A: -kʉ

POCKET (n)
   A: ò-kùrù; (ə̀)rù-

POINT (v)
   A: -ma
   EO: -sɔkɔñ
   Ku: -leriom ~ -tʉɔm
        -sɔɣɔɣɛnɪ̀   'point with comtempt'
   Od: -sʉɣoɣoon
   WO: ótɔ̀kɔ̀ñ

POLE (n)
   A: (à)ɗɪ̀-wà ; ɪ̀-

POMADE
    EO: ə̀bìsíə̀
    Ku: èl·ò
    Od: è-l·ò
    WO: èlò

POOR   cf. POVERTY
    A: ò-ɗíɣí úwēkūlòm   v. 'be poor' -méél ékùlòm 'become poor, fall into poverty'
    EO: -sor igo   mì̠ nésòr mìgó 'I'm poor'
         òñìgô   'poor person'
    Ku: ògòñ
         ò̠ñì̠gôñ   'poor person'
    Od: -kulom   'be poor'
         ùvékùlòm   'poor person'
    WO: (m-)íìgò   'be poor'
         ón·ìgo   'poor person'
         ~ òñígô

PORCUPINE
    A: (ə̀)ɗíílə̀
    EO: ə̀ɗìɓílə̀
    Ku: ókù̠rù̠
    Od: ə̀-ɗíílə̀; (ə̀)rì-
    WO: ə̀ɗìɓílə̀

POT
    A: (ə̀)-ɣùùɣ; (ə̀)s-ùùɣ
        ò-kò; (ə̀)rò-   'water pot, pitcher'
        òl·èmòm ókò   'potter'
    EO: ékúkù   'water pot'
         ə̀gù   'cooking pot'

Ku: èɓəɓə̀   'water pot'
     ə̀gùγ; r-   'cooking pot'
Od: ə̀-gùùγ; ə̀sùùγ
     ɔ̀ɔ́-n·ṳ̀; (à)rṳ́ṳ́-   'water pot'
WO: ɔ́-ɓɛ̀lɛ́; ɛ́-
     èkùkù   'waterpot'
     ~ èbɛ̀   'waterpot'
     ɔ̀nɛ̀mɔ̀nɔ́ɓɛ̀lɛ̆; ɛ̀-   'potter'

POUND (v)
A: -γum/-kum
     è-γúmûm   n. 'way of pounding'
EO: -gum
Ku: -γum
Od: -γum/-kum
WO: ə̀-gûm
     í-gúmə̀nə̀   'something pounded'

POUR
A: -saγaran
EO: -zu
Ku: -zu
     -za   'pour from one container to
                         another'
Od: -zu
WO: ə̀-zû
     -zuə   v.i. 'pour out'

POVERTY
A: èkùlòm
EO: ìgô
Ku: ìgôñ
Od: èkùlòm
WO: ìgô

PRAISE (v)

    A: -ɓoom

          -sɛβ   mí úsέβ ñòdí 'I praised him'

                                        òdí ásὲβá lóór ódì 'he
                                           praised himself'

    EO: -gelemen   also 'enlarge' cf. INCREASE
          -tutumen

    Ku: -tutumeni
          ǝðìèn έβà   n. 'praise name'

    Od: -sɛβ
          àlì-sêβ   n. 'praise'

    WO: ǝ-bómǝ̀n
          ǝ-tútùmǝ̀n   'favor, prefer, praise'
          ítútúmǝ̀n   n. 'praise'
          ǝðíén ítú   'praise name'

PRAWN   see CRAYFISH

PRAY (v)

    A: -ɓɛrɛγì (ɔɔ-)   also 'worship; beg
                                            forgiveness'

                                        mí úɓὲrὲγí ròdí 'I prayed
                                            with him'

                                        mí úɓὲrὲγí àŋó ñòdí 'I
                                            prayed for him'

    EO: -γalam
    Ku: -siseñ
          ǝ́sìsěñ   n. 'prayer'

    Od: -kpuluγu (oo-)
          ìí-kpùlùγǔ   n. 'prayer'

    WO: à-γálàm   also 'worship'
          ὲγàlàm   n. 'prayer'

PREGNANT

    A: -moromi (oo-)   v. 'make pregnant' cf. BURN
          ànìr èγùn   'pregnant woman' cf. WOMB

Od: -mor (oo-)   'be pregnant'
     -moromi (oo-)   'make pregnant'
     è-ɣùn; (ə̀)rù-   'pregnancy' cf. Abua 'womb'

PRESS (v)
  EO: -fị̀dị̀

PREVENT
  Ku: -kigəmə   àm'íkìgə̀m'ị́nà k'ị́ 'nɔδụ̂à 'I
                          prevented him from
                          escaping'

PRICE (n)   see COST

PRIDE
  A: ì-ɓó   personal name

PRISON
  A: ìkól·ī̀
  EO: ìkól
  Ku: ìkòlí
       ~ òtù ìkólí
  Od: ì-kólí
  WO: ìkólụ́árị́

PROFIT (n)
  A: àsụ́ɔ́
  EO: àsụ̀ɔ̀
  Ku: òwîl
  Od: à-sụ́ɔ́
  WO: ásụ̀ɔ̀má

PROSTITUTION
  EO: òδɛ́mà   cf. ADULTERY
  WO: ò-δə̀mɛ́mà   'prostitute'

PROTRUDE, STICK OUT
    A: -sɔl   v.t., v.i.

PROVERB
    A: (ə̀) δɪ̀-doγ; (ə̀)sɪ̀-
    EO: ə̀sɪ̀dò
    Ku: ə̀sɪ̀dòγ
    Od: ə̀sɪ̀dòγ   also 'riddle'
    WO: ə̀dò

PULL (v)
    A: -δur
    EO: -ña• ~-ñaγ
    Ku: -ñaγ   'pull back, withdraw'
    Od: -ñaγ   general term
          -δur   'drag (logs to water)'
          -γɔγ   'drag resisting animal or
                                     person'
          è δ ù γ é ə̀ n   'act of pulling'
    WO: à-ñâ

PURSUE   see DRIVE AWAY

PUSH (v)
    A: -ñu
    EO: -dụ
    Ku: -nu
    Od: -ñu
    WO: à-dụ̂

PUT AWAY
    A: -seere   'put away and keep'
          -gbɔlɛ   'put aside'
    EO: -sɪ̣ɛ
    Od: -tuγuneen

WO: à-sâ   'pick up and take'
      à-sá ìtènè   'remove'

PUT DOWN

   A: -seere

       -mʊnɛñ   'to put-- down flat'

       -mɛrɛmi̧   'to put-- down upright'

       -sereɣi   'put down together'

                      mə́séréɣi̧ 'have put together'

   EO: -soroñ ~ -soron

       -mɛrɛñ   'put down in standing
                           position, stand a child
                           on his feet'

   Ku: -soroni   'put something down flat'

       -gʊrɔm   'put someone down'

       -maramɛni̧   'stand on edge'

   Od: -soore

   WO: ə̀-sérèñ

       -sere   'keep down, lay down'

                      òwə́sèrè ɛ́mâ 'village
                         founder'

PUT IN

   A: -lɔɣ

       -lɔɣɔm   'put inside with...'

       -doɣodi   'put several things in
                         container'

   EO: -lɔ

   Ku: -lɔɣ

   Od: -lɔɣ

   WO: à-lɔ̂

PUT ON

   A: -ɓam   'put, place on something'

                      áɓámá 'placed him on'

A:	-lɔɣa	
	-lɔɣɔ̆ɟan	'put on several things'
EO:	-gbam	
Ku:	-guri	'put, place on'
	-soroni	'put, place on'
	-laɣa	'put on clothing'
	-zuomə	'put on hat'
Od:	-seeri	'put on' also 'keep'
WO:	à-gbómɔ̀m	'put on something'

PYTHON

A:	ògbóm óδíɣ	cf. ROPE
Ku:	ṵ̀gbɔ̀gbɔ́	
	~ ògbɔ̀gbɔ́	
Od:	òbòm òδìɣ	cf. ROPE
WO:	ébì	'long python (may be killed)'
	ɔ̀δṵ́m	'sacred type python (taboo)'
	à̀δṵ̂m	'female spirit, representing sacred python, water-dwelling'

Q

QUARREL
- A: ɔ̀-rʉ̀ɔ́nʉ̀   n.
- EO: -ɓulən   v.
- Ku: ɔ́ɓɛ̀m   n.
  - -ɓʉman   v.
- Od: ɔ̀-rʉ́án   n. masc. name
  - -rʉan/-tʉan   v. mɪ́ ʉ́rʉ̀án rɔ̀dɪ́ 'I quarrelled with him'
  - -rʉɔnʉ/-tʉɔnʉ   v. 'to pick quarrel with, be agressor'

    mɪ́ ʉ́rʉ̀ɔnɔ́m ñɔ̀dɪ́ ɔ́rʉ̀ɔnʉ̀ 'I quarrelled with him'

    ɔ̀dɪ́ rʉ́rʉ̀ɔnɔ̀mɪ́ɪmɪ̀ ɔ́rʉ̀ɔnʉ̀ 'he's quarrelling with me'
- WO: ɔ̀-βúlə́n   n.
  - ə̀-βúlə̀n   v.

QUESTION (n)
- A: (ə̀)δɪ́-púrù   cf. ASK
- Od: ɪ́pùrùə́n
- WO: ɪ́-pùrə̆n   'inquiry about witchcraft'

QUICKLY, DO
- EO: -kperegi   kpèrègé mə̀rù 'come quickly'
- Od: -kem   'do something quickly'

    àmɪ̀ tə́kĕmìnɪ́ àmɪ̀ɪ̀n án·à 'I'll see you soon'

QUIET
- A: -ɓoriən   v. 'be quiet'
  - ɓɔ̀rìə́n   'keep quiet!'
  - kpáɪ́   'be quiet' onomatopoeic?

    ɔ̀dɪ́ kpáɪ́ kpáɪ́ kpáɪ́ 'she kept very quiet'
- Ku: ɓɔ̀ɓɔ̀m   árɔ́ ɓɔ̀ɓɔ̀m 'he remained silent'

R

RABBIT
      A: (ə̀)ɗí-wòòr; (ə̀)sí-
      Ku: àgárà; r-
      Od: àgàrá; (à)r-
      WO: òkə̀tə́ éɗùm ìgbò   'Ibo rat'

RACE, RUNNING (n)
      Od: èɣììl   cf. RUN
      WO: é-yìlí

RAFFIA PALM
      A: ɔ̀ɣɔ́l
      EO: ɔ̀ɣɔ̀l
            òɗùɗúm   'palm used for making mats'
      Ku: ɔ̀ɣɔ́l
            òɗùɗùm   'wild raffia, used for
                                          thatching'
      Od: ɔ̀-ɣɔ́l; ì-   'tapped for palmwine'
            ɔ̀-gbɔ́; ì-   'raffia palm'
      WO: ɔ̀ɣɔ́l
            èɗúmɔ̀ɣɔ́l   'palm used for making mats'

RAIN (n)
      A: ɔ̀làβìá   -ɗiɣi ɔ́làβìà
            ~ɔ̀lɔ̀βìá   ɔ̀làβìá ràlɔ́β 'rain is
                                          falling'
      EO: ɔ̀lɔ̀βá
      Ku: ə̀ɗìɔ̀   ə̀ɗìɔ́ nàlɔ̆β 'it's raining'
            ~ ɔ̀lɔ̀βá
      Od: ὲ-lὲβὲ; (à)rà-   'repeated rain'
      WO: èmùə́ɗìɔ̀

RAINBOW
    EO: égwèlégwè
    Ku: égùlégù
    Od: àlàgbènáàn

RAINS [SEASON]
    A: ùn·ù; (ə̀)r-
    Od: ùn·ù; (ə̀)r-
          èlémú   'August break'
    WO: ɔ̀kókìmù ə̀ðìò

RAM (n)
    A: ò-dùɣúnə̀; ì-
    EO: òdùnə̀
    Ku: ódúɣúnə̀; r-
    Od: ò-dùɣùnə̀; ì-
    WO: ò-dùnə̀; ì-

RAT, MOUSE
    A: (ə̀)ðí-wó; ì- ~(ə̀)sí- 'rat'
    EO: òkétə̀   'mouse'
          àgárà   'bush rat'
    Ku: ə̀ðùɣɔ́ éðúm;
            ə̀sùɣɔ́ éðúm   'rat'
          ə̀βòtòβ; r-   'mouse'
    Od: ə̀l-ìvó; ìvó   'mouse'
    WO: ókə̀tə́; í-   'rat'

RAZOR
    A: ɛ̀lɛ̀gɛ̀ ɛ́mṵ   'knife for scraping head'
    Ku: ɓérípɛ́lɛ̀
    WO: ɔ̀kpɔ̀mə̂   'shaver'
          ~ ə̀rézè

REACH (v)   cf. ARRIVE; EXTEND; HAVE

    A: -si   also 'arrive'

        -tɛñ   'reach, arrive, happen,
                             catch up with, catch'

                        mí ú-sí Búə̀n 'I arrived
                             in Abua'

                        ə́-rú ə́-sí 'she arrived'

        -lool   'reach, equal, come up to
                             (desired point)'

                        mɛ́-nị́γɛ̀-lóòl 'it's all
                             right now'

    EO: -tɛñ

    Ku: -tɛị   -tɛ̀ị íkpòkì 'obtain money'

                        ɔ̀tɛ̀ị míkpòkì 'one who
                           always gets money'

    Od: -si   'arrive'

        -tɛñ   'reach with hand, catch up
                             with'

                        nɛ́ɛ̀tɛ̆ñ zàày mị 'it's my turn'

    WO: à-tɛ́ñ   'reach for'

READ (v)

    A: aal/-bal   cf. COUNT; MARRY

    EO: -sen

    Ku: -sen ə̀ðírè

    Od: -ɓal   'count'

        -γɔl (ɥ-)

    WO: ə̀-gô

        ə̀-gê ðìrì   'reading'

READY

    Ku: gwá   'come on, get ready'

                      àmị nə́kòkòðìə̀n ə́rŭ 'I'm
                         ready'

RECONCILE [TWO FACTIONS]

    A: -βɔmɔγị/-pɔmɔγị   cf. LOVE

RED

A:	ó-tótòɣ; í-	n.
	-tɔtɔɣ	v.
EO:	-ɓaɓam	
Ku:	ɔ̀ɓàɓăm	cf. RIPE
Od:	-kəɣ	
	-kə̀ɣə̀mi	'redden, make red'
	òkə̀kə̀ɣ	'red color'
	ə̀lìkə̂ɣ	'redness'
	élì-kə̂ɣ	'redness'

REFUSE (v)

A:	-kel/-ɣel	v.t.
	-ɣine/-kine	'refuse to do thing'
EO:	-ŋanana	rare; only when dealing with oracle
Ku:	-gin	v.t.
Od:	-gin	v.t.
	-gine	'refuse to do...'
	ì-gínè	n. 'refusal'
WO:	òβísì	v.t.
	òðúə̀sí	'refuse, not agree'

REJOICE (v)

A:	-bo	mí rèbó íbò 'I'm joyful'
	ì-bô	n. rejoicing
Od:	-bo	

REMAIN, STAY, BE [IN PLACE]

A:	-rɔl/-tɔl	ìkpókí íróllį 'there was money'
		ìkpókí ítôl 'there was no money'
		ìkpókí kɛ̀tóllį 'there will be money'

A: -suɣeñ   'remain, be left over'

íβɛ́dị̀βɔ́   n. 'remainder' íβɛ́dị̀βɔ́ ịnὑn 'the other birds'

EO: -sion   'remain, be left'

-siomǝ   'remain in place'

-ra   'stay in place, be'

Ku: -rɔ   'remain, be (in place)'

-rị̀la   'remain in place, be present'

- δìδíǝ̀   'remain, be left over'

Od: -rɔl/-tɔl   'remain, stay, be'

-sὑɣó   'remain, be left'

WO: à-rô   'remain, be in place, stay'

ǝ̀-síòmὲn   'remain, be left'

ìsìsìo   n. 'remains'

REMEMBER   cf. THINK

EO: -walama

-tụtụga

WO: íkìòmǝ̀ (m-)

REMIND

Od: -tụɛmị̀ (ɔɔ-)

REMOVE (v)

A: -muton   'remove one of many, completely'

òsôβ òmὑtòn 'didn't cut it through'

REPEAT   see AGAIN, DO

REPLY   see AGREE, ANSWER

RESEMBLANCE

A: ǝ̀ɣị̀ɣị̀ɣà

RESEMBLE

    A: -ɣịɣ/-kịɣ   á-kĪɣ 'resembles'

                                       ɔdị́ ákĪɣ ééɣè 'what does he look like'

    EO: -gụ̄ban

    Ku: -gụ̄ɓan

    Od: -gbaanan

    WO: à-gụ́bàn

REST (v)

    A: -poɣiən/-ɓoɣiən

    EO: -sirigə

    Ku: -sirepoɓ

    Od: -ɓooɣiə/-pooɣiə

    WO: élèmènòɓù (m-)

            é-lèmèn óɓù   'resting, peace'

RETURN (v)

    A: -tiɣeel/-riɣeel   'to return after long absence'

            -ɓulə   'return, if moving away'

    EO: -tibərə

    Ku: -mulə   m-ị́tŭn ə̀ðìázìm ə̀mùlə́ 'I went home because of darkness'

    Od: -ruɣeel/-tuɣeel   'return home'

            -mulə   'turn back, return'

            è-mùlúə̀n   n. 'return, turning back'

            è-rùɣéélə̀ə̀n   n. 'return home'

    WO: ítòkònə̀ (m-)

RIB (n)

    A: ịkálòkù

            ~ ɔ́ɔ́kpɔ́ ékpòrògààñ

    EO: ɛ̀gágá

      Ku: ɛ̀gɛ̀gà òkúròɣ
      Od: ɔ̀-kàlá; ì̀-
      WO: àgágá; ^zà

RICE
      A: àrừsự́
      EO: òrósì̀
      Ku: òrósì̀
      Od: àrừsự́
      WO: ɛ̀rósì̀

RICH
      A: òmóɣɛ̀ɛ̀l   'having wealth'
      EO: -l·àβ   v.i.
      Ku: ògbó ɛ́lì̀là
            ɔ̀lì̀là   'rich person'
      WO: -lâβ

RICHES, WEALTH
      A: ɛ̀ɛ̀l·à
      EO: àmàlàlà
      Ku: ɛ̀lì̀là
      Od: ɛ̀ɛ̀l·à
      WO: àmàlàlà

RIDDLE   cf. PROVERB
      A: (ə̀)ðì̀-kə̀r; (ə̀)sì̀-   start: kə̀r   reply: kə̀də́
            (ə̀)ðì̀-doɣ
      EO: ìdúm
      Ku: ə̀sừdừm
      WO: ə̀dừ̆m   cf. Ab. 'story, tale'

RIDICULE (n)
      Od: ì̀-gílāām   fem. personal name

RIGHT
    A: èlíòm   direction and 'correct'
        δɪ̰γááγ èlìòm
    EO: òδìóm
        òδìkə̀n   'right, correct'
    Ku: òɓéɓì   'correct'
        òδíòm
        yel   íyĕl àmɪ̰ 'I'm right'
    Od: òδìóm
    WO: òδíòm
        ~ ə̀δìòm

RING (n)
    A: (ə̀)-gúl·ù; (ə̀)sí-
    EO: ə̀gúlù
        ~ ə̀ríŋì
    Ku: ə̀gúlù; r-
    Od: ə̀-gúl; (ə̀)rù-
    WO: ə̀ríŋì

RIPE
    A: -ɓaal   cf. WHITE v.
                    óògìrí βɔ̄ máɓáàl 'orange
                        is ripe'
        -wil/-bil   v. cf. BLACK
                    ɔ́ñṵ̀bɛ̀ βɔ́ máwîl 'banana
                        is ripe'
        (à)δɪ̰-ɓààl   'ripeness'
    EO: -ɓam   'ripe, red'
    Ku: ɔ̀ɓàm   'ripe, red' cf. RED
        ɔ̀kpɔ̀   'ripe, mature, old'
    Od: -ɓáár   'be ripe'
    WO: àɓâm

RIVER
    A: ɔ̀-βį̃́ñ; (à)rį́-
    EO: ɔ̀-βį̂y; ɛ̀-
    Ku: ɔ̀-βį̂y; àrɛ̀-
    Od: ɔ̀-βį̂ñ; (à)rį̀-
    WO: ɔ̀-βį̂y; ɛ̀-

ROAD
    A: ètén; (ə̀)r-   also 'path'
    EO: ɔ̀bɔ̀dɔ̀   'road'
          ègbétěn   'path'
    Ku: ò-gbétěn; r-
    Od: è-bòòm; (ə̀)rə̀-
    WO: ɛ̀só; ˄zà

ROAST (v)
    A: -pɔγį̣/-βɔγį̣
    EO: -βụgụ
    Od: -βɔɔγį̣/-pɔɔγį̣   v.t.
    WO: à-βụ́gụ̀
          ɛ̀-βụ́gànà   'roast, something roasted'

ROBE
    A: (à-)dónį̣; (à)sį́-   'ceremonial robe'
    EO: ə̀rùə̀   'robe, gown'
    Ku: àkápà
    Od: à-kápà
         ~ à-sù̀ɔ̀mà

ROCK (n)   see STONE

ROCK (v)
    EO: -gbegele   'canoe rocking'
    Ku: -dikə
    WO: ə̀-wégèlè   v.t. 'rock, as in canoe'

ROLL (v)

    A: -kilə (oo-)   v.i.
          -kilemi (oo-)   v.t.
    EO: -kikilə
    Ku: -kikilə   v.i.
          -kikilegi   v.t.
    Od: -kilimiən (oo-)   v.i.
          -kilimi (oo-)   v.t.
    WO: ə̀-kíkìlə̀n   v.i.
          ə̀-kíkìlè   v.t.   'roll, as barrel'
          ə̀-kpôl   'roll up, as mat on floor'

ROOF (n)

    A: àñṳ̀-ótù   also 'ceiling'
    EO: àñṳ̀ òtú
    Ku: àñótù; àñṳ̀ ə̀rútù
    Od: àñṳ̀ ótù
    WO: àñṳ̀ótù

ROOM (n)

    A: ò-sòβ; ì-
    EO: ègúlə̀
    Ku: ɛ́·kpótù; r-
    Od: ɛ̀-kpɛ́; (à)rà-
    WO: ígùlə̆; ^zə̀

ROOT (n)

    A: (à) δ̣ì-nị̀; (à)sị̀-
    EO: ɔ̀gú (órérén)
    Ku: ɔ̀kàkà òrérén; ị̀-
    Od: ɔ̀ɔ̀-kà; ị̀ị̀-
    WO: ógwòrèn; ɛ́gwìrèn

ROPE (n)   cf. PYTHON
 A: ò-ðìɣ; ì-
 EO: òðìðì
 Ku: ò-ðìðìɣ; ə̀sì- òbòðìðìɣ 'big rope'
 Od: ò-ðìɣ; ì-
   ɔ̀-ɣɔ̀rɔ́ɣį̀ɔ̀m 'rope for tying firewood'
 WO: ò-ðìðì; ì-
   ~ ìðìðízə̀

ROTTEN, BE (v)
 A: -ɓɔr   v.i. 'be rotten, rot'
        cf. WET

 EO: -βụβ
 WO: à-βụ́βụ̀

ROUND
 A: ə̀ə̀ɣìərə̀ə̀n
 EO: òkò

ROW, PULL BOAT
 Ku: -zɔɣụ

RUB (v)
 A: -guñən   'rub against rough surface'
   -ɓul   'rub, as oil on body'
 EO: -si   'rub, as oil on body'
 Ku: -siɣ   'rub, as oil on body'
 Od: -siɣə   'rub, as oil on body'
 WO: ə̀-síə̀   'rub oil on oneself'
   -si   'rub oil on other'

RUN (v)
 A: -kiil/-ɣiil
 EO: -ɣil
 Ku: -ɣil

```
Ku:  -γìl ɔ́ɗʊ̀à          'run away'  cf. GO AWAY
      óγîl méγíl          n.  'runner'
Od:  -γiil/-kiil
     òkìil mèγìil         n.  'runner'
WO:  ə̀-yílì
     é-yìlí               'act of running, fear'
     ò-yìlòmòyìl          'runner'
```

RUST (n)
```
EO:  ɛ̀kpàkpà
Ku:  ɔ̀sàrí
Od:  ɔ̀sàrì̥
WO:  ɔ̀zàr
```

S

SACRIFICE

A: ị̀yáár ə̀γù̀δùm — n. cf. LIFE; THING
ɛ̀kị̀à — n.
-βịγịrɔn/-pịγịrɔn — v. 'make, perform sacrifice'
ɔ̀-βị́γị́rɔ̄n ɛ̄kị̀à 'let us perform a sacrifice'

EO: ɛ̀kɔ́l — n.

Ku: ị̀kɔ̂l — n.
~ àlụ̀kpɛ̀ — n.
-kɔl ị̀kɔ̀l — v.

WO: ɛ̀kɔ̀lâ — n.

SAD

Ku: -kụnụ — kɔ́kụ̀nụ̂ 'don't be sad'
àmị́ nàkụ̀nụ́ 'I'm unhappy'
ị̀kụ́nụ̀ — 'mourning'

SAIL (n)

WO: àbálị̀

SALIVA

A: ị̀-γɔ̀r — pl.
EO: ɛ̀γɔ̀r
Ku: ị̀γɔ̀r
Od: ì-γɔ̀r
WO: ɛ̀wɔ̀r

SALT (n)

A: (ə̀)-bɔ̀β
EO: ə̀bɔ̀β
Ku: úɓôn
Od: ə̀-bɔ̀β
WO: ə̀bɔ̀β

SALUTE   see GREET

SAME, THE VERY (n)
    A: o-ginə   òɡínə̀ ɔ̀dị̀ 'he alone'
           i   ìɡínə̀ 'the same'

SAND [SOIL]
    A: ị̀-sàr
    EO: ɛ̀sàsár
    Ku: ị̀-sàsâr
    Od: ɔ̀ɔ́-sàár; ị̀ị́-
    WO: ɛ̀sị́sàr

SANDBANK
    A: èɓúmị̄sāār   'sand hill'
    EO: èɓùm
    Ku: èɓùm ị́sị̀sár
    Od: èkpúɔ́sāār
    WO: èɓúm

SANDFLY
    A: ìgbírígìdì
    EO: ɛ̀kàkâñ
           ~ ɛ̀kàtàkótò
    Ku: ị̀kɛ̀kâñ
    Od: ị̀-ɣàyàkáị̀
    WO: ɛ̀kàkâñ

SARDINE
    Ku: ɔ̀ɓànị̀rî

SATISFIED   see TIRED

SAW

A:	-γ i̧γ/-k i̧γ	v. cf. RESEMBLE
	-γ i̧γ i̧ɔγ/-k i̧γ i̧ɔγ	'to saw back and forth'
EO:	à fɨ́kɨ́fɨ̀kɨ̀	n.
Ku:	à fɨ̀kɨ́fɨ̀kɨ̀	n.
Od:	à-fɨ̀γ í fɨ̀γ ì	n.
WO:	à fɨ́kɨ́fɨ̀kɨ́	

SAWFISH

EO:	ɔ̀kɨ́
Ku:	ɔ̀kɨ́

SAY (v)   cf. TALK; TELL

A:	-ɓɛm	
EO:	-rų (ɔɔ-)	also 'tell'
	-rų áβár	'to say something'
Ku:	-fuγ	also 'talk'
Od:	-γol/-kol	'to say that...'
	-kpɛtɛ	ɔ̀dɨ́ àkpɛ́tɛ̀ mɛ̀káráàn 'what did he say'
WO:	ə̀-sî	
	sìé	'tell it, say it'
	ón·ɨ̧ ɔ̀sì	'speaker'

SCALES [FISH]

A:	ì-βólópòl én·ə̀
EO:	ɛ̀fɛ́rɛ́fɛ̀
Ku:	ò-pólòm; ì-
Od:	ìíβō
WO:	ìgbîn·ə̀

SCAR (n)

A:	ètèdù
EO:	ɛ̀ɓákà̀

Ku: ɛɓâr
WO: èpíèsì

SCARCE (v)
   A: -ku   ò-kû 'thrift society'

SCHOOL (n)
   Od: òtù ìtų̀ų̀γá   cf. LEARN

SCISSORS
   A: (ə̀)sínzèrè; (ə̀)sí-
        sínzèrè
   EO: ɔ̀kpáβàmà
   Ku: ìkpápų́
   WO: ɔ̀-kpàβàmâ

SCOOP UP (v)
   A: -γɔβ/-kɔβ   óγóβáníàn 'to get fire'
                    mį́ ràkɔ́β ópōsɔ̀ 'I'm
                      scooping mud'

SCORPION
   EO: èɗéñ
      ~ ɔ̀kpɔ̀lɔ́dų̀   cf. PENIS
   Od: ɔ̀ɔ̀-kpɔ́lɔ̀dų́; ìì-   cf. PENIS
   WO: àdàmókòtò; àdàmíkòtò

SCRATCH (v)
   A: -rųβɛnaan/-tųβɛnaan 'scratch oneself'
      -zara   'scratch, as chickens'
   EO: -rɔβį̀   v.i., v.t.
      -salasal   'scratch, as chickens'
   Ku: -rɔβį̀   'scratch oneself'
      -zara   'scratch, as chickens'

Od: -suun ~ -roɓị   'scratch, itch someone'
     -roɓịa   'scratch oneself'
     -zara   'scratch like fowl'
WO: à-róɓịàn   'scratch oneself'
     ə̀-fə́fə̀lə̀   'scratch, as fowl'

SEAMSTRESS   see TAILOR

SEE
A: -mịịn
     í-mị́ị̀n   'clairvoyance'
EO: -bị
Ku: -bịγ
     -bịγan   'see, visit (durational)'
Od: -mịịn
     -mịịnan   'see each other, meet'
WO: ên·ị̀ (m-)
     ɛ́n·ị̀èsì   'act of seeing'

SEED (n)
A: è-kpò; ì-
EO: è-kpò; ì-
Ku: è-kpò (òrérén); ì-
Od: è-kpò; ì-
WO: èkpórén

SEIZE
A: -ziton   'snatch'
     -ɓol   'grab'
     goroɓ   'seizing quickly' ideophone?
EO: -wɔr
Od: -ɓum   'seize, grab by force'
WO: ó-kpàtàgàn   'grab'

SELF [NON-REFLEXIVE, EMPHATIC]
    A: ɔn·ɔ̂ ~ ñí̵nɔ̀   'he himself'
          bû̵nɔ́   'they themselves'
    Od: àmì̵ nì̵vɔ̀   'I myself'
          àmì̵ bě   'I alone'
          ɔ̀dí ̵nì̵vɔ̀   'he himself'

SELFISHNESS
    Ku: ɔ̀-kû̵kû̵

SELL (v)
    A: əəl/-bool
          əələ/boolə   'sell to...'
          əələnaan/boolənaa   'sell (thing) for (person)'
    EO: -wol   also 'sweep'
          -wolomə   'sell to...'
    Ku: -wol
          -wolomə   'to sell to...'
          ɔ̀wɔ̀lmɛ́   n. 'seller'
    Od: -ɓool
    WO: ɘ̀-wôl
          -wolomə   'sell to...'
          ɔ̀-wɔ̀lɔ̀m àrárà   n. 'seller of things'

SEND
    A: -ɣi̵əm/-ki̵əm   mí̵ úɣíɔ́m ñɔ̀dí̵ ðí̵ná 'I sent
                                    him a letter'
                                tèlé àɣi̵ɔ́m 'walk on'
                                ɔ̀dí̵ ɛ́lénÍ̄ aɣiɔm 'he ate on'
          -rom/-tom   mí̵ ú-rɔ́m ñɔ̀dí̵ dôm 'I sent
                                    him on errand'
                                mí̵ kɘ̀-tɔ́m ñɔ̀dí̵ dôm 'I'll
                                    send him on errand'

SEPARATE [CHAFF FROM GRAIN]   see also STRAIN
   A: -wuñon

SET TRAP
   A: -kpámį́ ə́ɗíβìl
   Od: -kpaarį̀
   WO: à-kpátì̦

SEW
   A: -kɔl
   EO: -kpo
   Ku: -kpoγ
   Od: -kɔl
   WO: à-kɛ̂ñ

SHADE (n)
   A: ùbə̀
   EO: ə̀ɓòɓò
   Od: ùbə̀
   WO: àɓàɓùə̀

SHADOW (n)
   A: òòγò; (ə̀)ròòγò
   EO: ògògó
   Ku: òkòkôγ; r-
   Od: ò-kóōγ; ì- ~(ə̀)rə̀-

SHAKE (v)
   A: -βiiγə/-piiγə   v.i.
         -βiγemi/-piγemi   v.t.
   EO: -zìgen   v.t.
         -nunu   v.i. ɛ́ná nɛ́nùnú 'he's
                             shivering'
   Ku: -ñegi
   Od: -ziγe   v.t.

WO: ə́-nú·nù   v.i. 'shake, shiver'
                      mí nə̀núúnù 'I'm shaking'
                        (fear or nervousness)

     ə́-zígè   v.t.

SHAKE HEAD (v)

A: -meeraam ɛ́mṳ̄   'shake head in agreement
                        (up and down)'

     -ɓoɣomomi ɛ́mṳ̄   'shake head in disapproval
                        (side to side)'

SHALLOW

EO: è-kpɔ̀kpɔ̀rɔ̀β   'shallowness'

Ku: -kpololo   v. 'be shallow' ɔ̀là̀ββɔ́
                        ə́kpɔ̀lɔ́lɔ̀ 'lake is shallow'

     é-kpɔ́lɔ̄lɔ̄   n. 'shallow, shallowness'

SHAME (n)

A: ùmùɣ ə̀lɔ́ɔ̀r   ùmùɣ ə̀lɔ́ɔ̀r rúsìβ íímì
                        'I'm ashamed'

     ùmùɣòlɔ́ɔ̀r   ùmùɣòlɔ́ɔ̀r rúsìβ íímì
                        'I'm ashamed'

EO: àlɛ̀ɣɛ̀l

Ku: àrị̀-ɣɛ̀l   àrị̀ɣɛ̀l nèδìɣí àmị̀
                        'I'm ashamed'

Od: (à)rɛ̀-ɣɛ̀r   àrɛ̀ɣɛ̀r nésìβ àmị̀
                        'I'm ashamed'

                      ùɣíílɣà rɛ̀ɣɛ̀r 'don't be
                        ashamed' cf. RUN

WO: íwɔ̀ɓù   cf. BODY; DIE

SHARK

A: ɔ̀fṳ́rṳ́má

     òkí   cf. SAWFISH

EO: ɔ̀fṳ́rṳ́má

Ku: ɔ̀-fṳ̀rṳ̀má

Od: áfṳ́rṳ́má

WO: ɔ̀fṳ́rṳ́má

SHARP, HOT   cf. BITE; WHET, SHARPEN
    A: -lom   'sharp, hot-tasting, like
                                        pepper'

          ə̀ðílòm   'hot, like pepper'

          -Toβ   v. 'sharp'

          (ə̀)ðí-ròβ   n. 'sharpness'

    EO: -γam   'sharp, painful, like pepper'

          ò-sù   'hot, as pepper'

          -sù   v.i. 'be, become sharp, hot'

          o-sùsùén; ì-   modif. 'sharp'

          ə̀lù-sù   n. 'sharpness, hotness'

          ə̀lù-sǔ   n. 'sharpness' also 'heat'

    Ku: ògâm   'hot, as pepper'

          -siβ   v. 'be sharp' ògyὲ β'ə́sĭβ
                                        'knife was sharp'

          ósísíβə̀n   n. òsìsìβə̀n ógyὲ 'sharp
                                        knife'

          ə̀lìsíβ   n. 'sharpness'

    Od: -roβ/-toβ   'sharp'

          -gam   'be hot, like pepper'
                                        also 'painful'

    WO: àgâm   'hot, as pepper'

          ò-sùsú; ì-   'sharp'

          -su   v.i. 'be, become sharp'

          ə̀-sû   n. 'sharpness'

SHAVE (v)
    A: -γul/-kul

    EO: -ti   'shave beard'

          -kpoton   'shave head'

    Ku: -gulə   'shave beard'

          -kpoton   'shave head'

          -kpur   'trim hair'

    Od: -γul   'shave other's beard'

          -bul   'shave other's head'

Od: -ɣulə   'shave own beard'
        -bulə   'shave own head'
WO: ô·kpò (m-)   'shave beard or head'

SHEEP
    A: ìyól ɔ́gà   cf. GOAT
    EO: àmɛrìgbɔ̀
    Ku: ɔnánǎ; r-
    Od: ɛ́ɛ́-nā; (à)ràá-
    WO: ɔ̀-náàná; ɛ̀-

SHELL (n)
    A: ò-kpòr; (ə̀)ró-kpór   'shell of animal, not marine'
    Ku: ò-βóβò ɛ́ɣɔ̀ɪ̀   'snail shell'

SHINE (v)
    A: -mụ   v.i.
    EO: -san   v.i.
    Ku: -mụ   'shine as sun'
    Od: -mụ   v.i.
         -mụa   v.t. 'shine, make shiny'
    WO: à-sánɪ̀   v.i.

SHIRT
    A: àsụ̀ma ~àsụ̀ɔ̀mà   cf. ROBE
    EO: àsótɪ̀   Engl.
    Ku: àkápà
    Od: à-kápà
    WO: ə̀rùə̀

SHOE (n)
    A: ò-kóró; (ə̀)ró-
    EO: àgbákà
    Ku: àgbàkà; r-
    Od: ə̀-kóró; (ə̀)rə̀-
    WO: àgbàká; 'zà

SHOOT (v)
   A: -taβ/-raβ
   EO: -teñ
   Ku: -raβ
   Od: -raβ/-taβ
          ὲ-ráβá   'act of shooting'
   WO: ə̀-têñ

SHORT
   A: -kperə
   EO: ò-kpèrèkpèr; ì-
          -kper   v. 'be, become short'
          ὲ-kpúkὲ   'short' fem. name
          ò-δùgúlú   'short and fat' masc. name
          -kperemen   v.t. 'shorten'
          ə̀lì-kpèr   n. 'shortness'
   Ku: òkpèrèkpěr   'be short' òkpèrèkpěr ɔ́nì̜
                                    'short man'
          -kper   'be short' ɔ̀nì̜βɔ́ ə́kpěr
                                    'man is short'
          -kperemeni   v.t. 'shorten'
          ə̀lùkpér   n. 'shortness'
   Od: -kper
          -kperemi   v.t. 'shorten'
          ə̀lì-kpêr   n. 'shortness'
   WO: òkpèkpér; ì-   modif.
          -kper   v.i.
          -kperemən   v.t. 'shorten'
          í-kpêr   n. 'shortness'

SHOULDER (n)
   A: ɔ̀-βá; (à)rá-
   EO: òβágwɔ̀   cf. HAND
   Ku: ɔ̀βá; r-
   Od: ɔ̀-βá; àrù̜-

WO: èmú ɔ́βáàgwɔ̀;
     [ɔ́βàgwɔ̀]

     ìmú ɛ́βáàgwɔ̀
     [ɛ́βàgwɔ̀]

SHOUT

A: -l·ɔ   v. kál·ɔ̀mṹn 'don't shout
                                 again (anymore)'

     ị̀-l·ɔ̀γị̀   'shouting'
     (à)δị̀-ɔ̀l·ɔ̂   n.

EO: -muluγu   v.

Ku: -muluγu   v.

     -muluγuom   v. 'to shout at person to
                                 make him ashamed'

Od: -muluγu   v.
     ì-mùlùγù   n.

WO: ókòkìə̀n(m-)   v.
     ìkòkìə̀n   n.

SHOW (v)

A: -δenaan

EO: -lorom

Ku: -leriom

Od: -δeeriom

WO: ôl·ɔ̀mə̂ (m-)

SHRIMP

Od: ɛ̂-zɔ̀l; ị̀-

SHRINE (n)

Ku: òtù érù

WO: ɔ̂-sẫ   'ancestral shrine, family
                        juju' masc. name

SIBLING

A: ùmòr; əb-

EO: ìmòr

Ku: ùmòr; ər-   ùmə̀rán·ị̀ 'sister'

Od: ùmòr; èbùrùmòr

WO: ìmòr   àδị̀z' ímòr 'sister'

SICK

A: -rụrụɣịan/-tụrụɣịan 'be sick'
       (ɔɔ-)

     éé-βìnè̩; (è̩)ríí-   'sickness'

EO: -w̃ɛr   'be sick'

     àsụ̀w̃è̩r   'sickness'

Ku: -w̃ɛr   v. 'be sick'

     àsụ̀w̃è̩r   'sickness'

Od: -w̃ɛ   'be sick'

     ɛ̀-zɛ́ɣ; (à)rà-   'sickness'

WO: à-w̃ê̩r   'be sick'

     àw̃è̩r   'sickness'

SIDE, EDGE

A: ɔ̀gbàl   'side' ógbàl óβîñβɔ̄ 'near
                                   the river'

                                á-mị́ná ógbàl ɔ̀dị̀ 'she lay
                                   down by her side'

                                mị́ ụ́-mụ̀nɛ́ñ ógbàl àmị̀ 'I put
                                   her down by my side'

EO: àkákà

Ku: àká

     δàká   'by the side of...'

     àk-óβị̂y   àkụ́bɔ̀ 'other side of river
                                   (inhabited)'

                                ɛ̀δɛ́ị̀ ɛ̀mà 'other side of
                                   river (uninhabited)'

Od: ɔ̀tụ̀   'side'

     ɔ̀gbàgị̀   'side, boundary, edge'

     àlàká   'side' as in 'go to the side'

                                ɛ̀δɛ́ñóm óβị̂ñ 'other side of
                                   river' cf. CROSS

WO: è̩kpòkpòm

SILK COTTON TREE
    Ku: òbòñókàɪ̤́
    Od: ɔ̀ɓààl òréñ
          òbòkáñ

SILK SCARF
    A: (à)sɪ̤́-lókō;
          (à)-lókō   cf. Engl. 'silk'

SING
    A: -mɔɔr
    EO: -mɔr
    Ku: -mɔr àsôr   'sing a song'
    Od: -mɔɔr
    WO: ôrṳ̀ (m-)

SINGE
    A: -tuβ/-ruβ

SINGER
    Od: òmòòr sòòr; ì̤-
    WO: ɔ̀-rṳ̀ɔ̀←màsṳ̀ɔ̀r

SINGLET
    A: ɔ̀fɔ̀rókɔ̀   cf. Engl. 'frock'
    EO: ɔ̀fɔ̀rɔkɔ̀ ~ ɛ̀fɔ̀rɔkɔ̀
    Ku: àf(ɔ̀)rókɔ̀
    Od: à-fɔ̀rókɔ̀
    WO: ófɔ̀rókɔ̀

SIT   cf. REMAIN
    A: -tɔl/-rɔl   mɪ̤́ á-tōl ūdè 'I'm sitting
                              down'
    EO: -tara
    Ku: -rɪ̤la

Ku: -rɔ(dèládì̞)   'sit down'
                         tɔ̀ déládì̞ 'sit down!'
                         àmì̞-rɔ̀dèládì̞ 'I sat down'

Od: -rɔl/-tɔl   also 'be in place, remain'

WO: à-tɔ́tɔ̀
        àpì̞tɔ̀β   'sitting down'

SKIN (n)

A: ò-zû(~jû); (è̞)rú-

EO: òzú-é̞lúzù

Ku: òβóβò ózù   'back of body'

Od: ò-zú; ì̞- ~ è̞rù-

WO: ózù òβù

SKIN, FLAY (v)

A: -kpan

EO: -kpor[ózù]

SKINK

EO: èté

WO: ègbélé

SKULL

A: ɔ̀ɔ́-kp(ɔ̀)ɛ́mū

EO: òkpókpó émú

Ku: òkpɔ̀kp'ɛmụ́

Od: òkpòkpɛ̀mú   cf. HEAD

SKY

A: àñụ̀(ákɛ̀)   also 'heaven'

EO: àñụ̀ ~ ɛnàñ

Ku: ụ̀tɛ́nàì̞

Od: àñụ̀; àrụ̀ñụ̀ ótù   also 'roof'

WO: àñụ̀   cf. MONTH

SLAP   cf. HIT

SLASH (v)
    EO: -sị̀
    Ku: -sị̀   'slash grass, bush'
    Od: -soβ   cf. CLEAR FARM
    WO: ə̀-sôβ

SLAVE
    A: ɛ̀-bɛ̀nɛ̀; (à)rɛ̀-
    EO: ò-gèní; ì-
    Ku: ɛ̀-bànà; àrụ̀- ~(a)rɛ̀-
    Od: ɛ̀-bànà; (à)rụ̀-
    WO: ògôn; ì- (A)

SLEEP (n)
    A: (à)rà-là
    EO: àdàlà
    Ku: àdị̀là
    Od: àràlà
    WO: àdàlà   àdàlá nə̀sú ə̀m 'I'm sleepy'

SLEEP (v)
    A: -naanị
          ò-mèèl rálà   'fall asleep'
    EO: -koδu
    Ku: -koδu
    Od: -koδi
    WO: ə̀-dû
         ~ ə̀sér ə̀dù
         ó-dúómàdàlà   'sleeper'

SLICE (v)
    A: -kị̀rị̀β   'cut into small pieces'

EO: -soβ   'cut' cf. CUT

-pal   'sharpen, cut sharpened end'

Ku: -ba

Od: -vɛlɛ   also 'split'

WO: ɛ̂kɪ̀rɪ̀(m-)

SMALL

A: -γom/-kom

ɛ̀-<u>bám</u>   n.

(ə̀)δí-γòm   'smallness'

EO: ɔ̀-gbàrà; ɛ̀-   n. ɔ̀gbàr ón·ɪ̀ 'small man'

                                ɛ̀gbàr ɛ̃́wúnòm 'small men'

-kɪ̀r   v. ə̃̀wúnóm mə̄ ɛ̀kɪ̀rɪ̀kɪ̀r
                            'the men are small'

                                ə̃̀wúnóm mə̄ wàkɪ́r 'the men
                                are small (few)'

àlɪ̀-kɪ̀r   n. 'smallness'

Ku: -kɪ̀r   v. òtùβɔ́ ákɪ̆r 'house was
                          small'

ɔ̀gbàrá   n. òtùβɔ́ ɔ̀gbàrá 'house
                          is small'

                              ɔ̀gbà ótù 'small house'

Od: -kio   òdí né̂ə̀kìó 'he's small'

                              ɔ̀bàm ɛ́nâm 'small animal'

                              òdí ɔ̀bám 'he's small'

ɛ̀γɛ̀ríkɪ̄r   'minute'

-kiemi   'make small'

ə̂lì-kìó   'smallness'

ɔ̀-bám   'small one' fem. name

WO: àdṳ́   modif. àdṳ́ ɛ́nṳ̀rṳ̀ 'small
                            bird'

(ɛ́)-kɪ̀rɪ̀   'be, become small'

ɛ́kɪ̀rɪ̀ (m-)   v. 'become small'

àδɪ́-kɪ̀rɪ́   n. 'smallness'

SMALLPOX
    EO: əfìlízə̀   'influenza'
    Od: ɛzɛ́gí ìbám ám̂ɲ̂ñ   euphemism
    WO: ítílà   cf. Hitler

SMELL
    A: -βurə (oo-)   v.i.
         -δu   v.
    EO: -βur   v.i.
         -βurə   v.t.
    Ku: èδù   n.
         -βur   v.i.
         -duə/-δuə   v.t.
    Od: èδú   n.
         -βur/-pur   v.i.
         -βurə/-purə   v.t., v.i.
    WO: ə̀-βúrù   v.i.
         ə̀-dúə̀   v.t.

SMOKE (n)
    A: à-mʉ̀ɣì̱
    EO: ɔ̀mʉ́gʉ̀
    Ku: àmʉ̀gì̱
    Od: à-mʉ̀gì̱; (à)sʉ̀-
    WO: àmʉ̀ŋgʉ̀

SMOOTH-SKINNED (v)
    A: -mʉnamʉna (ójʉ̀)   'to be smooth-skinned'

SNAIL
    A: ɛ̀-ɣɔ̀ñ; ì̱-
    EO: ɛ̀ɣɔ̀ì̱   'large, edible snail'
         ɛ̀kpárì̱ɔ̀m   'watersnail'
    Ku: ɛ̀-ɣɔ̀ì̱; ì̱-

Ku:	ɛ̀kpàrɪ́ɔ̀m	'watersnail'
Od:	ɛ̀ɣɔ̀ñ	'large, edible snail'
	ɛ̀bɔ̀ñ	'watersnail'
WO:	ɛ̀ɣɔ̀ɪ̰	
	ɛ̀bɪ̰ógɔ̀	'yellow snail'

SNAKE

A:	ɛ̀-kàràβ ɪ́yààr; (à)rà-	'bad thing'
EO:	ɔ̀-kàràβ àβár; ɛ̀-	
	ɔ̀ɗúm	'python'
	ɔ̀ɓíl	'black cobra'
	ɪ̰dɪ̰ákɔ̀	'non-poisonous watersnake'
	ɔ̀gbàràgbàrà	'large, green, rough- skinned, poisonous snake'
Ku:	ɔ̀-kàràβàbár; àsɪ̰kàràβɪ̰yár	
Od:	ɔ̀ɔ̀-ɗìɣ; lì-	
	~ ààr; àrɪ̰rɪ̰ár	'thing'
WO:	ɔ̀-kàràβàβár; ɛ̀kàràβàrárà	

SNEEZE (v)

A:	-jɪ̰a ~ -zɪ̰a	
EO:	-kpisə	
Ku:	-kpisən	
Od:	-fɪ̰ɪ̰ma	'blowing out nose'
	-za	reflex
WO:	íkpìsə̀ (m-)	
	í-kpìsə̆n	'repeated sneezing'

SNORE (v)

A:	-ɣɔn/-kɔn	
	ɔ̀ɣɔ́nɔ́ɣɔ̀n	n. 'snoring'
Ku:	-ɣɔn	
Od:	-ɣɔn/-kɔn	

SNUFF   see TOBACCO

SO   see THUS

SO THAT   see IN ORDER THAT

SOAP (n)
    A: (à)sábà
    EO: ɔ̀sɔ̀
    Ku: ósɔ̀
    Od: ɛ̀-sɔ́
    WO: ɔ̀sɔ̀

SOCIETY   see CLUB

SOFT   cf. WEAK; CHEAP
    A: -ɗuɣ
          -ɗuɣe   v. 'soften'
          (ə̀)ɗí-dùɣ   n. 'softness'
          ívùlə̀vùlə̀   'soft things'
    EO: -gʊr   v. 'weak, soft'
          ɔ̀ɓùrùɓùr   modif. 'soft, as meat, flesh'
          -gʊrɛmɛn   v.t. 'weaken, soften'
    Ku: ɔ̀dùdùɣə̀n
    Od: -duɣ
          -duɣe(mi)   v.t. 'soften'
          ə̀lì-dûɣ   n. 'softness'
    WO: ɔ̀-gùgúr; ɛ̀-   modif. 'soft, weak'
          -gʊr   v.i.
          -gʊrɔman   v.t. 'soften'
          ɛ̀-gʊ̀r   n. 'softness, weakness'

SOIL (n)   cf. MUD
    EO: ɔ̀bɪ̀bɪ̀

Ku: ìdóɣɔ̀l
WO: ɛ̀-tɔ́kɔ́lɔ́   'mud'

SOLE OF FOOT
A: ɛ̀dà ówòl
EO: ɛ̀ɓá-wèl
Ku: ɛ̀ɓáɓà ǵwêl
WO: ɔ̀dɛ́líkè
     ɛ̀zɛ́rɛ́mɛ̀lìkè   'top of foot'

SOME
A: òpól
EO: ə̀wídì ~ ìdí
Ku: ídì
Od: ɛ̀dɛ̌
WO: ə̀wídì

SON   see CHILD

SONG
Od: (à)sɔ̀ɔ̀r
WO: à-sʊ̀ɔ̀r

SOON
A: ónə́mêm   'little time, soon'

SORE (n)
A: ɛ̀-kɔ̀; (à)rɔ̀-   'wound'
     ~ è-sì   cf. PLACE
     ~ ɛ̀-ɓár; (à)rá-
EO: èsì
Ku: ɛ̀kɛ́tɛ́;r-
Od: è-sì; (ə̀)rì-
WO: èsì; ˋzə̀   cf. PLACE

SOUND
    A:?   ììtíə̀   'sound of drum'
    EO: -si   v.
    Ku: -si   v.i. 'sound, as drum'
                             also 'leak'
    Od: -ɓɛm   v.i. 'sound, as drum'
    WO: ə̀-sî   v. 'sound, as drum'

SOUP
    A: (ə̀)-móóbò̀β; (ə̀)sí-
    EO: àmụ̀bóβ
    Ku: ə̀múbò̀β
    Od: ə̀-mòbôβ; (ə̀)sù-
    WO: ófị̀ló́   Nembe

SOUR
    A: -sịkịrị̀   v.
    EO: è-gbə̀gbə̀mə̀   'sourness'
    Ku: égbə̄gbə̄m

SOUTH
    EO: àgò̀támàn   'side river flows down to'

SOW (v)   see PLANT (v)

SPARROW, SWALLOW
    A: (à)-mụ̀gɛ́ɛ́m; (à)sị̀-
          (àmị̀) (βó̀ò̀βò̀n)

SPEAK
    A: -ɓa   'speak Abuan'
          -ɣam/-kam   'speak non-Abuan'
    EO: -kpa   'speak language'
          -ɣoroɣo   'talk, speak'

```
    Ku:  -fuɣ
    Od:  -δεγε                  'speak, talk, converse'
         -kpɛtɛ                 'speak Odual'
         -kpa                   'speak other languages'
         ɔ̀kpɛ̀tɛ̀máár            n.  'speaker'
    WO:  à-kpâ
         ~ ə̀-sî                cf. SOUND
```

SPEAR (n)
```
    A:   ɔ̀-sɔ̀β; (à)rɔ̀-
    EO:  àβɛ̀gɛ̀rɛ̀
         ɔ̀sɔ̀β                  'fish spear'
         ~àgàñ                  'fish spear'
    Ku:  ɔ̀sɔ̀β; r-
    Od:  ɔ̀-sɔ̀β; ị̀-
    WO:  ɔ̀-sɔ̀β; ɛ̀-
```

SPECIES   see GROUP

SPIDER
```
    A:   ɔ̀ɔ̀-tákụ̀; (à)ràà-
    EO:  èkùlétò
    Ku:  ə̀bùrùkókò
    Od:  ò-bònɔ́ɔ̄kɔ̄; ì-
    WO:  ɔ̀tókɔ̀lôtù; ìtókɔ̀lîtù
```

SPIRIT   see GHOST

SPIT (v)
```
    A:   -sị̀n
         -sị̀nɔɣɔm íɣɔr         'to spit on-- many times'
```

SPLIT (v)
    A: aa̤i/-baa̤i   'saw plank, split yam'
          -pol   'split wood'
    EO: -ba
          -pol   'split firewood'
    Ku: -gu̯lɛ
          -pol   'split firewood'
    Od: -vɛlɛ   also 'slice'
          -pol   'split wood'
    WO: ə̀-pû

SPOON (n)   cf. LADLE
    A: ɔ̀-kàŋi̤; i̤-
    EO: ɛ̀gyàsi̤
    Ku: i̤gàzi̤   'small spoon'
    Od: i̤-gàsi̤
    WO: ɛ̀gyási̤

SPOTTED
    A: ɛ́-kpɛ́mɛ́nà

SPREAD (v)
    A: -leñ

SQUEEZE (v)
    A: -miim
    EO: -mimiom
    Ku: -mumoγ
    Od: -miiβ
    WO: îmi̤ (m-)

SQUIRREL
    A: é-γèrékè; (ə̀)ré-

    EO: èkórókò   'smallest squirrel'
         èwúrúrū   'medium squirrel'
         èkókò   'largest squirrel'
    Ku: é-kērēkè; èsí-
    Od: è-γérèkè; (è)rè-
    WO: ɛ́kòròkò; ˋzà

STAB (v)   cf. PIN
    EO: -gim
    Ku: -gim
    Od: -gim
    WO: à-gúsì

STALK (v)
    A: -sɔβɔγụ
    EO: -lịa
    Od: -sɔβ òγụ̀m
    WO: êl·ὲ à-gị̀ (m-)   'go stealthily'

STAND (v)
    A: -mɛɛra
    EO: -mara
    Ku: -mara
    Od: -mara
         ὲ-márá   'act of standing'
    WO: ɛ́ὲrà (m-)

STAND UP (v)
    EO: -βètènê
    Ku: -βetinə   àmị́ nὲβètínὲ 'I'm
                                  standing up'
    Od: -βetunu
    WO: à-δúɛ́ɛ́rà

STAR (n)

    A: ɛ́ɛ́-nààn; (à)ráá-

    EO: ɛ̀n·ànân

    Ku: ɛ̀-nànáḭ ~ ɛ̀nḭnáḭ; ḭ-

    Od: ɛ̀-nân; (à)rḭ-

    WO: ɛ̀nànááḭ

STARCH [POUNDED]

    EO: ìgúmə̀nə̀ éδìə̀

    WO: òsú ~ òsṹ

START   see BEGIN

STAY   see DWELL; REMAIN

STEAL (v)

    A: -mi

           ì-mí   n. 'stealing'

           lɛ̀ɛ̀βlɛ̀ɛ̀β   'stealthily' ə́-δíɣí lɛ̀ɛ̀β
                                     'she did stealthily'

    EO: -ɓi

    Ku: -ɓiɣ

           ə̀ɓìɣ   n. 'stealing, theft'

    Od: -miiɣ

           ə̀vììɣ   n. 'stealing, theft'

    WO: íyì (m-)

           íyì ə̀ɓì

           í-yə̀ɓì   n. 'stealing, theft'

STERN [OF BOAT, CANOE]

    A: ètí òɣùùɣ

    EO: ètì òwú

    Ku: ètí óɣùɣ

    Od: è-tĭ

    WO: èδúmòwù

STICK (n)
    A: see TREE
    Ku: é-kùδí(órérén); í-
    WO: ò-sìsì   'walking stick' fem. name

STICK... ON (v)
    Ku: -gbi

STING
    A: (à)δí-ràr   n.
        -rar/-tar   v. míràr íímì 'something
                                      has stung me; I've
                                    been stung'

STIR (v)
    A: -kirion
    EO: -tibren   'stir, turn'
        -gbogoro   'stir in pot'
    Ku: -gbu   'stir, turn'
    Od: -γir/-kir
        -γireni/-kireni   'turn over'
    WO: ə̀-pígìrì   'stir, as soup in pot'
        ò-pìgìròmê̂   'stirrer, thing to stir with'

STOMACH
    A: ɔ̀kúrúbākà
    EO: òbògùnùgùn
    Od: ʊ̀bɔ̀ɔ̀là; íbíílà
    WO: òbògùgùnù

STONE (n)
    A: (ə̀)δì-γììγ; (ə̀)sì-   also 'rock'
    EO: ìkpútú
    Ku: ɔ̀gbíɔmá; r-   'stone for grinding'
    Od: ɔ̀-βàràkpǎr; ì-
    WO: ìkpútú; ʼzə̀

STOP (v)
    Ku: -wɛlɛ   ịn'áwèlɛ́ mògìr 'he stopped
                                       working'

STOPPER [BOTTLE]
    A: è-ɓùlùɣìòm   n.
         -ɓuluɣi   v.
    Od: òɓùlùɣìòm   n.
    WO: íɓùlùgòm (m-)   v.

STORM (n)
    A: òò-loɣ; (ə̀)ròò-
    EO: èbìrì
         òkùkù   'wind'
    Ku: ògìm
    Od: ògìm
    WO: èbìrì

STORY
    EO: ègbèrìbə̀
    Ku: àsụ̀gbàgbà
    WO: ègbèrìbə̀

STRAIGHT
    A: òsél   'straightness'
    EO: -selə
    Ku: òsèl
    Od: -sel   'be straight'
    WO: ə̀sélə̀

STRAIN, MAKE EFFORT (v)
    A: -kparaɣa   'strain oneself'
    EO: -kparamɛn   'make effort'
    Od: -kparam   'strain, make effort, try'
    WO: à-kpáràmàn òɓù

STRAIN, SEPARATE (v)
    A: -sal   'strain, as liquids'
    EO: -kịa   'separate'
    Ku: -mumoγ   'squeeze through cloth'
         -kịa   'strain through weight, without effort'
    Od: -ziγi
    WO: à-kị́à   'strain, separate, filter'

STRENGTH   cf. HARD
    EO: àlị̀-kpár   also 'hardness'
         ὲkpàr
    Ku: ə̀lị̀-môn
         -monomeni
           ~ -kparamɛnị   'strengthen'
    Od: ὲ-kpàr   masc. name

STRETCH (v)
    A: -gbụrịon   v.t. 'stretch a coiled thing'
    EO: -selemen   v.t.
    Ku: -mịnịnị   v.i. 'stretch after sleep'
    WO: àñáà   v.t.

STRONG   see also HARD
    Ku: -mon   òmòmə̀nə̀n ónị 'strong man'
                   ɔ̀nị̀βɔ́ ə́mǒn 'man was strong'

STUDIES (n)
    A: í-tōōγə̄   no sing. cf. FACE; FORWARD
                   ìtóóγə́ á·mị rὲkị́nị rísíγ 'my studies are progressing'
                   ìtóóγə́ ánnà ὲγị̂nị rìsíγ 'may your studies progress'

STUDY   see LEARN

STUMP (n)
   Ku: èsìn óγ̂ɔlβɔ́   'stump of raffia palm'

SUBMERGE (v.t.)
   A: -δiñe   'submerge thing under water'
       -δiñeγi   'submerge forcibly'
       -δiñeγi òγìlγ   'to drown someone'

SUCK (v)
   A: -pi̧β
   EO: -pi̧pi̧ɔβ
   Ku: -pi̧pi̧ɔβ   'suck bones'
       -mam   'suckle, suck'
   Od: -pi̧i̧β (ɔɔ-)   'suck bones'
       -maam   'suck breast'
       -mɔɔβ   'suck bottle'
   WO: ɔ̂fi̧fi̧ɔ̂β(m-) (A)   'suck bone'
       ɔ̂pi̧pi̧ɔ̂β (O)   'suck bone'
       -mɛmi̧   'suck liquid, breast'

SUFFER (v)
   A: -mi̧i̧nɔm
       -mi̧i̧nɛ   'make suffer'
   Ku: -yɛ   'suffer from loneliness'

SUFFERING
   A: èmèrèméèr
   EO: ìgbèr ~ ɛ̀γɛ́γà
   Ku: àli̧gàm ə̀rúzù   also 'trouble'
       ɛ̀γɛ́γà ~ ɛ̀γɛ́γɛ̀
   Od: ɔ̀-mi̧i̧nɔ̀m
   WO: òδ îgbèr

SUFFICIENT, BE (v)
    A: -kasịan   cf. LOCK
                                     mɛ́-kásị̀àn 'it's sufficient'
          -geni   ɔ̀géní 'it's not sufficient'

SUFFOCATE
    A: -ɣụrụɣi/-kụrụɣị   v.t.
          -ɣụrụɣan/-kụrụɣan   v.i.
    Ku: -βụr   v.t. 'strangle'
          -βer   v.i. 'suffocate'

SUGARCANE
    A: ụ́gwɔ̀
    EO: ə̀lùkpó
    Ku: ókpŏɣ
    Od: ụ̀kpɔ̂ɣ
    WO: ókpɔ̀

SUIT (v)   see FIT

SUN
    A: ógɔ̀gɔ̀ ~ ɔ̀mụ̀
    EO: ə̀ɣózɔ̀n
    Ku: ɔ̀gógó
    Od: ɛnàm ə̀δíɔ̀
    WO: ógɔ̀gó

SURPASS (v)
    A: -pu
    EO: -pu
    Ku: -pu
    Od: -pu
          -puom
    WO: ə̀-pû

SWALLOW (v)

    A: -mį̀n

           -mį̀nɔm   'swallow up, cover
                                                  completely (of liquids)'

           -mį̀nɔɣɔm   'swallow up completely'

    EO: -mį̀n

    Ku: -mį̀n

    Od: -mį̀n

    WO: -mį̀nį̀

           ɔ̀-mį̀nį̀   'act of swallowing'

SWAMP (n)

    A: ìɣɔ̀ɔ̀l

    EO: àpį̀pį̀

           ɔ̀làβ

           àbàrà   'extensive; cultivated area
                                                    next to river, covered
                                                    during flood'

    Ku: ə̀ɓɔ̀ù

    Od: ìɣɔ̀ɔ̀l; ì-   'land alternating with
                                                    wet spots'

           àbàrà; (à)rà-   'land adjacent to river'

    WO: ɔ̀l·àβ (A)

           apį̀pį̀ (O)

SWEAR (v)

    A: -ɣuniən

    EO: -worogi

    Ku: -ɣaδįan

    Od: -ɣìrį́zɔ̀

    WO: ə̀-gúrù

SWEAT (n)

    A: èlómə̀n

    EO: ènóβórə̀

Ku: ònùmôr
Od: ìnùmán
WO: ínòβòrə̆

SWEEP (v)
A: -ɓeer
EO: -wol
Ku: -gber
Od: -ɓeer
WO: ôwòl(m-)

SWEET
A: -dụ̯ɣ   v. also 'good tasting'
                 rὲ-dụ́ɣ ígēñ 'it tastes good'
                 ị́-dụ̂ɣ 'it isn't good tasting'

EO: -mɛlmɛl
    -roβ   'be sweet, pleasant'
                 ə̀róβ ə́m mə̀lùzú 'I enjoyed
                    myself'
    ὲ̀-mɛ̀lmὲl   'sweetness'
Ku: -mɛmɛm   v. àlso 'pleasant'
                 ìmὲmὲmɛ́mὲn éδìèn 'good food'
    -mɛmɛmɛnị   v.t. 'sweeten'
    έmέmɛ̂m   n. 'sweetness, pleasant-
                    ness (food)'
Od: -mɛl   v. 'sweet, good tasting'
                 ὲnàm òβó àmɛ̆l 'the meat
                    was sweet'
                 ɔ̀mὲlàn ὲnâm 'sweet meat'
WO: -dụ   v. òl·ógékpó ə̄mìnì nàdụ̂
                 'I'm happy, my mind
                  is sweet'

SWELL (v)
A: -bụ̯ɣɛ   v.i.
EO: -fu   v.i.
    -fuemen   'make swell'

Ku: -wuβ
Od: -βuuɣ/-puuɣ
WO: ə̀-fúgù   v.i.
       ə̀-fúgòmə̀n   v.t.

SWIM (v)

A: -mʉɣɨ
EO: -mɔβɨ
Ku: -mʉɣɨ
Od: -mʉɣɨ
WO: ɔ́·ɨ̀ (m-)
       ɔ̀-yɛ̀mɔ́ɔ́ɨ̀   'swimmer'

SWORD

A: èlóòl ɛ̀ɣàm   cf. MATCHET
       ɔ́-pɨ̀à   'curved sword'
EO: àlápógídí
Ku: àɓɛ̀gɛ̀rɛ̀
       ~ àlápógídí
Od: ʉ̀-bà-mʉ̀gɛ̀m;
          ɨ̀-bà-sʉ̀-mʉ̀gɛ̀m   cf. KNIFE
WO: àɓɛ́gɛ̀rɛ́

T

TABLE (n)
    A: ìdáàbìlì
    EO: àdɛ́fì
        ~ àgbàd-óδè   'bed for eating'
    Ku: àdɛ́fì
    Od: ì-zébèlè
    WO: àgbádôδé
        àdɛ́fì   Nembe

TAIL
    A: ɛ̀-sɔ̀β; (à)rɔ̀-
    EO: ɛ̀pɛ̀pɛ̀
    Ku: ó-dʉ̀; àrʉ́-
    Od: ɔ̀-dʉ́; ì-
    WO: ìkólòm; ˇzə̀

TAILOR (n)
    Ku: ò-kpòɣmə́
    Od: ɔ̀kɔ̀l mɨ́kɔ̄l   also 'seamstress'

TAKE
    A: -sɨ̲ɣɛ   cf. ACCEPT
        -sɨ̲ɣɨ̲ɔɣ   'take several things'
    EO: -βin
    Ku: -βin   'take, obtain'
        βìné ~ pìné   'take!'
        -wɔr   'take by force'
    Od: -sɛɣɛ
        -βin/-pin   'receive, marry'
        -ɓum   'take by force'
    WO: ə̀-βî

TAKE AWAY
    A: -aar/-bɔr   'take from, get from'
                                 mí áár ñɔ̀dí íkpòkì 'I got
                                    money from him'
                                 mí ràbór ñɔ̀dí íkpòkì 'I'm
                                    taking money from him'
          tíìn   'take!' (what's offered)
          tíìnààní   'take one, have one!'
    Ku: -sɛɣɛ   'take away, remove'
          -da óβìn   'receive'

TAKE CARE OF (v)
    Od: -ko (oo-)

TAKE HOLD, CARE (v)
    A: -βam/-pam
          -βamanaan/-pamanaan   'hold for...'

TAKE OFF HAT
    Ku: -kperinə èɣóì
          -zurunə èɣóì   'take off hat in greeting'

TAKE PART OF...
    A: -βoor/-poor   mí úβóór ílɛ̀l βɔ 'I took
                                    portion of the yams'

TALE
    A: (ə̀)δì-dùm; (ə̀)sì-
    EO: óbà
    Ku: óbà
    Od: ə̀sù-dùm
    WO: ɔ̀bá
          ɔ̀-gbàm ɔ̀bá   'story-teller'

TALISMAN
    WO: ɛ̀-gbà   masc. name

TALK (v)   see also SAY; SPEAK
    A: -ɓa   ɔ̀ɓàánáán óyὲ 'to talk to
                         someone'

       -ɣaaβ/-kaaβ   kááβ 'say!'

                     kákāāβ 'don't say!'

    EO: -ɣòròɣórò
    Od: -si   ὲzòòr nósì mí̩kàñà 'we'll
                         talk a lot'

    WO: óɗùkò (m-)

TALL, BE (v)   see also LONG
    A: -βoβ/-poβ   mí̩ ɛ́pòβnī 'I'm tall'
                     mí̩ úβóβnī 'I was tall'

TALLNESS   see LENGTH

TAP [PALM TREE] (v)
    Ku: -gbo   cf. DIG

TASTE (v)
    A: -nɛma (ɔɔ-)   v.t.
    EO: -δɛδɛma
    Ku: -δɛδɛma
    Od: -n·ama (ɔɔ-)
    WO: ə̀-δə́ə̀βò

TEACH
    A: -tʉɣɛmi̩
    EO: -tʉɛmɛn
    Ku: -tʉɣʉmɛni̩
    Od: -tʉʉɣʉmi̩om

    WO: à-rų́àn
         ɔ̀-rų̀ànàmâ   'teacher'

TEAR (v)
    A: -βaar/-paar   ɛ́pāār ókùrù 'tears pocket'
    EO: -gɔgɔñ
    Ku: -gɔ
    Od: -ba

TEARS (n)
    A: ì-zín   èkpó ézīn 'a tear'
           j

TELL
    A: -ɓɛnị
    EO: -rų...ña   cf. SAY
         -gba óbà   'tell a tale'
    Ku: -gba
    Od: -gba
         -ɗum ə̀súdùm   'tell story'
    WO: à-gbâ
         à-gbêgbèrìbə̀   'tell story'

TERMITE
    A: ó-ɣárà; (à)rá-
    EO: ɛ̀kàkà
    Ku: áádɔ̀ñ; r-
    Od: ɔ̀ɔ̀-ɣàrà; ị̀ị̀-
    WO: ɛ̀kàkà

TESTICLES
    A: ị́ị́-kpà
    EO: ɔ̀pɔ̀rópɔ̀
    Ku: ų̀kpàsų́kpà

    Od: ɪ̀kpàβýaɣ; àr-   sing.
    WO: ɔ̀βỳlỳ; ɛ̀- (-zà)

TESTING-FRAME [FOR WITCHES]
    A: ɔ̀-nɛ̀m

THANK   see BLESS

THAT
    A: -ɔpɔ   -abɥɛ
          -ɛpɛ   -ɪ̀pɛ
          -δɪ̀βɛ   -mɥβɛ
    EO: ɔ̀βə́; ɪ́yɛ̄
    Ku: ɔ̀βə́; ɪ̂yɛ̌
    Od: ɔ̀pó
    WO: ɔ̀pâ; zizuə

THAT [INTRO. DIRECT DISCOURSE]
    A: mɔ́   mɔ̀nɔ̂ 'that he/she...'
                          máàmɪ́ 'that I...'
    Ku: mə́ ~ mə́ə̄

THAT (conj)
    A: dɪ́   'that, which'
    WO: ɓɛ   mɪ́ wālāmā ɓê ènɔ́ nə́rù 'I
                          think that he'll come'

THAT WHICH
    A: ìdɪ́

THAT'S WHAT...
    A: pɔ́ kwìdɪ́   pɔ́ kwìdɪ́ mɪ́ á-ɓɛ́nɪ̀ ñɪ́nə̀
                          'that's what I told you'
                          pɔ́kwɔ̄ ɪ̀yáárβɔ̄ 'that's why'

THATCH (n)

    A: ɔ̀kàm

    EO: àkáñ

    Ku: ákǎñ

    Od: à-kâm; (à)rà-

    WO: àkáñ

THATCH (v)

    A: -zá ɔ́kàm

         ~ -já

    EO: -zu

         ~ -l·o   'weave'

    Ku: -l·o

    Od: -zá ótù

    WO: ə̀-zû

THEN

    A: pɔ̀dɪ́

         kṳ́ɔ́ ɪ́dḭ̀ɔ́

    Ku: ɔ̀βɛ́sà

         yṵ́máā   '...then (result of
                          consequence)'

THERE

    A: ɛ̀pɛ́

    EO: ìgwé

    Ku: ḭ̀βá ~ èβə́   kpònè méβə́ 'look there'

    Od: èpə́

    WO: ɛ̀gɪ́lḭ̀

THEREFORE

    Ku: bə́lə̀né   'since, hence, therefore'

                       ɔ̀kwá ə̀δìɣì bə́lə̀né 'therefore,
                       hence it is so'

THEY

    Ku: ì-ɗìm   'crafty and deceiving,
                                              perhaps supernatural'

THICK

    A: égbìkìrì

    EO: ògbógbòm

    Ku: ògbógbòm

    WO: ógbōgbòm   'thickness'

THIEF

    A: ɔ̀-ɓà; (à)rʊ̀-

    EO: òɓìòmèɓì   cf. STEAL

    Ku: ɔ̀-gbà; àrʊ̀-

    Od: ɔ̀-ɓà; (à)rʊ̀-

    WO: ɔ́n·ị̀ɘ̀ɓì; ɘw̃únòmèɓì cf. STEAL

THIGH

    A: ɔ̀-gbɔ̀; (à)rʊ̀-

    EO: òbèdú

    Ku: ʊ̀gbɔ̀

    Od: ʊ̀gbɔ̀; àr-

    WO: ò-bédù ɘlìkè; ì-

THIN

    A: -kɔlɔlɔ
          ~ -kɔgɔnɔ   also 'narrow' cf. NARROW
          -ɣɔlɔɣɔlɔ

    EO: -kị̀r

    Ku: ɔ̀βɛ̀rɛ̀βɛ̀r   'like leaf'

    WO: ɔ̀βɛ̀rɛ̀βɛ́rɛ̀

THING

    A: ị̀yáár; (à)ráráár

    EO: àβàr; ìbú

Ku: àbár; èɗíə̀r
Od: àár; ɔ̀kpɔ́
WO: àβár; àrárà

THINK

A: -tʉɣịan (ɔɔ-)   'think, remember'
                           mị́ ráátʉ́ɣíā̄n mɔ́... 'I think
                             that...'

   -gbi   'count, reckon, think'
                           mị́ ùgbî mɔ́... 'I don't
                             think that...'

EO: -tʉtʉga
Ku: -rʉrʉan   also 'remember'
Od: -tʉa (ɔɔ-)   'think, remember'
   -ɣedi   'reckon, think that...'
WO: à-wálàmà

   -tʉtʉga   'consider'
   ɛ̀-wálám ól·ògì   'thinking' Oloibiri

THIRST

A: ɛ̀-ɗɔ̀ɣ ámʉ́ʉ̀m   n.
   ~ àɗíβʉ̀ àmʉ̀ʉ̀m   n.
EO: ɔ̀l·ɛ̀   'be thirsty' cf. MELT
Ku: ɛ̀ɗɔ̀ɣàmʉ̂m   ɛ̀ɗɔ̀ɣàmʉ̂m nèɗìɣí àmị̀
                            'I'm thirsty'
WO: ɛ̀-ɗáámʉ̀   n. cf. THROAT
                          ɛ̀ɗáámʉ́ nèsú ə̀m 'I'm
                            thirsty'

THIS

A: -ɔβɔn   -abʉɛn
   -aɗịɛn   -amʉɛn
   -ɛβɛn   -sịɣɛn
   -atʉɛn   -ịβɛn

EO: òn·ón; íñēn
Ku: ònón; íñĕn (íñĕn?)
Od: òβó
     (ò)βóβó
     (ə̀)βíβə́
WO: ɔmana; zizənə

THORN
A: óò-tòr; íì-
EO: òtòtól
Ku: ò-ɓùɓúlə̀m; ì-
Od: ò-ɓúlōm; ì-
WO: ò-tótòl; ì-

THOUGHT (n)
A: ɔ́ɔ̀tṳ̀γḭ́án
Od: ḭ́ḭ́tṳ̀á   'thinking, thought'

THREE DAYS BACK
WO: àmálḭ̀ɓɔ̀l

THROAT
A: è-kpóòkò   also 'gluttony' 'long throat'
EO: è̩ðɔ̀   'throat, gullet'
Ku: è̩ðɔ̀γ; r-   ɔ̀ðɔ̀γɔ́ðɔ̀γ 'glutton'
Od: è̩-ðɔ̀γ; àrà-   'throat, greed'
                              ɛ̀ðɔ̀γ àmṳ́ṳ̀m 'greed for water'
WO: è̩ðɔ̀   'gullet'
     è̩kpókòròkò   'windpipe'

THROW (v)
A: -toβ/-roβ
EO: -roβ

Ku: -roβ
Od: -roβ/-toβ
WO: ə̀-rôβ

THROWING
Od: ə̀lì-rôβ   'act of throwing'
                                   also 'sharpness of knife'
      èròβôm   'throwing'
WO: ò-ròβ   n. 'throwing (abstract)'

THUNDER
A: ɔ́ɔ́mààñ
EO: àgbàràrà   also 'lightning'
Ku: àgbàràràn   n.
WO: àgbàràrà   n.

THUS
A: ị́dūōn   'in this way'
     édìβɔ̄   'in that way, exactly'
EO: ɔ̀kų́nɔ́n
Ku: ɔ̀kɔ́nɔ́n   gìré mɔ́kɔ́nɔ́n   'do thus!'
     ɔ̀kwá; ɔ̀kų̀á   'it's so'
Od: èkúɛ́
WO: árɔ̀βàpɛ̀

TIE (v)
A: -kpɔ   'suspend by rope'
    -ɣɔrɔɣị/-kɔrɔɣị   'tie bundle'
    -muunə   'tie cloth'
    -kaɣa   'tie head-tie' cf. KNOT
    -βaδị   'tie up hand and foot'
    -kaɣ   'tie rope' cf. KNOT
EO: -munə   'tie cloth'
    -kpe   'tie head-tie'

EO:	-kpɔ	'tie bundle, rope'
Ku:	-munə	'tie cloth'
	-kpiə	'tie head-tie'
	-ɣɔrɔgi̤	'tie bundle'
	-kpɔ	'tie rope'
	-kpy̤a	'tie oneself, with rope'
Od:	-minə	'tie cloth'
	-ɣɔrɔɣi̤/-kɔrɔɣi̤	'tie bundle, wood, rope' 'tie after wrapping'
	-βuruɣi (-p)	'wrap'
	-kara	'tie head-tie'
	-kpy̤a	'tie rope around self'
	-kpɔ	'tie cloth; moor boat'
	-kaɣa	'tie head-tie'
	-kuɣə	'tie wrapper loosely around chest'
WO:	ə̀-zínì	also 'moor boat'
	à-ɣórɒ̀gi̤	'tie head-tie, bundle, rope'
	ínṳ̀ə̀(m-)	'tie cloth'

TIME

A:	(ə̀)-mèm	ə̀mém étúm mêm 'from time to time' cf. FOLLOW
		mêm 'once'
		i̤yàl ə̀mêm 'twice'
		έβὲl ə̀mêmmɔ́ 'the first time'
		ékùnə̀ ə̀mêmmɔ́ 'the last time'
		mémmèm 'one by one'
EO:	ὲɣi̤ri̤	
	~ ìfíè	Nembe
Ku:	óβêl; r-	
	-lèì	'to be time'

Ku: néléî 'it's time, time's
up'

néléî óβêl δámí 'it's my turn'

kóbìgèl 'a long time'

Od: èmèn   òtèmên 'sometimes'

     ~ àsákí   Kalabari

WO: òkókò   n.

     -le   'to be time for...' .

élē 'it's time'

élē ēm ágî 'it's time for me to go'

élēākēnè 'it's time to do it'

TINDER (n)

  WO: éékà

TIRED

  A: -βεr/-pεr   v. impersonal 'be tired, satisfied (ref. to food)'

òδìγì múβέr ími 'work has tired me; I'm tired of...'

míβèr íímì 'I'm tired'

méβèr ñòdí 'he's tired/ satisfied'

kèpêrrí ñòdí 'he'll be tired'

    (à)δí-βèr   n. 'tiredness, satiety'

  EO: -βεr   v. 'be tired'

nááβèr âm 'I'm tired, satisfied'

àβέr ám 'I was tired'

  Ku: -taβ   v. 'be tired'

nέtáβ àmí 'I'm tired'

ìtàβ δǒ àmí 'I'm not tired'

Od: -βɛr/-pɛr   v.   'tire, be tired'
'nɛ́ɛ̀βɛ́r àmʲ̀   'I'm tired'
ɛ̀βɛ́r àmʲ̀   'I was tired'
nɛ́pɛ̌r àmʲ̀   'I'm getting tired'
 òðìɣì òβó nápɛ̌r àmʲ̀   'the work tires me'

WO: ə́-gbēβ ə̄m   'I'm satisfied, tired'
cf. WEAK

TOAD

A: ɛ̀gbìrímə̀
EO: òβòm
Od: ɔ̀-fɔ̀kʊ̀fɔ́kʊ̀
WO: ówɔ̀   cf. FROG

TOBACCO

A: (ə̀)ðìrɛ̀
EO: ìrɛ̀
Ku: ìrɛ̀
    ɛ̀gbíàn írɛ̀   'snuff'
Od: ɨ̀-βɛ̀rɛ̀ɛ̀r   also 'snuff'
WO: ììrɛ̀
    ɛ́gbànììrɛ̀   'snuff'

TODAY

A: ródòn   ðúɣùl éródòn   'tonight'
EO: ə̀dòdôn
Ku: ə̀dídòn
Od: ə̀dôn
WO: ə̀dôn

TOE (n)   cf. FINGER

EO: ɛ̀kpàlɨ́ ə́wèl; ɛ̀kpàsɨ́...
WO: ɛ̀kpásálə̀lìkè   ònóβírɛ̀kpásálə̀lìkè 'big toe'

TOMATO
    A: óbìə̀n ə̀ɓèkèñ   cf. PEPPER
    WO: ə̀tòmátò(sì)

TOMORROW
    A: íɓùènéén
    EO: èlègên nə́rú
    Ku: èlègyên
    Od: èδìé
    WO: èlègén

TOMTOM
    A: ò-kíríkó; ì-   also 'slit drum'
    EO: èkéré   'wooden slit drum'
          òzè   'tomtom with skin'
    Ku: òkpókpó   also 'wooden slit drum'
    Od: ɛ̀-kṳ́ɛ́r; (à)rṳ̀-
    WO: òkpókpó

TONGUE
    A: (ə̀)-nễm; (ə̀)sí-
    EO: ə̀l·èm
    Ku: ə̀nèm; r-
    Od: ə̀n·èm; ə̀r-
    WO: ə̀nèm; -́zə̀

TOO   see ALSO

TOOTH
    A: ó-làà̧; (á)rá-
    EO: àl·à̧
    Ku: ò-ɓùɓúrà; ì-
    Od: àl·àà̧; àr-
    WO: àl·à̧; ˝zà

TOPS [GAME]
    EO: ìkòsò
    WO: èwúlìkòsò

TORTOISE
    A: ù-békù; (è)rú-
    EO: èδùlè
         àn·ì ápútà   'wife of tortoise'
    Ku: èδì-γûl; èsùγûl
         ~ èδùγùl
         ànípété   'wife of tortoise; foolish
                                          woman'
    Od: è-δùγùl; (è)rù-
    WO: èdùlè; ˋzè

TOUCH (v)
    A: -ɓɔγ
        -ti
    EO: -tiə   also 'dash, present some-
                                   thing'
    Ku: -kulən
    Od: -kuləən
    WO: è-tîè

TOWN   see VILLAGE

TRADE, BUY AND SELL (v)
    A: -muul
        -muulən   'argue about price'
                                mí úmùùlén ròdí

TRADER (n)
    A: òmùùlδíγí
       ~ òmùùlòm èδíγí

EO: òmùl mə̀ɓùə̀
Ku: ɔ̀n·ɪ̰ ə́ɓúə̀   cf. MARKET
Od: ò-ɓòmə́ɓò; ì- ~(ə̀)rù-
WO: ɔ́n·ɪ̰ ə̀ɓùə̀

TRAP (n)

A: (ə̀)δɪ̀βɪl
EO: àlɪ̰kpàtɪ̰   general term
     àɣɪ̰lέ   'deadfall'
     ògùgù   'pit trap'
     àgwáñ   'trap catching foot of
                            animal'

     -kpatɪ̰   v. 'trap, set trap'
Ku: έwɔl
     ὲgwέñ   'trap for rats'
Od: ὲβûm   'deadfall'
WO: ɔ̀kpàtɪ̰
     àɪ̰lέ   'deadfall'
     ὲtì   'enclosure type trap'

TRAVELER
Od: òtὲlὲmὲrélé   cf. WALK

TREE

A: ò-réñ; ì-   also 'wood; stick'
EO: ò-rὲrén; ì-
Ku: ò-rὲrén; ì-
Od: ò-rĕñ; ì-
WO: ò-rén; ì-

TRIBAL MARK
WO: ìgwə́nə̀

TRIBE   see GROUP

TRICK (n)

    A: ègbèrì

    Ku: íkòí

        ~ èpèlè   cf. DRAUGHTS

    Od: ì-pὲlì

    WO: ôβòkò   'deceit'

        èmàŋgàlà   'trickiness' masc. name

TRICK, DECEIVE (v)

    EO: -lὲγὲ

TROUBLE (n)

    A: ìβàγàmì

    Od: àràákpὲ   also 'case'

    WO: ə̀bôlògì

TRUNK

    A: ò-gbókù; ì- ~(ə̀)rò- 'trunk of tree or human'

    EO: èɡùm òrérén

    Ku: è-gùm (òrérén); ə̀rù-

    Od: è-ɡùm; (ə̀)rù-

    WO: èɡùmórén

TRUTH

    A: ì-gèñ   also 'good things'

                    é-gèñ 'it's true'

                    ~ é-gèñnī 'it's true'

                    kə̂-géñ 'it's not true'

                    è-gèñ ὲjō 'good character'

                    ò-gèñ óyè 'honest man'

    EO: ə̀gêñ

    Ku: ə̀gyə̀géì

    Od: ə̀gèì

    WO: ὲdìgí   ὲdìgáβàr 'true thing'

TRY (v)

    EO: -kparamɛn   cf. STRAIN

    Ku: -wiən   'try, attempt'

          -kpar   'try, accomplish, manage'

    WO: à-kɛ́nə̀βò   'do and see'

TSETSE FLY

    A: ɔ̀sɔ́ɔ́β

    EO: òwòṛ

    Ku: òwóṛ

    Od: àsɔ́ɔ́β; (à)r-

          òbùmə̀ɓóṛ   'large tsetse'

    WO: òwóṛ   cf. Abuan ə̀ɗíwóṛ

TUMBLE DOWNWARD

    A: βèléβèlèβèléβèlè   'turning end over end
                                    while falling'

TURN (v)

    A: -kiton

    Ku: -tibəreni   'turn over'

    Od: -ɣireni/-kireni   v.t.

          -kiton   'go round'

                          kìtŏn 'turn around'

          -kireən   kìrè̝én 'turn around'

    WO: à-βí̞rɛ̀   v.t. 'turn'

          à-βí̞rà   v.i.

TURTLE

    EO: ɔ̀bŏ

    Ku: òwɔ̀í̞   'salt water turtle'

           ṳ̀ɓŏ   'fresh water turtle'

    WO: ɔ̀ɓɔ́

TWIST (v)
    A: -pu̧r/-βu̧r
    EO: -βu̧ru̧βu̧r
    Ku: -βɔr
         -za   'twist rope'
    Od: -βu̧r/-pu̧r
    WO: à-fáŋgàlà
         à-βí̧βi̧rì   'twist rope'

U

UGLY   cf. BAD

    A: ə́bē̄ē̄β

    EO: -gurom   'become bad, ugly'

          -guremen   'make bad, destroy, spoil'

          ə̀lì-gùròm   'ugliness'

    Ku: -gurom

          -gurumeni   'make ugly'

          ə̀δù-gùróm   'ugliness'

    WO: ìgóróm   'bad looking'

          -gorom   v.i. 'be, become bad'

          -goromen   'make bad, destroy'

          ɔ̀kàràβ   modif. 'bad'

ULCER

    EO: èpùm ə́wèl   'ulcer on leg'

    Ku: ɛkɛ́tɛ́

    WO: èsì   cf. PLACE

UMBRELLA

    A: òγóβààm

    EO: àbi̥lâr

    Ku: óblári̥

    Od: àbàláàri̥

    WO: àbu̥làr

UNDERNEATH

    A: ɛ̀ɛ̀ni̥ùm

    EO: àgə̀dé

    Ku: δə́dè   cf. EARTH

          δ-ékpúkù

    Od: ɛ̀δí̥àn   'below'

    WO: ɔ̀dɛ̀

UNDERSTAND (v)
    Od: -mɔɣɔñan

UNDOUBTEDLY
    A: ɔ́bɔ̀   ɔ́bɔ̀ múɣííɣ íímì 'no doubt,
                               I could have been killed'

UNDRESS (v)
    A: -katanaan   cf. UNTIE
    EO: -ɓutonə
    Ku: -sɛɣɛgyan íbùrə̀
    Od: -kpɔrɔna   'undress self'
          -kpɔri̭ɔn   'undress someone'
    WO: ítènègì
          íbùɛ̀ðɔ̀

UNITY
    WO: ə̀ðí-ònìn   masc. and fem. name

UNPLEASANT TO EYE
    A: ò̀ðíɣísə̀

UNTIE
    A: -katan
    EO: -ɓuton
    Ku: -kɔtɔn
    Od: -kɔrɔna   'untie something on oneself'
          -kɔtɔn   'untie (boat)'
          -kɔri̭ɔn   'untie (many boats)'
    WO: ɔ̂·kpɔ̀kpɔ̀ (m-)

UP TO
    A: gùrùβ   'right up to'

URINE

    A: ə̀-mùnùm   (ə-monom?)
         -mùnùm   (-monom?) v. 'urinate'
    EO: ə́mínòm
         -minom   v. 'urinate'
    Ku: ə̀mìnòm
         -minom   v. 'urinate'
    Od: ə̀-mònòm; (ə̀rə̀-)
            [n·]
         -monom   v. 'urinate'
    WO: ə́mínòm
         înòn (m-)   v. 'urinate'

USELESS PERSON
    Ku: ò-δìm

V

VAGINA

    A: è-kpíδíγ; (ə̀)rí-

    EO: ə̀δìßò

         ~ ὲpὲl   euphemism

    Ku: ὲγàr

    Od: ə̀δì-ßò; ə̀sì-

    WO: ὲßὲ; ´zà

VEIN

    EO: ò-gíβ; ì-

    Od: ò-gĭβ; ì-   also 'artery' B *-kîpa

    WO: ò-gîβ; ì-

VERANDAH

    EO: ɔ̀gbàgbà

    Ku: òbúrú

    Od: à-pέ; (à)rà-

    WO: óbùrú

VILLAGE

    A: ὲὲ-má; (à)ráá-

    EO: έmà   'town'

         ɔ̀gbàr έmà   'village'

    Ku: ὲmà; r-

    Od: ὲ-má; (à)rǎ-

    WO: ὲmà; ^zà

VISIT (v)

    Od: -δiγənəən

VOICE

    A: ὲ-δɔ̀γ; (à)rɔ̀-   'human voice' cf. THROAT

         (à)δị̀-àßâ   'animal noise'

EO: òkórókò
Ku: ókòròkò
Od: ù̀-ɣúrúkò; (à)rà-
WO: òkóròkò

VOMIT (v)
A: -zuɣi
EO: -ɓị̀ɔ
Ku: -zugi
Od: -zuuɣi
WO: óòlènì (m-)
     ólèní

VULTURE
A: ò-dèlè; (à)rè-
EO: òdèlè
Ku: òdèlè; r-
Od: ò-dèlè; ị̀- ~(à)sù̀-
WO: ò-dèlè; è-

W

WAIST

    A: è-sìn; (ə̀)rì-   (ámì̤)(βέ̤ὲβὲn)

                              ànì̤r ébōōm ésî̤n 'wide-hipped woman'

WAIT, WATCH (v)

    A: -kori   'watch' 'wait'

                          ú-kòrí í·mì̤ 'wait for me'

            -gon   'to wait'

            gón   'watch, look out'

    EO: -poñ   'be on look-out'

            -koδom   'wait'

            ɔ̀ròkóδù   'wait'

            òkòké̤δí̤ó   'nightwatch'

    Ku: -ɓərə   'wait' àmí̤ nə̀ɓərə́ ì̤nà 'I'm waiting for him'

            -gòn   'watch'

    Od: -ɓərə   'wait'

            -gon   'watch for something expected'

            -βəɣə/-pəɣə   'watch event taking place'

    WO: ə̀-kôδì̤   'wait'

            ə̀-pópònòm   'keep watch'

            ôkòδì̤ (m-)   'keep awake, night'

WAKE UP

    A: -sụma   v.i.

            -sụmɛñ   v.t.

                        mí̤ ụ́-sụ́mɛ́ñ ñɔ̀dí 'I woke him'

    EO: -sụma   v.i.

            -sụmɛñ   v.t.

    Ku: -sụma   v.i.

            -sụmɛnì̤   v.t.

Od: -sụma   v.i.

-sụmeɛn   v.t. cf. GET UP

WO: ôsụ̀mà (m-) v.i.

ó-sụ̀mɛ̀dàlà 'awakening'

ósụ̀mɛ̀ñ (m-) v.t.

WALK

A: -tele/-rele   v. 'to walk'

-sumuɣiən   'walk through bush (no path)'

ò-tèlìòm èrèlè n. 'walker'

EO: -rere   v.

Ku: -rele   v.

Od: -rele/-tele   v.

òtèlè mèrélé n. 'walker' cf. TRAVELER

è-rélé   n. 'walk, journey'

WO: à-dôn   v.

ɛ́dǒn

WALKING STICK

A: ị̀kpárá

EO: ókpétì

Ku: òkpètì ị́kị́ón·ị̀ cf. ụ̀kị̀ón·ì 'old man'

ị̀kị̀éw̃únòm (pl.)

Od: ɛ-ɓụ̀; arụ̀-

WO: ɛ̀kị̀ànị́

WALL (n)

A: ìì-kpè

EO: ɛ̀ɣ-òtú

Ku: ɛ̀ɓáɣótù; r-

Od: ɛ̀-ɓǎɣ; (à)rà-

ɛ̀ɓàɣótù

WO: ə̀kígótû; ə̀kígítû

WANT   see WISH

WAR
    A: ὲ-γàm; (à)rà-
    EO: ὲŋàm
         ìwéyὲ   'fight between two'
         ìwὲyágwò   'wrestling'
    Ku: ὲγàm; r-
    Od: ὲ-γàm; (à)rà-
    WO: ὲγ̃àm; ʹzà
         òsùmὲ   'small-scale war between
                                     villages'

WARD, QUARTER (n)
    A: èkòòl
    EO: ̀əpòló
         òmàr   'group of related families
                                     (extended family?)'
    Ku: òγôl
    Od: ò-kòòl; (ə̀)rə̀-
         almost [u̥kɔɔl]
    WO: ̀əpóló

WARM (v)
    A: -lεl   mí ú-lέl έlὲlβ̄ ú-nі̥̀àn
                                   'I warmed yam by fire'
         -ŋa(ɔɔ-)   'warm oneself'
                                   mí ráŋá ní̥àn ~ mí ràlέlá
                                     ní̥àn 'I'm warming myself
                                     by the fire'

WARMTH   see HEAT

WASH (v)
    A: -tol (oo-)   'wash thing'
         -wurə   'bathe'

EO: -totol   'wash pots'

       -fɔ   'wash cloth'

       -wurə   'bathe'

Ku: -titol   'wash pots, cloth'

       -wurə   'bathe'

Od: -tol (oo-)   v.t.

       -ɓur   'bathe someone'

       -tələ (oo-)   refl. 'wash oneself'

       -ɓurə   refl. 'take bath, bathe
                                 oneself'

WO: ə̀-tótòl   'wash pots'

       à-pʊ́ɛ̀   'wash cloth' also 'get lost'

       -sisili   'wash cloth, not clothes'

       ə̀-wúrə̀   'bathe'

WASP

   Od: ɔ̀-gáʊ́

WATCH   see WAIT

WATCHMAN

   WO: ɔ̀kòɓòm mə̀ɓìò   'watch-night'

WATER (n)

   A: (à)-mʊ̀ʊ̀m; [(à)rʊ̀-]

   EO: àmʊ̀m

   Ku: àmʊ̀m

   Od: àmʊ̀ʊ̀m

   WO: àmùw̃

WATER LETTUCE

   EO: ìpòpŏβ

   Ku: ópòpôβ

   Od: òó-fō; ìí-

   WO: ə́pòpōm

WATERSIDE
     EO: àkákóβí
     Od: èsìδíǝ
     WO: àmóβí

WATERSNAIL   see also SNAIL
     A: ɛkpòríòγ
     Od: ɛ̀-bɔ̀ñ

WAVE (n)
     EO: ɔδừgɔ̀
     Od: èé-kpǎ(mú̀ừm); (ǝ̀)rǝ̀ǝ́-
     WO: ɔ̀-δừgɔ̀; ɛ̀-

WEAK   see also SOFT; TIRED
     A: -duγòγ
     EO: -gừr   'become weak'
          àlừ-gừr   'weakness'
          ɔ̀gừrừgừr; ɛ̀-   modif.
     Ku: -duγ
          òdừdừγɛ̀n   adj.
          -duγumeni   'weaken'
          ǝ̀lừ-dừγ   'weakness'
     WO: -gừrừ   v. 'become weak, tired'
          ɛ́-gừr óβừ   'weakness, fatigue'
                               òβú émìnì á-gừrừ 'I'm
                                   tired, my body is weak'

WEALTH   see RICHES

WEAR (v)
     A: -zuǝ éγóòñ   'wear hat'
          -murinǝ úkpè   'wear cloth'

WEAVE (v)

   A: -lo

       òlòmìl·ò   n. 'weaver'

   EO: -l·o

       òl·òmìbú   n. 'weaver'

   Ku: -lo

       òlòmə́   n. 'weaver'

   Od: -lo

       ò-l·ùə̌; ì-   n. 'weaver'

   WO: ə̀-l·ô

       ò-l·òmíkpè; ì-   n. 'weaver'

WEAVERBIRD

   A: à-mṵ́tḭ́à

WEED (v)

   A: -ruβ/-tuβ árɔ̀ɔ̀ɣɔ   'removing grass by hand'

       -sam   'with matchet'

   EO: -fɔfɔ

   Ku: -papaβ

   Od: -ruβ/-tuβ   'weed, uproot'

   WO: ə̀-rûβ àdḭ̀ɔ̀   'remove weeds'

WEEK

   A: éé-δī̄ō   'four-day week'

WEEK DAYS

   EO: 1. ɔ̀nṵ́n ə́δúmə̀   free day

        2. ə̀sóδ ə̀δúmə̀   free day

        3. ìkùñ   holiday

        4. àkɛ́   holiday masc. name

   Ku: 1. àkɛ́   masc. 'day of rest'
                        god day masc. name

        2. òδùènì   fem. wife of àkɛ́

Ku: 3. àtɔ̀ɣɔ̀lɔ̀   masc.
     4. ògùrù   fem. 'day of rest' wife of
                                àtɔ̀ɣɔ̀lɔ̀ fem. name

Od: 1. ògùrù   fem. wife of àtóɣóló
     2. òδùènì   fem. wife of ààkɛ́
     3. àtóɣóló   masc.
     4. ààkɛ́   masc.

WELL (n)
   A: (ə̀)-ɣùδìə̀; (ə̀)sì-
   EO: ògùgàmûm
   Ku: ògùgwà àmûm
   Od: ə̀-ɣùδìə̀; (ə̀)sù-
   WO: ò-gùgù; ì-

WELL, BE   see HEALTHY, BE

WEST
   A: èméélòm (ògògò)

WET, BE (v)   cf. ROTTEN
   A: -ɓɔr   B *-ɣûnda; <u>v</u>ola 'rot'
       -ɣunə/-kunə   'get wet from rain'
                         -ɣúnə́ ólàβì̀à 'to get
                            drenched by rain'
                         -ɣúnə́ ómù̀ 'to be in sun
                            for long time'

   EO: -ɓɔrɔm   'become wet'
        -ɓɔrɔmɛn   v.t. 'make wet'
        ɛ̀-ɓɔ̀rɔ̀m   n. 'wetness'
        ɔ̀-ɓɔ̀rɔ̀mɓɔ́rɔ́m; ɛ̀-   modif.
   Ku: -ɓɔr   'be wet, rotten'
   Od: -ɓɔr   'wet, rotten'
        -ɓɔrɔmì̀ ~ -ɓɔrɛ v.t. 'wet, make wet'
        àlì̀-ɓɔ́r   'wetness'

WO: -ɓórɔ̌m   v.i. 'be, become wet'

      -ɓorɔman   v.t. 'make wet'

      ɔ̀-ɓórɔ́m; ɛ̀-   modif.

      ɛ́-ɓɔ̀rɔ̌m   n. 'wetness'

WHAM!!

  A: ɓwáɪ́

WHAT?   cf. WHY?

  A: ééɣē   'what?' 'why?'

      ìkə́ kʉ̀íδìɣì   'why'

                       ìdʉ̀ón ɓō ìkə́ 'what's this?'

                       B *-ṅga 'how' *-ki 'what?'

  EO: èèrè ~ érê   ɛnà kə̀δí mérè 'what did
                          he do?'

      ékə̀   mɪ́ nə̀δí ékə̀ ɛ̀ 'what shall
                          I do?'

  Ku: ê·rê· (ê·rê·)

  Od: ééɣè

      ~ ɛ̀káráàn

  WO: èríə̀ ~ kéèríə̀   ɔ̀mánà kéèríə̀ 'what's this?'

                       àw̃ kw̃nàkɛ́nɛ́ èríə̀ 'what are
                         you doing?

      àkà   'why, what indeed'

                       àmɪ̀ kʉ́mɪ́ nákɛ̀n àkà 'what
                         shall I do?'

WHATEVER

  A: ɛ̀ló; ɪ̀ló

WHEN?

  A: pʉ́rə̀mèn

      mém mō   'the time that, when
                      (indirect discourse)'
                      cf. TIME

  EO: (à)kárɛ́ɣɪ́rɪ̀

Ku: àkɛ́rɔ́βèl
    ìgyèl β...   'during time when...'
Od: ókə̀rə́mèn   'which time'
WO: ə̀kɛ́rɔ̀kɔ̀kɔ̀

WHENEVER
A: mémlɔ́

WHERE?
A: ɛ́ɛ́ɣn̄
EO: ə̀kérésìn   ɛnà kòlɔ́ kérèsì   'where
                                      is he?'

    àkárágàɛ   ɛnà kòlɔ́ káràga   'where
                                      is he?'
                                   w̃ nàgì kárágà̀   'where are
                                      you going?'
Ku: δɛ́kên
Od: (tɛ́)δíɣèn   ò-δíɣèn òdì   'where is he?'
                                   ì-δíɣèn èdì   'where are
                                      they?'

WO: ə̀késì ~ ə̀kérésì   cf. PLACE

WHEREVER
A: èkpìsí lɔ́

WHET, SHARPEN
A: -ɣolə/-kolə   B *-nola
EO: -ɣolə   'whet, grind, sharpen'
    ~suemen   'sharpen'
Ku: -ɣələ
Od: -ɣələ/-kələ
WO: ə̀-ɣélə̀   'grind, whet, sharpen'
    à-pâl   'sharpen stick'
    ò-ɣèlə̀mə̂   'sharpening stone'

WHETSTONE

    EO: əδìlì

    Ku: ògbí ́ómà   'grinding stone'

           òɣólòmə̀   'whetstone used by older
                                    people'

    WO: òɣòlòmə̂

WHICH?

    A: pṹrō̄   also 'what'

                          pṹrō̄ əδìò 'which day'

                          pṹrəmèm 'when, what time'

    EO: òkə́rè   w̃íwòl mòkə́r ɛ́lɛ̀l 'which
                                  yam did you sell?'

           àkárà   'what kind?'

    Ku: ə̀kə́r ~ àkə́r

           ókên; íkên

    Od: ò-kə̀r; ì-   òkə̀r ótù 'which house?'

                          òβó òtù òkə̀r ɔ́ì 'whose
                                house is this?'

                        òtù òβóβó òl-òkə̀r-ɔ́ì 'this
                              house is whose?'

    WO: ə̀kə́r(è)   ə̀kə́r òtù 'which house?'

WHIRLPOOL

    WO: ó-gìrí   cf. WORK

WHISPER, TALK SOFTLY (v)

    Ku: -βoβolə

    Od: -βə̀lə/-pələ

WHITE

    A: -βalaɓaal   v. 'be white'

    EO: -ɓalaɓal

    Ku: ɔ̀ɓàlàɓâl

Od: -ɓaal   èvèl òβó à-ɓàál 'the goat
                       was white'
                 èvèl òβó ɔ̀ɓààl 'the goat
                       is white'
                 ɔ̀ɓààl évēl 'white goat'

WHO?

A: ánį́ɛ̀n   B *nî
    àbụ́ánį́ɛ̀n   pl.
EO: ə̀nên
Ku: ə̀ñén
Od: òkə́róóị̀
WO: àn·į́ɛ̀n ~ kànį́ɛ̀n   sing. ɔ̀mánà kànį́ɛ̀n 'who
                       is this?'
                 ànį́ɛ̀n kínə̀rù 'who is
                       coming?'
    ə̀wéì   pl. ə̀wéì kíìrù 'who
                       (many) came?'

WHOEVER, PERSON WHO

A: ɔ̀-ló   'he who...'
                 ɔ̀ló āmɔ̄ɔ̄γ Ìkpòkì 'he who
                       has money'
     bụ̀-ló   'they who...'
                 bụ̀ló ōmɔ̄ɔ̄γ Ìkpòkì 'they
                       who have money'
                 ñínə̀β̄ ēmɔ̄ɔ̄γ bɔ̀ íkpòkì 'you
                       (pl.) who have money'
                 bụ̀β̄ɛ́ órú bɔ̀ 'they who come'
                 ɔ̀pó érú bɔ̀ 'he who came'
WO: ówə́   sing. 'he who...'
     ígú   pl. 'they who...'

WHOSOEVER

A: òyéláárú   'whosoever came'
       [=òyè̂ ló érú]

WHY?   cf. WHAT
    A: ééɣē   'why, what'
         ~ ìkə́ kừíδìɣì
         δíɣí kúɔ́   pókwɔ́ ìyáárβɔ̄ 'that's why'
    EO: ìδíékə̀   'why, what'
         ~ èkə̀   'why, how'
         ~ èèré
    Ku: èzìnkêrê
         ~ èrê
    Od: èbùmééɣē   èbùmééɣē k-án-ə̀rù 'why did
                                      you come?'
    WO: àkákɛ́nì̧
         ~ ɛ́kēn àkà

WIDE
    A: -Tɛɣ   v. 'be wide'
         -rɛɣɛ/-tɛɣɛ   v. 'widen'
         ɛ́rɛ̀ɣɛ́   'width'
         ~ àδí̧-rɛ̄ɣ   'width'
    EO: -rɛñ   v. 'be, become wide'
         -rɛɣɛmɛn   v.t. 'widen'
         ɛ̀-rɛ́ɣɛ̀   'wideness'
         ɔ̀-rɛ̀rɛ̀ñ; ɛ̀-   'wideness'
    Ku: -rɛɣ   v.
         -rɛɣɛmɛnì̧   v. 'widen'
         ɛ́rɛ̀ɣɛ́   'width'
    Od: -rɛɣ/-tɛɣ
         -rɛɣɛ/-tɛɣɛ   v. 'widen'
         àlì̧-rêɣ   'width, wideness'
         ~ ɛ̀rɛ̀ɣɛ́   'width, wideness'
    WO: ɔ̀-rɛ̀rɛ́ñ; ɛ̀-   modif.
         -rɛñ   v.i. 'be, become wide'
         -rɛñman   v.t. 'widen'
         ɛ́rɛ̆ñ   'width'

WIFE
    A: ànír   cf. WOMAN
        òβìnèñ   'favorite wife'
                                personal name
    Ku: án·Ị̈
    WO: àδịzà

WIN [CASE]   see GO HOME

WIND (n)
    A: óókùùγ
    EO: òkùkù
    Ku: ò·gìm
    Od: òpịβà   no pl.
    WO: òβíβìlòm

WINE
    A: èmíìm
    EO: èmìn
    Ku: èmìn ~ èmìm   'distilled' also 'gin'
        ùdè   'palmwine'
    WO: è·mì   also 'gin'

WING
    A: ò-βéèβ; (è)ré-   B *vava -pupa,-papa 'flap
                                      wing'
    EO: ìβòm
    Ku: àpàbà; r-
    Od: ùβòm; (è)s-
    WO: ìβòmέn·úrụ́; ´zà

WIPE (v)
    A: -ɓuroγ
    EO: -gbidi
    Ku: -ɓul
    Od: -gbul
    WO: è-gbídì   'clean off'

WIRE (n)

    A: (à)wáyà

    EO: àwáyà

        ~ òδìδì

    Ku: àwáyà

    Od: à-wáyà

    WO: àwáyà

WISH, WANT (v)

    A: -wa   also 'seek, look for'

    EO: -fɛl

    Ku: -βɔrɔɣan

    Od: -va

        ~ -gbeel   'desire'

        -ral/-tal   'need, want, feel need'

                           mɛ́tăl àmɨ̀ mɔ̀βɔ̀ɣɔ̀l àmʉ̀ʉ̀m

                              'I need to drink water'

                         àmʉ̀ʉ̀m nɛ́tăl àmɨ̀ mɔ̀βɔ̀ɣɔ̀l

                              'I need to drink water'

    WO: à-sɔ̀   also 'look for' 'have

                                intercourse with woman'

WITH   see AND

WITHER (v)

    EO: -ɣaɣara   'become dry'

    Ku: -ɣaɣara   cf. DRY

    Od: -ɣal/-kal

WOMAN

    A: à-nɨ́r-èβòβ;

          àɱárɨ́r-èβòβ

    EO: àn·ɨ́; àw̃àn·ɨ́

    Ku: ànɨ́éβòm; àw̃ánɨ́

    Od: ànɨ́; àrà·nɨ́

        ànɨ́éβōōβ; àrànɨ́éβòōβ

    WO: àδɨ̯zà; àwâr

WOMB

    A: è-ɣùn; (ə̀)rù-   B *-v̱ûma 'belly'

    EO: òtù-ɛ́màrà   ɛ̀màrà 'delivery'

    Ku: ɔ̀lị́màrá [≈ɔ̀là ị́màrá]

    Od: ɔ̀là

    WO: ɔ̀màrɔ̀màw̃ị̀

WOOD   see TREE

WORK (n)

    A: ò-ðìɣì; (ə̀)rì-
          ò-ðìɣìnòm óðíɣí   'worker'

    Ku: ògìr; r-
          -gir   v. 'to work'

    Od: ò-ðìɣì; (ə̀)rì-

    WO: égìrí   also 'wrestling'
          ón·ì èɡìrí   'worker'

WORLD

    A: ə̀ɓìrínì

    EO: àmàrə̀w̃únòm   'mankind?'

    Ku: àmàr ə̀w̃únòm

    Od: ɛ̀màrə̀réī̀
          ~ ə̀ɓìrínì

    WO: see EARTH

WORM

    A: (ə̀)-síléègbèm; (ə̀)sí-

    EO: àsị́gà

    Ku: àlɛgâ; àsɛgâ

    Od: ɛ̀-ɓàl; ị̀-

    WO: àlị́-gà; àsị́- ~àlị́gàzà

WORSHIP (v)   cf. PRAY

    EO: -ɣalam

WOUND (n)

    EO: ɛn·ɛ̀m

    Ku: ɛ̀nɛ̀m

    Od: èsì

         ɛ̀nɛ̀m   'fresh cut'

    WO: ɛ̀βṵ̀

WRAP (v)

    A: -βuruɣi/-puruɣi

    EO: -βurugi

    Ku: -βurugi

    WO: à-ɣɔ́rɔ̀gḭ̀   also 'tie, as headtie,
                               bundle, rope'

          ɔ̀-ɣɔ̀rɔ̀gɔ̀mâ   'wrapper, thing used for
                               wrapping'

WRESTLE

    A: -gba ḭ́nṵ̄ɣ   v.

          ɔ̀-kpárà   n. 'champion wrestler'

          òtùmɔ́kpàrà   n. 'champion wrestler's
                                    assistant'

    EO: -wèwé āgwɔ̀   v.

          ìwè ágwɔ̀   n. 'wrestling'

    Ku: òwêgèlègè   v.

          òmòmə̀nə̀n   n. 'wrestler'

          ɔ̀-dàmá   'champion wrestler'

          ḭ̀pàlḭ́   'second ranked wrestler'

          èɡèlèɡé   n. 'wrestling'

    Od: -gba éɡèlèɡè   v.

          èɡèlèɡè   n. 'wrestling'

    WO: ə̀-wê [òsùmə̀]   v. cf. WORK

          òsùmə̀   n. 'wrestling, fight'

WRIST

    Ku: ḭ̀kpɛ̀ɣɛ̀rɛ̀β ágwɔ̀

WRITE (v)
   A: -gɛ
   EO: -gɛ
   Ku: -gɛ
   Od: -gɛ
       ɛgḭá   'writing, something written'
       ɔgὲmɔ̀βrὲὲr   n. 'writer'
   WO: ɛ̂gɛ̀ (m-)
       ɛ̂gɛ̀ɗḭrḭ   'writing'
       ɛgὲmə̀ɗírí   'writer'

WRONG
   Ku: -βum   éβŭm ḭnà 'he was wrong'
                      íβŭm ḭnà 'he's wrong'
                      íβŭm áw̃à 'you're guilty'
   Od: -pḭɔm   'be wrong'
   WO: ὲβḭlὲ̀

X Y Z

XYLOPHONE
    Od: ìgélégé

YAM
    A: ɛ̀-lɛ̀l; ị̀-
    EO: ɛ̀l·ɛ̀l
    Ku: ɛ̀-lɛ̀l; ị̀-
    Od: ɛ̀-lɛ̀l; ị̀-
    WO: ɛ̀l·ɛ̀l; ʼzà

YAM HEAP
    A: ègú ị̄lɛ̀l
    EO: ɛ̀bɛ́l·ɛ̀l
    Ku: èsìn ɛ́lɛ̀l
    WO: ə̀túr ɛ́l·ɛ̀l

YAM STOREHOUSE
    A: èkùè ílɛ̀l
    WO: èdènì
          èdénɛ́l·ɛ̀l

YARD (n)
    A: èɓùɣótû   'backyard'
        ɔ̀mánótū   'back of house' cf. BACK

YAWN (v)
    A: -maaɣa   B *-aɣu 'yawning'
    EO: -maaŋaŋa
    Ku: -maɣa
        í-màɣǎ   n. 'yawn'
    Od: -maaɣa
    WO: à-ɣɛ̂kpòtì
        à-ɣâ   'to open mouth'

YAWS

    A: ùké

    EO: ɛ̀kàrà

    Ku: ɛ̀ɓɛ̀

    Od: ùké

        àráɓḷ   'sores of yaws'

    WO: ɛ̀kàrà

YEAR

    A: ààlà; áásḭ́à   B *-ɣaka

    EO: ààl·à

    Ku: ààlà; r-

    Od: ààlà; àsḭ̀à
           ~ àsṳ̀mṳ̀sḭ̀à

        àlàɓó nétùòɓó   'next year'

        ə̀ə̀n·ə́   'last year'

    WO: àl·à; ʼzà

YEAR'S END

    Ku: ò-zé   'feast at end of year,
                            marked by shouting
                            spirits out of village'

YELLOW (v)

    A: -dor   'very bright yellow'

YELLOW FEVER

    Ku: ákàm égúə́dè

    WO: òróbḭ́ (A)

        ìgwámàlàlà (O)

YESTERDAY

    A: ɔ̀mán ìδùè

    EO: ə̀lègên nétén

    Ku: ə̀lègyên étén   cf. PASS

Od: èδùé
WO: èlègénè̠

YOUNG

    A: òpúɣ   'young and tender (not male)'
    EO: òkùβ
    Ku: òkúβ
    WO: òkûβ

YOUTH

    A: òñ-úɣèèl; úɣèèl   'youth, young man'
    EO: ò-yèl; ì-   'young person'
    Ku: òñúyèl; àw̃ìyúyèl   'young person'
    Od: òñùɣéél(ɔ̀ñ); úɣéél 'youth, young man'
    WO: óyêl; í- (A)   'youth, young person'
          òyélî (O)

ZINC

    Od: à-gbừbà

PERSONAL PRONOUNS

I		subj.	obj.	poss.	
	A:	àmí̧	mí̧	í̧ími̧	ami̧
	EO:	àmi̧	àmi̧/mi/m-	am	δAm
	Ku:	àmi̧	ami̧/am-/m-	ami̧	δámí̧
	Od:	à·mi̧	ami̧/am-	zami̧	ami̧
	WO:	àmi̧	mi̧/m-	Am	AmInI sg.
					zAtUm pl.

YOU (sg.)		subj.	obj.	poss.	
	A:	n·â	n·a	ñíne̖	an·a
	EO:	àw̃á	aw̃a/w̃A/w̃-	ma/maw̃a	δíóm/δíyóm
	Ku:	áw̃à	aw̃a/aw̃/a-	aw̃a/maw̃a/ñam	δóñóm
	Od:	án·à	an·a/an·-	zana	onume̖
	WO:	àw̃	w̃-/w̃ũ-	dA	An·A sg.
					zAtA pl.

HE, SHE, IT		subj.	obj.	poss.	
	A:	ɔ̀dí̧	ɔ̀dí̧~ø	ñɔ̀dí̧	ɔdi̧
	EO:	ɛnà	ɛna/ɛn-	yɔ	δí̧ó/δí̧yó
	Ku:	i̧nà	i̧na/i̧n-	i̧na	δóyó
	Od:	ɔ̀dí̧	odi	zodi	odi
	WO:	ɛnɔ̀	ɛnɔ/ɛn-	dɔ	ɔlɔ sg.
					zɔtɔ pl.

WE		subj.	obj.	poss.
A: [excl.]				
	yóór	yóór	í̧yɔ̀ɔr	ə́yoor
A: [incl.]				
	yíre̖	yíre̖	í̧yìre̖	əyire̖
EO:	i̧yàr	yar	i̧yar	δi̧yár
Ku:	i̧yàr	i̧yar	i̧yar	δí̧yár
Od: [excl.]				
	èzɔ̀ɔr	ezoor	zezoor	ezoor

Od: [incl.]	subj.	obj.	poss.
èzìré	ezirə	zezirə	ezirə
WO: àrɨ̀	arɨ/ar-	arɨ	aarar sg.
			zaatar pl.

YOU (pl.)	subj.	obj.	poss.
A: ñínè̀	ñínè̀	íñìnè̀	əñinə
EO: ìnì	inin/ini/nin-	nin	ðíní
Ku: ìñîn	iñin	iñin	ðíñín
Od: èñìné	eñinə	zeñinə	eñinə
WO: ìnî	ini/in-	din	iinin sg.
			ziitin pl.

THEY	subj.	obj.	poss.
A: bɨ̀dɨ́	bɨ̀dɨ́	bɨ̀dɨ́	abɨdɨ
EO: àwà	awa/aw-	awa	ðáwá
Ku: àwà	awa	awa	ðáwá
Od: èdí	edi	zedi	edi
WO: àwɔ̀	awɔ/aw-	awɔ	aalụwɔ sg.
			zaatụɔ pl.

HE

    Ku: ò-ðìm   'crafty, deceptive, possibly supernatural'

EMPHATIC PRONOUN (subj.)

    A: kú

           mɨ́ kúùpù 'I won'
           ɔ̀dɨ́ kúə̀pù 'he won'
           n·â kúùpù 'you won'
           yóór kúùpù 'we won'
           ñínè̀ kúìpù 'you (pl.) won'
           bɨ̀dɨ́ kúùpù 'they won'

NUMBERS

ONE

    A: ò-níɪ̄n   òníɪ̄n mēm mèm 'one at a time'

    EO: ònîn

    Ku: ònîn

    Od: òñíín

    WO: ònîn

TWO

    A: i̱yàl   i̱yàl i̱yàl 'in sets of two'

    EO: i̱wàl

    Ku: i̱wàl

    Od: i̱zàl

    WO: i̱wàl

THREE

    A: i̱rààr

    EO: i̱sàr

    Ku: i̱sàr

    Od: i̱rààr

    WO: i̱sàr

FOUR

    A: ìñè̱

    EO: ìñè̱

    Ku: íñè̱

    Od: íñé̱

    WO: íñè̱

FIVE

    A: óòɣ

    EO: ɔ̀w

    Ku: óóɣò

Od: òòɣ
WO: òwù

SIX

A: ódíĩ́ñ   òdììñdììñ 'in groups of six'
EO: òdîn
Ku: ódîn
Od: ódíín
WO: ódîn

SEVEN

A: óδúə̂l
EO: òδùə̀n
Ku: óδūə̄n
Od: óδúə̂l
WO: óδúə̂l

EIGHT

A: ɔ̀βàànâ
EO: énə̌
Ku: ɔ̀βáñà
Od: àβὲñá
WO: wàl bə́ δíòβ (A)
       ɛ́ñǎn (O)

NINE

A: ésùɣə́
EO: ísìó
Ku: ésùɣ̄
Od: èsúɣó
WO: ònîn bə́ δíòβ (A)
       ísìó (O)

TEN

    A: ðíòβ
    EO: ðíòβ
    Ku: ðìòβ
    Od: ə̀ðìòβ
    WO: ðìòβ

ELEVEN

    A: ðíòβ nòníìn
    EO: ðíòβ nònín
    Ku: ðìòβ nònín
    Od: (ə̀)ðìòβ nòñíín
    WO: ðìòβ nònîn

TWENTY

    A: ðìsíβ
    EO: ə̀rùsùβ
    Ku: ə̀ðùsúβ
    Od: (ə̀)ðìsíβ
    WO: súβ

THIRTY

    A: ðìsíβ rìðìòβ
    EO: ə̀rùsúβ nìðíòβ
    Ku: ə̀ðùsúβ nìðìòβ
    Od: ə̀ðìsíβ ðìòβ
    WO: ɔ̀dàβár

FORTY

    A: èrúbààl   ~ ị̀yàl ə̀rìsì ə̀ðísìβ
    EO: wàl pó
    Ku: èrúbə̀l
    Od: èrúbàl
    WO: wàl pó

SIXTY

    A: ɛ́ráβáràr ~ ɔ̀ɔ̀nɪ̀r

    EO: sàr pó

    Ku: ɪ̀sàr ɛ̀wálá

         ~ ɛ̀ráβaràβ

    Od: èrúbàl ə̀ðìsíβ

    WO: sàr pó

EIGHTY

    A: ìnə̀ ə́rúkúrɔ̀n   cf. IRON

    EO: ìñ pó

    Ku: ɪ̀wàl ɛ̀wálá

    Od: ɪ̀zàràráálā

    WO: ìñ pó

ONE HUNDRED

    A: ɔ̀ɔ̀ɣə́rúkúrɔ̀n

    EO: ɔ̀w(ʋ̀) pó

    Ku: ɪ̀wàl ɛ̀wálá nə̀ðùsùβ

    Od: ɪ̀zàràráálá nə̀ðìsíβ

    WO: òwù pó

TWO HUNDRED

    Od: ɔ̀nɪ́r

FOUR HUNDRED

    A: ɔ̀nɪ̀r

    EO: ɔ̀dɛ̀

    Ku: ɔ̀nɪ́r

    Od: ɪ̀zàl ɔ̀nɪ́r

    WO: ɔ́dɛ̀

FIRST
    A: ɔɓɛ̀l
    EO: ɔ̀pùrṵ̀
    Ku: ɔ̀pùr
    Od: ɔ̀ɓɛ̀l
    WO: ɔ̀pṵ̀rà

SECOND, THIRD, ETC.
    A: ɛ̀dí èmùnènìòm ị̀yàl
          ɛ̀dí èmùnènìòm ị̀rààr
    EO: òlèlèmèn wálị̀
          òlèlèmèn sárị̀
    Ku: wòléɣéméní ị̀wàl
          wòléɣéméní ị̀sàr
    Od: ògbèɓìòm ị́zăl
          ògbèɓìòm ị́rāār
    WO: òlélémə́n wàlị̀
          òlélémə́n sàrị̀

ETHNIC NAMES

ABUA
    A: (ə̀)-búə̂n   'Abua people'
    EO: əbúə̂n
    Ku: ə̀-búə̂n
    Od: ə́-búə̂n
    WO: əbúə̂n

AHOADA
    A: ɛ̀kpáβɪ̄ā   'Ahoada people'
    EO: ɛ̀kpàβɪ́ɔ   (Ɛkpɛyɛ)
    Od: ɛ̀-kpàβɪ́á
    WO: àhṵ́dà

AKASSA (NEMBE)
    EO: àkàsà
    WO: àkàsà

ANDONI
    WO: ìfìngì

BENIN
    EO: ɛ̀mɔ́bà   'Oba's town, land of fables'
    WO: əbìní

BONNY
    EO: òkólóɓə́
    Od: òkólóɓə́
    WO: òkólóɓə́

BRASS
    Ku: àtṵ̀ɔ́

DEGEMA

    EO: ìðékémà

    Od: ə̀-ðékémà

    WO: ə̀dégémà

ENGENNI

    EO: ɛ̀gɛ̀nɛ̀

    Ku: ɛ̀gɛ̀nɛ̀

    Od: ɛ̀gɛ̀nɛ̀

    WO: ɛ̀gɛ̀nɛ̀

EPIE-ATISA

    A: ɔ̀l-épíè   'Epie person'

    EO: àlɛ̀βíàr

    Ku: àtísà

    WO: àðíɓàr

EUROPEAN, WHITE PERSON

    A: ɔ̀ñ-ə́βèkèñ

    EO: ə̀βèkèñ(ỹ)

    Ku: ə̀βèkêy

    Od: ə̀-βèkě̃ỹ

HAUSA (NORTHERNER)

    EO: ə̀wùsə̀

    Od: àwʊ̀sà

    WO: ə̀wùsə̀

IBIBIO

    A: ùɓɔ̀ɣɔ̀

    EO: ɛ̀ɓɔ̀kɔ̀

    Ku: ị̀ɓɔ̀kɔ̀

    Od: ị́ɓɔ̄kɔ̄   'Ibibio, Efik'

IGBO

    A: (ə̀)-bèn

    EO: ìgbò

    Ku: ìgbò

    Od: ə̀bèn   cf. LIE

    WO: ìgbò

IJO

    A: ɔ̀l-íjɔ̀   'Ijo person'
           z

    EO: ə̀kùmèn

    Ku: ị̀zɔ̀

    Od: ị̀-zɔ̀

    WO: àɓúmàn

IKWERRE

    A: ə̀bén ị́nɔ̄ɣ

KALABARI

    A: (à-)kálábàrị̀

    EO: àkálábàr

    Ku: à-kálábárị́

    Od: à-ŋvɔ́m

    WO: àkálábâr

KOLO (E.O.)

    EO: ə̀ɣòlò

    Ku: ə̀-ɣólò

    Od: ə́-ɣólò

    WO: ə̀ɣòlò

KUGBO

    EO: ɛ̀màgɔ́   largest of four Kugbo
                          villages

Ku: à-gbôy
              i
Od: àgbóỹ

NEMBE
A: ɔ̀l-ə̀lébé   'Nembe person'
EO: ə̀tèɓù
Ku: ə̀- δèbé
Od: ə̀-lèbé
WO: ə̀tèɓù

ODUAL
A: ɔ̀l-óδùə̀l
EO: òδùə̀n
Ku: ó-δúə̀n
Od: ò-δúə̄l   òlòδúə̄l 'belonging to Odual'
WO: òδùə̀n

OGBIA (WO)
A: ógbḭ̀à
EO: ògbḭ́à   (Oloibiri)
Ku: ògbḭ́à
Od: àráásɛ   'Ogbia and Kolo'
WO: ògbḭ́à   òtélèl̄ 'Oloibiri'
                       òtúkpésī 'Anyama'
                       àyákóró ▪Sangatama'
                       ókḭ̀kḭ̀ 'Amaḏụgoama'

OGONI
WO: ògònì

OKRIKA
A: (à)-γḭ̀rḭ̀kà
EO: ɛ̀kḭ̀rḭ̀kà

Ku: ìkị̀rị̀kà
Od: ị̀-γìrị̀kà
WO: ὲkị̀rị̀kà

PORTUGUESE
A: ɔ̀ñ-épɔ̀tòkìrì
Od: ɔ̀pɔ̀tòkìrì

URHOBO, ISOKO
A: ɔ̀l-ágbɔ̀ñ   'Urhobo, Isoko, etc.'
EO: ìsɔ̀bɔ̀
Ku: ɔ̀sɔ̀bɔ̀
Od: ɔ̀sɔ̀bɔ̀
WO: ìsɔ̀bɔ̀

YORUBA
WO: ə̀yórɔ̀bə́